Praise for Oh Mexico!

"Every so often a young writer comes along who can open up a special place to us, and at the same time remind us all of the way we were. This is what Lucy Neville has done in this enchanting travel memoir."

Carmen Callil

"Lucy takes you along as she deals with public transport, shopping, the endless doubles entendres of the local language (almost everything has a secondary, sexual connotation) male machismo, local politics, a hilariously fraught visit by her parents and sister and much more. Anybody who has ever been a 20-something traveller should enjoy this engaging read – think *Holy Cow* in Mexico."

Bookseller and Publisher

"Mexico City is famous for decapitations and gang violence. So announcing you are moving there would worry most parents – even Lucy's 'unshockable' father Richard Neville, once tried for obscenity in the infamou⸱
Lucy's comic observation and eye for the l
a classic coming of age romantic travel me
Almost French with *Like Water for Chocolₐ*

"Neville's first book is a travel memoir w
the panache the pizzazz, the characters an
a good novel."

Adelaₐ⸱ ⸳⸳⸳⸳⸳⸱⸳⸳ₗₐₑᵣ

"At its very best, travel writing has the capacity to illuminate not only the heart of a traveller, but of a country, too. The page-turning journey that is *Oh Mexico!* manages to do both things with considerable skill and frequent hilarity... Neville has the canny reserve of a born story-teller, capturing the dissonances as well as the melodies of expatriate life in a country like no other."

Weekend West

"...a vibrant account of life in Mexico. It is a typical tale of an adventurous twentysomething... excellent when describing the challenge of finding a place to live, being overwhelmed by the sex appeal of her handsome flat mate, responding spontaneously to new and alien experiences, finding a job teaching English to a group of women she calls the 'First Wives' Breakfast Club', struggling with the complexities of speaking a foreign language, unraveling the nuances of class in Mexican society and learning the subtleties and texture of daily life in Mexico City... Neville is a talented writer whose easy, warm style and very 'non-chick lit' calmness in the presence of glamorous men makes for an entertaining account of two years and two loves in a city little known to many."

Sydney Morning Herald

"Part love story, part adventure, *Oh Mexico!* is a fun, light read, ideal for those eager to run away."

Courier Mail

OH MEXICO!

Love and adventure in Mexico City

LUCY NEVILLE

NICHOLAS BREALEY
PUBLISHING

London • Boston

First published in the UK and USA by
Nicholas Brealey Publishing in 2011

3–5 Spafield Street
Clerkenwell, London
EC1R 4QB, UK
Tel: +44 (0)20 7239 0360
Fax: +44 (0)20 7239 0370

20 Park Plaza
Boston
MA 02116, USA
Tel: 888 (BREALEY)
Fax: (617) 523 3708

www.nicholasbrealey.com

ISBN: 978-1-85788-572-9

British Library Cataloguing in Publication Data
A catalogue record for this book is available from the
British Library.

p. 313: Texcoco Netzahualcóyotl poem from J.M.G Le Clézio, *The Mexican Dream:
Or, the Interrupted Thought of Amerindian Civilizations*, translated by Teresa Lavender
Fagan, reproduced with kind permission of The University of Chicago Press © The
University of Chicago 1993. All rights reserved.

pp. 232 and 278: quotations from *The Conquest of New Spain* by Bernal Diaz, translated with an introduction by J.M. Cohen (Penguin Classics, 1963). Copyright © J.M.
Cohen, 1963. Reproduced by permission of Penguin Books Ltd.

Text design by Lisa White
Maps by Ian Faulkner

Printed in the UK by Clays Ltd, St Ives plc.

𝒮 CONTENTS 𝒮

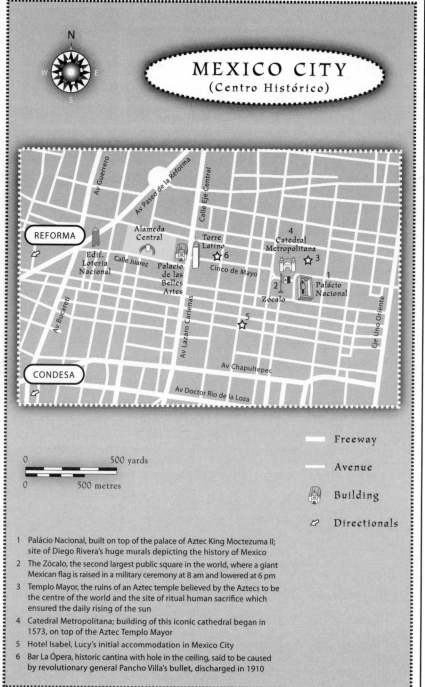

MEXICO CITY
(Centro Histórico)

N
W · E
S

REFORMA

Av Guerrero

Av Paseo de la Reforma

Calle Eje Central

Alameda
Central

Edif.
Loteria
Nacional

Calle Juarez

Palacio
de las
Belles
Artes

Torre
Latino
☆ 6

Cinco de Mayo

Catedral
Metropolitana
☆ 3

4

2

Zócalo

1

Palácio
Nacional

Av Bucareti

Av Lázaro Cárdenas

5
☆

Eje Uno Oriente

CONDESA

Av Chapultepec

Av Doctor Rio de la Loza

0   500 yards

0   500 metres

——— Freeway

——— Avenue

🏢 Building

↵ Directionals

1 Palácio Nacional, built on top of the palace of Aztec King Moctezuma II;
   site of Diego Rivera's huge murals depicting the history of Mexico

2 The Zócalo, the second largest public square in the world, where a giant
   Mexican flag is raised in a military ceremony at 8 am and lowered at 6 pm

3 Templo Mayor, the ruins of an Aztec temple believed by the Aztecs to be
   the centre of the world and the site of ritual human sacrifice which
   ensured the daily rising of the sun

4 Catedral Metropolitana; building of this iconic cathedral began in
   1573, on top of the Aztec Templo Mayor

5 Hotel Isabel, Lucy's initial accommodation in Mexico City

6 Bar La Ópera, historic cantina with hole in the ceiling, said to be caused
   by revolutionary general Pancho Villa's bullet, discharged in 1910

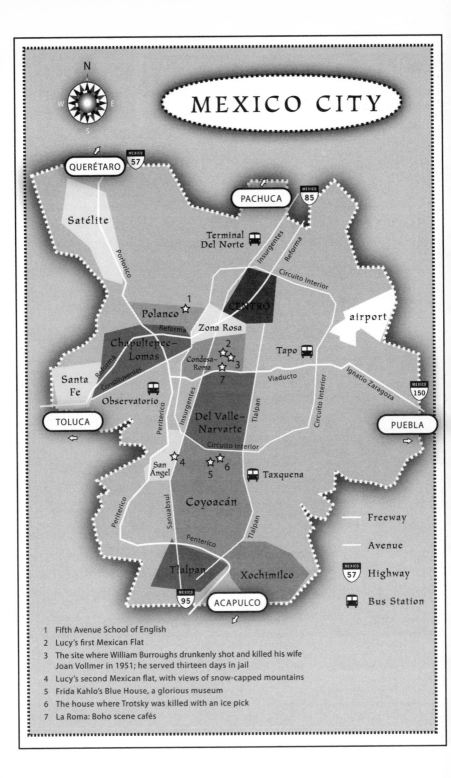

MEXICO CITY

QUERÉTARO

MEXICO 57

PACHUCA

MEXICO 85

Satélite

Portorico

Terminal Del Norte

Insurgentes

Reforma

Circuito Interior

CENTRO

airport

Polanco

1

Reforma

Zona Rosa

Chapultepec–Lomas

Tapo

Reforma

Condesa–Roma

2

3

7

Santa Fe

Constituventes

Viaducto

Ignatio Zaragoza

MEXICO 150

Observatorio

Periterico

Insurgentes

Del Valle–Narvarte

Tlalpan

Circuito Interior

PUEBLA

TOLUCA

Circuito Interior

San Ángel

4

6

Sanuabsul

5

Taxquena

Coyoacán

Periterico

Penterico

Tlalpan

Tlalpan

Xochimilco

Freeway

Avenue

MEXICO 57 Highway

MEXICO 95

ACAPULCO

Bus Station

1 Fifth Avenue School of English
2 Lucy's first Mexican Flat
3 The site where William Burroughs drunkenly shot and killed his wife
   Joan Vollmer in 1951; he served thirteen days in jail
4 Lucy's second Mexican flat, with views of snow-capped mountains
5 Frida Kahlo's Blue House, a glorious museum
6 The house where Trotsky was killed with an ice pick
7 La Roma: Boho scene cafés

To Nan

Prologue

At six in the morning I'm catching the subway at Barranca del Muerto Station, which translates as 'Cliff of the Dead'. Wrapped in a black shawl I ride the steep escalators deep deep down into the tunnel. The hot air hits my cheeks as I get closer to the platform. As I wait for the train I buy the only paper that's on sale, *El Gráfico*, a graphic tabloid newspaper. More pigs' heads have been sewn onto the decapitated corpses of policemen.

On the train, a strong mix of chemicals – hairsprays, perfumes and disinfectant – envelops me. A tiny brown-skinned child tiptoes barefoot across the recently mopped grey floor and hands me a carefully lettered note on coloured paper. It reads: 'We are farmers from the mountains north of Puebla. The price of coffee is too cheap. We are hungry. Please help us.' A blind woman is selling pocket-sized illustrations of the Virgin of Guadalupe.

At Mixcoac (pronounced 'Mixquack') Station, two dwarfs enter the train. They are lugging an amplifier, a bass and a rhythm guitar, and playing the Doors' song, 'People Are Strange'. A deep, pulsating voice resonates through the carriage. The old man next to me wakes up and begins singing along. The rest of the carriage remains asleep.

By Polanco Station, the number of bodies has multiplied and physical movement is challenging. I thrust my way out of the door here, using my elbows. As I exit the station, the sun is rising and golden light is shining through the oak trees. Walking through a leafy plaza, lined with circular pools of illuminated water and neatly cut rose bushes, I turn the corner into Calle Descartes. It's 6.45 am – poodle-walking hour. Women with ancient faces, dressed in frilly uniforms, are accompanying freshly groomed dogs for their morning poo.

I greet the security guards outside my work building. They are standing to attention with their guns cocked. *'Buenos días, güerita. Buenos días, huesita,'* they say to me. Good morning, white girl. Good morning, little bone girl. In Mexico I am considered unusually skinny.

I buy a plastic-tasting cappuccino from the 7/Eleven at street level in our building, and then run up the stairs to my class on the second floor. 'Hi, Coco,' I greet the receptionist. She is curling her eyelashes with the back of a teaspoon in front of the portable magnifying mirror on her desk. She's having a pink day today: pink shirt, pink nails, pink eye shadow.

'Hello, Lucy. Jour estudents are waiting for jou.' (One of the hardest sounds for Mexicans to make is the 'y'.) Two women and a man are sitting expectantly in the classroom: Elvira, Reina and Oswaldo. Elvira grabs my arm and guides me to my chair.

'Look, I buy tamales! They are hot, eat them quick. Here, the red one is for you – no have chilli.' A little parcel wrapped in corn husks is waiting for me on the desk.

'But I like chilli,' I protest. They all laugh.

'No! Gringos can't eat chilli.' (For Mexicans, it's a source of national pride to be the only country in the Americas that is brave enough to eat chilli.)

'I am from Australia. You know, CROCODILE HUNTER! We are not wimps, like the gringo Americans are,' I explain to them again.

'Okay, next time I buy chilli for you.' Elvira is forty-five. She works as a marketing assistant for Gatorade. She has long dark hair, which she gets curled at the beauty parlour every morning at 6 am. She is elegantly voluptuous, wearing tight, brightly-coloured low-cut tops to draw attention to the enormity of her breasts, and dark, baggy pants to hide the enormity of her behind. She moves around the room as if she is dancing the cumbia, swinging her hips and breasts rhythmically in every direction. I notice Oswaldo is having problems averting his eyes as she bends forward to get her notebook out of her bag.

'So, Oswaldo, did you finish the exercises I gave you on reported speech?' He snaps back to reality and gives me his full attention.

'Ah, well, you know, actually no have time . . . I was three hours in de traffic de last night and I arrived to my house at two in de morning.' (The sound 'th' is another big problem for Mexicans.) Oswaldo's excuse is probably true – he works as a computer programmer for a large pharmaceutical company and he often does twelve-hour shifts. He's plump and looks uncomfortable in his tight suit. He smiles cheekily, pleased with his excuse.

'I did – I completed the exercises,' Reina bursts out frantically. 'But I didn't really understand.' Her small dark eyes flash with desperation as she looks at me for help.

She works as an accountant for the telephone company in the building next door, and has just been told that if she doesn't improve her English soon she will lose her job. She is a 35-year-old single mother with four children to support. I brace myself to get the class going before she starts talking about her long and painful divorce.

'Me too,' says Elvira. 'Can jou explain?'

I decide to make them do a role play, so they can understand the context of the grammatical structures they are learning. One student could report a stolen car to the police, who could then report the details to the detective. To introduce this topic, I ask if anyone has ever had their car stolen.

'Jes,' Reina answers.

'Ah, really? Where was it when it was stolen?'

'It was on the Periferico.'

'Periferico?' I ask. 'But that's a highway . . . ?'

'Jes, I was driving to work in the traffic and a man comes and he took my car . . . '

'But you were in the car?'

'Jes, he breaks my window and hit me on the head. Then he took me out of the car.'

'Oh.'

'. . . But I don't remember that. I just wake up in the hospital and they tell me what happened.'

I look around at the others. They don't seem to be particularly surprised by this.

'Well, you are lucky they only took your car,' Elvira comments unsympathetically. 'You know, the same happen to my uncle, and they take his car *and* his wife.'

'What? What do you mean they took his wife?' I ask.

'Yes. They took his wife. But all the family gave money and they bring her back.'

'Oh. Well, ah, what about the car? Did either of you get the car back?' (I am trying to avoid getting sidetracked with kidnapping stories.)

'What?'

'Did the police find your car?'

They look at me strangely. Then Elvira begins to laugh. 'Probably the police *stole* the cars!'

'Yes, but anyway, if your car is stolen, you never get it back anyway. Dey sell de different parts at Colonia Buenos

Aires,' Oswaldo explains, mentioning a notorious area to the south-east of the city centre.

'Really?'

'Yes, actually I went dere last weekend to buy . . . how do you say de light on de back of your car?'

'You bought a stolen tail-light?'

'Yes, of course. Imagine to buy a new one . . . Oofa, I could never have money for dat.'

'Okay, so let's imagine that we live in Canada, where the police help you to find your car and there is no stolen car parts market . . .' I try to get the class back on track.

'Really? The police help you in Canada?' Elvira looks at me puzzled.

'Yes. The police try to find your car and return it to you.'

'And in your country too?'

'Yes.'

'And if they steal someone in your family, like in the case of my uncle, the police help you also?'

'In Australia it's not very common for people to be stolen from their cars on the way to work,' I explain. 'But if this was to happen, I imagine the police would try to help.'

Oswaldo is still thinking about the car situation. 'So dere is not stolen car market?'

'No.'

'But where you buy parts for your car?'

'I don't know. I guess we take it somewhere to be fixed – and they provide the missing part.'

'Isn't dat expensive?'

'Well, I think a computer programmer like you could afford it.'

Then Reina looks at me thoughtfully and asks: 'So, in jour country the police help jou and don't steal from jou? Jou can make enough money to buy new car parts if jou need them, and the people are not stolen from the traffic?'

'Well . . . no.'

The three of them stare at me in silence. Then Elvira asks the next logical question . . .

'So why – *why* you come to live here in Mehico?'

I think about it for a few minutes and then I reply, 'To learn Spanish.'

'Why not you go to Spain?' Reina asks.

'Well, I don't like European winters . . . and they speak with a lisp.' (Mexicans are always making fun of the Spanish accent – they should understand.)

'Ah, yes. But why no Chile or Arhentina?'

'Look, Mexico has great cultural diversity and a colourful history. And the people are really warm,' I explain. They look back at me blankly. 'Come on, Mexico is very rich, culturally speaking . . . What about the music? The art? The architecture? The food?'

'Ah yes, de food is very good,' agrees Oswaldo finally. But I can tell they're not satisfied by my answer. Somehow these things don't seem as important to them as their everyday reality of economic insecurity, their constant fear of being kidnapped, the corruption innate in their criminal justice system and in all layers of government.

'So you came all the way here – away from your family – just because you like the music and the buildings here?' Elvira inquires.

'Well – in Australia it's perfectly normal for people to go and live in other countries after university, just for the experience and challenge.'

It's difficult for them to understand this. Generally, when Mexicans go to live in other countries, it's because of the necessity of finding a job. In my case it was the necessity of *avoiding* getting a job.

I thought back to the moment when I decided to leave Australia. I was nearing the end of an Arts degree, majoring in politics and international relations and Spanish and Latin American studies. The last lecture was compulsory – it was about 'careers'.

A young woman with spiky silver hair and a tight-fitting grey suit gave us the run-down on real life. There were not enough jobs for those who graduated from university each year. So the question was: how could we make ourselves attractive to employers? She talked about writing CVs. Show them that you are ambitious. Show them what you have achieved in your past jobs, how you moved up from waitress to manager to general director. (I had never been promoted, nor wanted to be. Why would you want more responsibilities in a juice bar?) She described in detail the recruitment process of corporations. How 600 graduates would apply for any attractive position and how they narrowed it down to one person through psychometric tests, psychological examinations and integration dynamics.

Now – after we had spent three years debating political economic systems and had come to the conclusion that neo-liberal capitalism was both unethical and environmentally unsustainable – they were telling us that, if we were lucky, we would get a job working for a multinational corporation.

So at the prospect of looking for a real job, a step up from working at the juice bar in the Broadway Shopping Centre, I decided that what I needed to do next, while I absorbed all the knowledge I had just taken on board, was to live in Latin America for a year to improve my Spanish. After all, the thing about living overseas is that even if you don't manage to do anything at all while you're there, it still seems as if you are achieving something. If, say, you lived in Uzbekistan for a year . . . even if all you did was work at a bar and watch cable TV in your hotel, it doesn't matter. You lived in *Uzbekistan*!

At some point in my childhood I had begun to formulate a Latin American fantasy: salsa, magical realism, a history that was rampant with brave revolutions against brutal dictatorships. I am unable to pinpoint exactly what it was, only that it was Latin America that most appealed to my sense of the exotic, that was the most removed from my own reality, plus it was geographically the furthest away and one continent to which my hippie traveller parents hadn't ventured.

Originally I had my heart set on Colombia. But my mother said that if I went to Colombia she would commit suicide (she takes emotional blackmail to a whole new level). So I compromised and booked a round-the-world ticket, last stop Mexico City, which was considered to be the second most dangerous city after Bogotá. I would be there for one year; long enough to learn the language and gain an understanding of a different way of life.

A year before I had been there briefly, in a desperate attempt to improve my Spanish during my Australian summer holidays, and had fallen for the place. The people walked slowly, expressed their emotions, swore a lot, danced seductively, sung comically and had domestics in public. They ate a lot of fat and chilli, and hadn't heard of skinny soy decaf lattés.

On my first trip, I had bypassed Mexico City and taken a two-week course in Oaxaca (which is pronounced wa'haka). It is the poorest but one of the most culturally rich states of Mexico. Oaxaca City is full of artists, poets, stylish bars and cafés in crumbling colonial buildings with courtyards and live music. And it's the home of mezcal, an unruly cousin of tequila. It's cheap and addictive; they give it out free in little plastic cups as you're walking down the street, to lure you into their specialty shops which sell hundreds of different brews. Like tequila, mezcal is made from the agave cactus but it's distilled only once, whereas tequila is distilled twice.

Accordingly, my memories of that trip are limited, as was my learning of Spanish. But I do remember falling desperately in love with a Zapoteca man, culminating in a terrifying ride up a mountain on the back of his motorbike and watching the sun set over the city. Two days later I fell out of love, when I discovered that every other girl in my Spanish class had had the same experience.

So that was why I had decided to come and live in Mexico. However, there was still the question of how I would sustain myself in a country where a large percentage of the population risked their lives walking across a desert or swimming across a river to the United States to work like slaves, due to the lack of employment opportunities. As many people in my position had previously realised, teaching English was the obvious answer. Thanks to our forward-thinking British ancestors, it is now considered essential for almost every human being who wants to be part of the formal economy to learn English. This is convenient for Arts students like me, who graduate lacking any practical skills but feel the need to live in a developing country. So I enrolled in an intensive English language-teaching course. One of the cheapest places to do this happened to be in Valencia, Spain, which would be a good warm-up to Mexico, I thought when I booked the round-the-world ticket to Mexico City and scheduled a two-month stopover in Spain along the way.

A panic had descended over me on the last leg of my journey, flying from Madrid to Mexico. My finances were meagre after a few months in Spain. I would quickly have to find a job and somewhere to live, and create a social network – and all of this in Spanish. Sure, I had a basic handle on intermediate-level grammar, but that didn't seem to help much when it came to communication. And my speaking had hardly improved in Spain where I had spent most of the time cooped up with Scots and Irish classmates learning how to teach English.

But what if I couldn't find a job? I would have to ask my parents for money, or come back home to work in the juice bar, I worried, slipping the airline's complimentary packet of salted peanuts into my backpack in case I needed them later. To distract myself from my rising panic, I started up a conversation with the thirty-ish platinum-blond German who was sitting next to me. He was wound-up, because he was on his way to an annual refrigeration conference. He had been to Mexico City before, but only on business, and he had never left his hotel. The city was dangerous and polluted he said, advising me to stay one night and get the hell out of there to Cancún. Warming to his subject, he cautioned me against getting into a taxi due to the risk of getting robbed, raped and murdered. He offered to take me in the chauffeur-driven limo he had waiting for him. I lost him at the baggage claim carousel.

Once out of Customs, I headed directly to the pre-paid taxi booth, as advised by *Lonely Planet*'s section on 'pirate taxis'.

My taxi driver looked about fourteen. I gave him the name of the cheap hotel I was heading for in the historical centre of the city and tried to speak to him in Spanish, but he insisted on practising his English. 'Jou don't miss jour family?' he asked. He was surprised and concerned that I was travelling alone.

When we got to the hotel, he waited until I was safely booked in, and gave me a note with his name and phone number and his mum's phone number, just in case I had any problems or needed some advice. His name was Jesús. He told me he would be there for me if I had any problems and then invited me to stay at his grandmother's house in Acapulco that coming weekend. 'Jou must to know de bitches here!' he exclaimed.

'Bitches?'

'Jes, the bitches of Mehico are very famous. Cancún is the most beautiful, but it's very far from here.'

He took my bags to the reception and told the hotel staff that I was travelling alone, and to please look after me. As I was shown to my room, I felt a burning in the back of my throat and behind my eyes as I remembered my earlier arrival in Spain, where I had never found Jesús.

When I arrived at Madrid Airport, the friend of a friend I was supposed to be staying with was nowhere to be seen. I had jumped into a taxi and told the driver to take me to a cheap hotel. He dumped me in what was obviously the red-light district.

All the pay-by-the-hour hotels had been booked out. Trudging along with a suitcase that I could barely lift, plus a backpack and a laptop, I didn't exactly blend in. It started raining. I found another taxi. The driver asked me (in Spanish) if I could speak Spanish. I told him (in Spanish) that I was learning. Then he asked under his breath, 'Well, why didn't you learn before you got here?' After many miserable hours and various unhelpful taxi rides, I eventually found somewhere inhospitable and expensive to stay.

Now I was in Mexico City, where the taxi drivers are supposed to kidnap you before you even get from the airport to your hotel. But instead I felt like I had been picked up by a family member.

My hotel room was on the rooftop, looking out over Calle Isabel la Católica and twelve storeys up. I dumped my suitcase on the single bed and made my way to the window. It was dusk and the sky was greyish yellow. Directly opposite, circular Moorish steeples were covered in blue and white tiles. Below, street sellers were packing their unsold goods into carts, pulling them along behind them. I had made it at last. Exhausted and elated I was drawn outside to absorb the atmosphere. I took the creaky lift to the ground floor and wandered out into the crowds on the street, entering the first cantina I saw. I sat at the bar and ordered a Corona, glancing at the black-and-white photos lining the wall. They included the iconographic General Zapata with his sombrero and belt of rifle bullets. In one corner, a stout elderly woman missing one of her front teeth was serenading a table of old men. The only words I could understand were *blood, virgin* and something about a burning maize plantation. I recognised the little guy at the next table. He had been one of the hotel receptionists who had promised Jesús he would look after me when I checked in. His name was Panchito, a rotund adolescent with golden-brown skin and bright eyes. He had thrown a faded Metallica t-shirt over his work shirt. Panchito introduced me to his friend, Nacho, who smiled at me timidly. Neither of them had facial hair yet. 'Where are you from?'

'Australia.'

'Ah yes, lots of snow. Arnold Schwarzenegger.'

'No, not Austria – Australia. *Canguro*.' I hopped like a kangaroo. As I had learnt many times before, this was the only way to confirm my national identity.

'Ahh, Australia. Crocodile hunter. You like *lucha libre*?'

'Ah, I don't know. What is it exactly?'

'You mean, where you come from, there is no *lucha libre*?' They looked horrified. 'Come with us tonight!' They explained that it would be Místico (who could really fly!) against El Satánico, and then El Felino against Apocalipsis.

How could I say no? The fact that Panchito worked at the hotel made me feel safe. So we took the metro to the Arena Coliseo. Panchito insisted on paying for my ticket, even though it would amount to more than a whole day's wages. The streets were lined with stores selling *lucha libre* paraphernalia. My new friends were so excited that we had to stop to buy some Místico masks.

The arena was packed. It was a family event – mainly fathers with their sons – but the atmosphere was exhilarating. First came the women – bleached-blonde, shiny-breasted bimbos strutting across the stage in string bikinis. The men hissed and growled like animals. The women in the audience were hysterical – '¡PUTA! ¡PUTA!' (Whore!) Led onto the ring by the models came the thickly muscled *luchadore*, who bounced and sprang around in their masks and colourful lycra superhero costumes, threatening each other with backward somersaults.

The fights themselves were like a combination of sumo wrestling and trapeze flying – a choreographed boxing tournament, complete with dwarfs dressed as monkeys – a disturbing image. After a few beers, this formula becomes completely riveting. '¡*Chinga tu madre! ¡Pinche pendejo!*' I yelled, imitating my companions. 'Fuck your mother! Fucking moron!'

Legend has it that the Inuits have an unusually large number of words for snow and, equally, that the Ancient Greeks had many words to express love. This may or may not be true, but unquestionably in Mexico City there is a disproportionately large number of ways of saying, 'Fuck you!'

It would soon become clear why this was.

❦1❧

To-do List

The next morning after arriving in Mexico City I woke up and began writing a to-do list. Not that I am an organised person, but I was feeling overwhelmed – and I always find that a to-do list gives me a sense that there is potential to cope with the situation.

1. Find something to eat
2. Wash undies
3. Learn Spanish
4. Get a job
5. Find somewhere to live

Food first. With the map given to me by the hotel, I made my way north towards the central plaza, known in Mexico as the Zócalo. The air was still humid after last night's rain, and the earthy aroma of damp stone emanated from the grand dark grey palaces which stood either side of the street. During the colonial period, this place was referred to as 'the city of the palaces', palaces which the Spanish had built from the very stone of the conquered Aztec city of Tenochtitlán.

I turned right into Avenida 5 de Mayo. Pirate videos, CDs, lacy underwear, cosmetics, Armani sunglasses, vacuum cleaner parts, dried pig skins. Each street stall was playing its own music, competing in volume with the stalls next door, so that every few steps the background music changed: salsa, Britney Spears, *reggaetón*, Frank Sinatra, ranchero.

The formal shops also had their own music. Their speakers were placed outside on the street, as if attempting to capture customers with the rhythm. An old couple danced cumbia outside one of the shops. Ageing men dressed in faded army uniforms wound up old-fashioned organ-grinders that emitted groaning noises meant to resemble romantic ballads. They asked for money. There were far too many people on the street. So I gave up on the footpath and ran along the road, dodging the traffic. Horns were honking. Beside me was a truck full of riot police equipped with helmets, shields, and batons – ready for battle. A small girl carrying a baby held her hand out for change.

The street came to an end and an enormous paved open space appeared in front of me. To the north is the cathedral, built on top of a buried Aztec temple. Flanking the entire east side of the Zócalo stands the National Palace built from the ruins of the palace of King Moctezuma the Second.

The square was filled with thousands of people. Nearly all of them were wearing yellow raincoats. Some were carrying yellow flags, and banners, which read 'Smile, we're gonna win'. They stood facing a small stage, which had been placed in front of the cathedral. I crossed the road and pushed my way into the sea of yellow. On the big screens which stood on either side of the stage, a grandfatherly-looking figure was making his way towards the microphone. Mexico was in the midst of a presidential election and I assumed this was the warm-up.

'Obrador, Obrador!' The crowd was chanting his name. The noise was deafening. It resonated through my bones, making me feel dizzy. Then, a few seconds of silence before he took hold of the microphone and projected his strong high-pitched voice across the Zócalo. I stood still and listened – listened so hard I stopped breathing. And after a while, through a haze of verbs, articles and prepositions, some solid nouns began to stand out: 'poverty', 'solidarity', 'economic justice', 'neo-liberal imperialism'.

Then the sky opened. Yellow umbrellas burst open and I ran for cover. The crowd didn't move.

Back on Avenida 5 de Mayo, I followed the smell of frying meat. *Tacos de bistec* sounded like it wouldn't be brains or entrails. Fried beef chopped into tiny pieces placed inside a maize tortilla with red salsa and lime juice.

Mission One was now complete. I headed back to the hotel to address Mission Two.

§

I was walking across the hotel rooftop, on the way to the communal bathroom to wash my undies, when I first encountered Buck. He was in the lotus position, seemingly engaged in deep meditation. But when he saw me he began making slurping noises and yelled, '*Ay mamacita güerita*', imitating the Mexican men on the street. I told him to '*Chinga a su madre*', putting to use the vocabulary I had learnt the night before. He raised his eyebrows in an exaggerated manner as if in complete shock. Balding, with a shaved head and large comical mouth, he must have been in his early forties. On my way back from the bathroom, he suggested we go for a beer. I agreed. From his perfect simulation of Mexican macho patois, I figured he'd been here a while.

We went to the Opera Bar – a cantina about two blocks away, famous for the bullet holes in its ceiling left by the great revolutionary general, Pancho Villa. The walls were decorated with larger-than-life portraits of significant Mexican musicians and performers. Buck had worked as a mime-artist in New York, a park ranger in Colorado, a jazz saxophonist in San Francisco and a left-wing radio announcer in LA, before having become addicted to the creative energy of the Centro Histórico. He had now been living in the hotel room next door to mine for over seven years, keeping himself busy by working on his anti-Bush blog, going on regular Vipassana meditation retreats and openly taking advantage of the low prices of Mexican sex workers.

Buck was the first of many wacky North Americans I would come across living in Mexico City. I later realised that Mexico serves as a refuge for misfit gringos who can live well on their First World savings while enjoying a less rigid reality.

After a few Coronas, Buck mentioned that a friend of his was having an exhibition opening that night. We wandered down the road until we came to a graffiti-covered garage door. We banged against the tin and soon a small door opened on the right. Standing at the bottom of a dark, narrow staircase was a young woman. A black cocktail dress clung to her petite hour-glass figure. Buck introduced me to Amor, the artist of tonight's exhibition.

We followed her silky, long brown hair up the stairs into an open white space with a bare cement floor. The place was packed with immaculately groomed designer punks – asymmetrical haircuts, tattoos and surprisingly placed body piercings – dressed in luxurious evening wear. Our companion had painted delicate pink flowers onto everyday objects such as dinner plates, kitchen stools and toilet brushes, which at closer inspection were actually life-like depictions of vulvas.

Buck saw someone he knew and I was left to make conversation with Amor. I began in Spanish but she politely switched to English when she registered my stress level. Amor lived in the block of apartments above. It had taken six months for her application to be processed. Because the building was 'socially designed', she had had to compete with several other artists. Each 'member' was especially chosen by a board of government bureaucrats associated with Carlos Slim's foundation to revive the Centro Histórico. The board was obliged to select artists, scientists and intellectuals to create a stimulating environment.

Carlos Slim at that time was considered to be the richest man in the world, with business interests focused on telecommunications in Mexico and the rest of Latin America. He owned one quarter of the buildings in the Centro Histórico, Amor explained. That was basically the whole of its north–west quadrant. He had restored the fifteenth-century buildings and, with the help of specially trained incorruptible policemen, had gentrified the area by clearing away the black market economy and encouraging tourism with the establishment of boutique art galleries and cafés. Only five years before, it had been one of the no-go zones.

'You can trust the policemen in light-blue uniforms,' Amor told me. This was as opposed to the police in dark-blue uniforms found in the non-Carlos Slim area, who hadn't undergone special anti-corruption brainwashing.

Amor introduced me to her boyfriend, El Negro, a tall man with a shaved head and rat's tail. He saw that I was struggling to articulate my thoughts in the local language. 'I can speak English,' he told me, 'but I don't. It's the language of the fucking imperialist gringos. But you can speak in English, I understand.' El Negro was an electronic sound artist.

Three shots of tequila later I found Buck again, and it was evident he too had taken full advantage of the complimentary drinks. Addressing a small group of amused-looking youths, he was arguing the benefits of drinking one's own urine. 'I'm telling you,' he slurred, 'it's a natural antibiotic.' I interrupted his speech to tell him I was leaving.

'Noooooo!' he wailed, grabbing my shoulder. 'It's too dangerous to walk at this time.' And with a surge of alcohol-induced confidence, I decided to continue our conversation in Spanish. After all, I didn't want to be seen as an imperialist.

'Don't worry,' I replied. '*Voy a coger un taxi.*' But Buck didn't respond. He just stared back at me grinning. Then one of Buck's companions shouted; '*Hey!* She's going to *COGER un taxi!*' This caused an eruption of uncontrolled laughter. Finally, Buck pulled himself together and explained that, in Mexico, you cannot *coger* a taxi, only a taxi driver. The giggles continued. I got the idea. Your Spanish dictionary will tell you that *coger* means 'to take', but in Mexico it's just another synonym of the verb 'to fornicate'.

§

I woke up the next day feeling vaguely hung over and glanced at my to-do list. *Get a job.* Now this was getting urgent. With just 4000 pesos in the bank – that was about A$400 – I estimated I could survive for about ten more days.

I bought the morning paper and went through the job section. I went to a nearby internet café and searched the web. From there I sent out dozens of copies of a heavily exaggerated CV. On returning to the café that night, I found I had received a response from a school called Fifth Avenue.

The next day I attended an interview. My clothes had been squashed into my bag for the last three months and were beginning to take on a mouldy smell. I didn't have an iron. Neither did Buck. My naturally light-brown hair had been dyed black, but was starting to go pinky orange, topped off with light-coloured roots, which looked grey by contrast. I wouldn't hire myself.

But the interview was less stressful than I had antici-pated. 'I'm from Australia,' I said.

'Ah, jou spik English there?'

'Yes.'

'Dat's good, because we only hire de native speakers. Now let me tell jou about our company.'

Did this mean that he had given me the job? Apparently so. I would start attending training sessions next week and start work a few weeks later. Another one down. Now I turned my attention to finding somewhere to live.

I bought a map of the city. Sixteen *delegaciones*, each containing hundreds of *colonias* or neighbourhoods. Panchito had already offered me a room in his family home, sharing with his aunt and her three children. 'I told them about you. Only 35 pesos a week. My grandmother has never seen a foreigner.' But I declined after learning that his colonia, Ciudad Neza, wasn't even on the map, in fact it was actually in a different state.

'How long does it take to get there from here?' I asked.

'About two hours.'

'Thanks, Panchito, but I would prefer to live closer to my job,' I explained.

Polanco was the suburb I would be working in. But Buck informed me that this was an elite area of the city, and like most elite areas, it was boring, sterile and expensive.

I searched in the 'To Rent' section of the paper – Ixtapalapa, Xochimilco, Milpalta, Chapultepec – really the Centro was the only safe bet. One ad caught my eye. *'To Rent, Centro Histórico, Calle República de Bolivia, 500 pesos per month'*. That was only fifty bucks. As I made my way north, past the cathedral, the buildings began slowly falling into themselves. Stray animals emerged from piles of rubbish; graffiti covered the dilapidated stone walls. Eventually, I came across a small plaza where a group of teenagers appeared to be sniffing intoxicants. This must be Plaza Santo Domingo. The room for rent was here – '*Rentar depa*'. I banged on the door, nervously constructing sentences in my head as I waited. A hunched-over elderly woman opened the door.

'*¿Disculpe, está rentando un departamento?*'

But she looked shocked. 'You're not from here?' she asked.

'No.'

She led me through a moss-covered courtyard. A cat with kittens was asleep in the corner. The room she showed me was empty. High ceiling, a view looking over the plaza. But the windows had been smashed and shards of glass were scattered across the floor. Electrical cords sprouted down from the roof. No electricity and no water she explained. Although I was impressed by its post-apocalyptic poetics, it was lacking on the practical side.

As I walked past the plaza on my way back, I noticed that the teenagers had formed a circle around an older man. They were holding something to his throat. What could I do? Nothing. Heart pounding, I hurried on my way and it started to pour with rain. Rubbish began flowing down the street, riding on sewage. A rat clung for its life onto a piece of debris. Back towards the cathedral, I tried to tell one of the light-blue policemen what I had seen. 'Santo Domingo?' he laughed. 'That's not my area.'

My search would have to be extended to some other zones. And so my flat-hunting routine began. Every day I would buy the paper and circle all the options which fell under my wage, and then attempt to locate the suburb on the map. If I managed to do this, I would then call and arrange to see it. That was the terrifying part. Over the phone, communication depends on perfect pronunciation and correct grammatical structure. You cannot bluff with mime, or with smiles that say, 'Isn't it funny that I can't talk properly'. And there are only so many times you can ask someone to repeat something.

I spent hours constructing a flat-renting script only to hang up the phone in a panic when the other party didn't stick to their designated part in our dialogue.

§

It was during this period that I got to know the underground. I was constantly fascinated by taking the metro. The passengers would stare at me and I would stare back at them. A different kind of people existed in these tunnels than above ground. The metro is cheap – 2 pesos (about 20 cents) for unlimited distance. It connects the outer marginalised circles of the city with the commercial centres.

Traders heaved huge baskets of vegetables and bags of animal carcasses. The blind sold pirate music, promoting their wares with miniature speakers installed in their backpacks. Barefooted peasants from faraway villages begged for money. Buskers entertained in any way they could. Farmers played fiddles, street children sang songs. One man performed a magic trick by rolling around bare-chested on shards of glass, only to emerge unscathed. I was sometimes reminded of paintings by Goya. Fluorescent tubes lit up the dark faces, which were often deformed by deep scars and medieval teeth.

After a few days of solid searching, I began to find some liveable options. But the next step – bonds and payment terms – was fraught with complex bureaucracy. Firstly, I would need a *fiador* – a person who owns real estate in Mexico City – to write me a letter verifying that I was responsible and to sign legal documents agreeing to pay the rent if I failed to. On top of this, I required several different forms of ID that are unobtainable by foreigners.

It was now becoming clear why Buck was still living in a hotel after seven years. I continued my search, hoping that if I smiled enough, someone would just decide to trust me and rent me their flat without all the paperwork. But after two weeks of searching, about 47 encounters concluded in a repeatedly disheartening fashion, the only option was to find somebody who had already gone through this process, and go and live with them. I immersed myself in cyberspace once again, and attempted to navigate the Mexican flatmate-finding websites. Most of the ads seemed to be posted by foreigners, and that was one thing I definitely wanted to avoid, living with expats. But I did find one ad that appeared to be put up by a Mexican. It read: 'Art deco style, opposite Mezcalaria, all races, all religions welcome, Colonia Roma'. It was written in four different languages: Spanish, English, French and Portuguese. I sent an email and left my mobile number. The next day I received a call.

'*Buenas tardes*, Lucy? Yes . . . I'm Octavio, I posted the ad about the flat in La Roma.'

'Ah, *hola* . . . ah . . .' He picked up my phone anxiety and asked where I was from, and then he began speaking to me in fluent English. He gave me the address. I asked him for the nearest metro station.

'Metro? Ah, sorry, I'm not so familiar with the subway stations of this city – perhaps I could pick you up?'

'No, no. It's okay, I'll get there.'

'Do you have a *Lonely Planet*?'

'Yes,' I admitted.

'. . . Well it's just a few doors down from the house in which William Burroughs was living when he shot his wife.'

With this information, I located it exactly. As the *Lonely Planet* recounts, the beatnik writer who had been living in Mexico to escape the law had accidently shot his wife dead when aiming for the martini glass on her head during a drinking game.

Emerging at metro station Insurgentes, I found myself in the middle of a circular plaza with several different exits, none of them with visible road names. After walking down about four of them, I found it – Calle Orizaba. It was wide and quiet and lined with ash trees. Plants crept down from small Juliet balconies with arched windows. It was almost Italy; the difference was that many of the buildings were violently crooked, some with parts missing and huge cracks in the stone.

I crossed a little park which contained a replica of Michelangelo's statue of David. I gazed up at his enlarged thigh muscles. On every corner was some sort of art gallery. There were also art gallery cafés and an abundance of second-hand bookshop cafés.

I located the number of the building. It was painted bright yellow, and the large iron door had been left open. I was beginning to get curious – who was this Mexican who reads *Lonely Planet*, speaks four languages and doesn't know where the metro station is? As I climbed the stairs, it suddenly occurred to me that I wasn't wearing deodorant – it had run out a few days ago. I had been walking in the sun for at least an hour. I got to the fifth floor and banged on the door. And then the door opened and I saw Octavio for the first time. He was tall and gangly, with long dark curly hair and had the kind of handsomeness – almost perfection – that you might find in a Calvin Klein ad, if it wasn't for the nose, which was grand and full of character. Without that nose he would have been just another good-looking guy, and I would have assumed that he was arrogant and uninteresting.

'Hi. Come in. Can I get you a drink: coffee, tequila? Please make yourself at home.'

I stared dumbfounded around the room. The beauty of both the flat and my companion was a stark contrast to the dusty difficulties of the previous weeks. White walls, high ceilings, parquet flooring. The flat was almost empty. He began to show me around: 'This is the kitchen – just a fridge and a sink at this stage. My room . . .' Various guitar-like instruments were leaning against the walls. '. . . the bathroom. And this would be your room . . .' Empty, but full of light. Spacious and clean. 'Of course I can help you get any furniture you may need.'

We walked back to the living room. On the wall was a map of Mexico dating from before the 1846 Mexican–American War, when Texas, New Mexico and California were still part of Mexican territory.

It was dusk. Beams of orange light were shining through the window and illuminating the giant maguey cactus that stood in the corner. It was the only item in the room, other than a high-tech stereo and a bookshelf. I gave the bookshelf a furtive once-over, to try to get more of an idea of whom I was dealing with. An antique collection of *Encyclopaedia Britannica* printed in French, Hegel's *Philosophy of History*, Heidegger's *Being and Time*, Rousseau's *Du Contrat Social* (in French), a guide to ancient instruments, and *Lonely Planet* guides in various languages covering Mongolia, Ukraine and Bhutan.

'I hope you don't mind sitting on the floor.'

We sat down face to face, his long gangly legs stretching halfway across the living room floor. He was wearing a t-shirt featuring the image of Picasso's *Guernica*. Although he was thin he had quite a broad chest. We learnt each other's stories.

Being the son of a diplomat, Octavio had grown up in Argentina, Brazil, Switzerland and Canada. After having studied for a degree in international relations in Paris he had returned to Mexico in order to follow his father's, and grandfather's, footsteps. But after putting one foot inside the door of Mexican politics, he had become demoralised and decided instead to devote himself to what he was really passionate about – music. Against the wishes of his father, he had gone to live in Montreal and studied music. It was only recently that he had returned to Mexico and had found a job teaching music at a private university. Now he was in the process of putting together a band. He spoke to me about his life with a sort of eloquence mixed with a superficial modesty.

I asked him what he thought of Obrador, the candidate of the PRD, Partido de la Revolución Democrática (Democratic Revolution Party). Hordes of his disciples had been marching past my hotel room every day, screaming 'Obrador, the leader of the poor'. With the election coming up, I was wondering whether he signalled a radical change in Mexican politics.

Not according to Octavio. 'Obrador is simply a dema-gogue,' he informed me, 'who has a knack for blurting out tedious and outdated Marxist rhetoric at the right moments. What's more, he is uneducated and lacks the tools to come up with a vision sufficient to govern the various interests within the system.' He told me with so much assurance that I almost believed him. If only I had the tools to come up with a clever response to his critique.

'And what about Calderón?' I referred to the right-wing candidate. 'Surely he's just a puppet of the US government?'

'Well, he's certainly aligned with Bush, but that's the least of our worries. All that will happen is that he will de-nationalise petroleum. My deepest concern about the Nationalist Action Party now that they've got power, is the increasing prominence of the Yunque in its ranks,' he sighed, as he brushed his hair back with his long musician's fingers.

'Yunque?'

'Yes, a secret ultra-right Franco-esque Catholic organisation.'

'So, who will you vote for?'

'Vote? How absurdly futile that would be.'

I changed the subject. 'Hey, this area is really beautiful.'

'Yes, it was constructed in the era of Porfirio Díaz, the president who was overthrown during the revolution. He wanted to make Mexico like Europe. I've always wanted to live in this area and then, when I found this flat . . . Well, you can imagine. It was all meant to be.'

'Yes, it's beautiful.'

'And it has great feng shui. Have you noticed? It's full of direct natural light, and we're not in the way of any negative energy paths.'

'Well, that's good.'

'So, tell me, what type of furniture do you imagine for this room?'

After talking furniture for a while, and both of us agreeing that as little as possible should be introduced into the space, I decided it was time to go. Just as I was walking out the door, he looked at me. 'I am left with no doubt that we could live together amicably. The decision is in your hands – I imagine you need some time to reflect.'

He was right. I knew that I wanted to see him again . . . But I didn't know whether I wanted to live with him. How could I concentrate on my Spanish when his curious and inviting presence was already so destabilising?

❦ 2 ❦

The Turquoise Serpent

In the Zócalo, the semi-naked Indians were performing their daily rhythmic dance and drumming ritual for the tourists. Headdresses of exotic feathers resembling fountains flashed in the sun. Dazed, I stood watching them having come for a walk to think about the Octavio apartment situation. The drumbeat was now accelerating into a crescendo and the movements of the muscular red bodies adorned with animal skin and fur had become a hypnotic blur.

I felt a tap on the shoulder. It was the shaman drug addict whom I had noticed watching me earlier. His hollow dark eyes were staring directly into my own. Yellow skin stretched tightly over his sharp cheekbones, giving him an emaciated skeletal look. Tattoos of serpents spiralled around his bony arms.

'Want me to clean you?' he asked me in English.

'What?'

He asked me again in Spanish. Prompted by his bag of incense and crystals, I understood that he was trying to sell me a purification ritual. 'I'm busy.'

But he persisted until I gave in. I tried to look composed as he chanted and waved incense around my body in front of a bunch of curious Japanese tourists. When it was over, I gave him 10 pesos and moved away quickly. But he chased after me.

'I see your energy and it is very weak.' He grabbed my shoulder and looked me directly in the eyes. 'Here is very strong energy area . . . Is dangerous for you.'

'Okay, thank you, yes – I'll take that into account.'

The closest safe policeman in the vicinity stood guarding the entrance of the archaeological site, Templo Mayor.

I had read about this place. It was a section of the ruins of the Aztec city Tenochtitlán, which had been uncovered about twenty years before when they were building the subway. The main temple is still buried beneath the cathedral but there is a segment of the site behind the cathedral which is excavated and open to the public. I wandered around the maze of ancient volcanic stone walls, past the bases of small pyramids with their staircases leading to a dead end. The shape of a serpent emerged out of the stone.

'This here is the feathered serpent god Quetzalcóatl, whom the Aztecs believed to be the creator of the universe and humanity.' The tour guide seemed to have appeared out of nowhere. He was leading a group of North American tourists in khaki shorts, laden with camera equipment as if they were a film crew. I moved quickly in the other direction, my mind churning over. I hated the idea of Octavio seeing me in the mornings. I'd have to sneak into the shower before he woke up, so I could be sprightly and fresh before meeting for coffee in the kitchen and discussing archaeology. As for sharing a bathroom, I could keep my pimple cream and any other unromantic products in my room. And what if there wasn't a lock on the bathroom door?

A series of potentially awkward moments flashed through my mind. Could I ever relax with this faultless being lurking around the living room? I tried to imagine what sort of girls he would like, visualising coming home after a hard day's work and being confronted by a bevy of Brazilian supermodels with PhDs in philosophy.

'Oh my gud – what's this?' One of the American tourists was pointing to a wall which appeared to be lined with human skulls.

'Yes, this here is a replica of the "*tzompantli*", a large rack used to display the skulls of the victims of human ritual sacrifice.'

'And, ah, how did they do it?'

'Well, the victims were stretched over a sacrificial stone,' the guide explained, 'and then, while they were still alive, they would rip out their hearts with sharpened obsidian stones.' The group went silent and listened attentively. 'The heart would continue to beat as they drained the blood through specially carved channels. And then they would decapitate them and chop off their arms and legs. Yes, some estimates affirm that the Aztecs sacrificed twenty thousand people per year,' the guide went on.

Apparently most of the sacrifices were made to appease Huitzilopochtli (pronounced 'wi-chee-lo-pot-st-ly'), the sun god and god of war, who depended on human blood to rise every morning. At birth he had murdered his older sister Coyolxauhqui (pronounced 'coy-ol-shouw-ky') and multitudes of his half brothers that had been planning to kill their mother, the earth goddess Coatlicue. Using a large turquoise serpent, he had chopped off Coyolxauhqui's head, as you do, and hurled it into the sky to create the moon. Then he'd flung her body over a hill, where it broke into many pieces.

The ritual sacrifices had been re-enactments of these events and necessary to ensure the continuation of the daily battle between the sun and the moon, the light and the dark.

§

The sun was strong at this time of the morning and I felt a bit shaky after my introduction to the Aztec religion. Perhaps the shaman drug addict was right; perhaps I did have 'weak energy' – all the more reason to move into a clean, safe apartment with a sane flatmate. As I left the Zócalo, I noticed a line of people stretching along Calle Madero leading to a canvas tent, which was set up opposite the Palacio Nacional. Most people in the line were wearing yellow raincoats. It wasn't until I walked past the newspaper stand that I realised what they were doing. They were voting. It was Election Day. Felipe Calderón and Andrés Manuel López Obrador, the two electoral candidates, stood side by side on the front cover of the serious newspapers.

But on the front page of the tabloids, politics was ignored in favour of photos of the latest exploits of the narcotics gangs. Five decapitated heads sat in separate blood-stained portable iceboxes, with duct tape around their eyes. So much for the Spanish putting an end to human sacrifice.

☙

Later on that night, Buck and I walked down the road to the nearest cantina to watch the election results unfold. Inside its swinging doors, the fluorescent-lit room was alive with tipsy laughter and joyful shouting. The political persuasion of the pub owners was made obvious by their choice of decorations. Tonight everything was yellow – yellow streamers, yellow balloons, yellow flags. And most of the customers were wearing yellow. Every so often a middle-aged couple would get up, find a salsa track on the jukebox and dance. Then they would sit down again wearing huge smiles.

But the main source of joy was coming from the large television in the corner of the room. Obrador had already won in several states. Of course Obrador was going to win – who was this Calderón guy anyway? I had barely seen his picture, yet Obrador's image was so widespread that his grandfatherly features had been embedded into my psyche. His face was on posters strung across every building and on banners carried down the streets by thousands of people. It was on leaflets and booklets which had been handed to me every day, and which explained how he would transform a country with one of the most unequal distributions of wealth in the world into a Latin American Sweden. His victory had been clearly predicted in nearly all the polls. It all fitted in nicely with this so-called 'Wave of Pink' in Latin America, the rise of social democratic governments across the continent. Octavio's political insights would be interesting as all this unfolded.

All I knew about Calderón was that he represented the right-wing Nationalist Action Party, which was currently in power and headed by 'the approachable cowboy', President Vicente Fox, ex-president of Coca-Cola, Mexico. Fox was now hugely unpopular and endlessly ridiculed by the media. His diplomatic blunders had become fodder for comedians – he once told Fidel Castro to 'eat and then leave', so as not to offend the visiting US President George W. Bush. This created a diplomatic crisis between

Mexico and Cuba, who until this point had enjoyed a solid friendship. There was no way Calderón could win this election.

It was almost midnight as we walked back in the rain along the crowded streets towards the Zócalo. As we stood on the edge of the massive crowd gathered there, we could see a giant video screen. Obrador was striding onto the stage in front of thousands of ecstatic supporters, who were chanting '¡Se ve, se siente, Andrés es Presidente!'. You can see it, you can feel it, Andrés is the President! He waited for his audience to calm down and then shouted, 'I come here to tell you that we have won the presidency of the republic.' The crowd went wild.

The following morning, I switched on the TV to find Felipe Calderón's beaming face. He seemed to be making a victory declaration. Then Obrador's face flashed on the screen, speaking rapidly, and I caught the words 'fraude electoral'. Out in the streets it was uncannily silent. I felt it would be a good time to leave the Centro Histórico, so I called Octavio and told him I was ready to move in.

≋

Octavio lugged my suitcase up the stairs, then demonstrated his perfect manners by leaving me alone to get acquainted with my new space. He gave me a set of about twenty keys and showed me where each of them went and how they worked. He was going to his grandmother's house for lunch and would be back later on that night.

When he left I felt relieved. In his car on the way over, I had managed to ask him about the elections and whether he thought there had been electoral fraud. He didn't think so – it was just Obrador's populist tactics, which were now going to polarise the country. But I was unable to concentrate on what he was telling me, having been too busy thinking about a clever response. Just as I had feared, this had resulted in a disproportionate amount of smiling and nodding. Life would become absurdly complicated if I was going to fall into a nervous panic at the sight of my flatmate.

Lying down on the sunlit wooden floor next to the giant maguey cactus, I looked around at my new home. The few pieces of furniture and ornaments were thought-fully placed – I wouldn't change a thing. The flat was immaculate. And then the realisation hit me, what sort of man reaches such heights in interior decoration, keeps his apartment spotless, is worried about feng shui, is carelessly well-groomed and styled . . . Of course! Octavio must be gay. He was utterly out of my reach. I could relax – we could be friends.

Breathing a sigh of relief tinged with regret, I wandered into my room. It was empty except for a bare mattress in the corner. I didn't have sheets or blankets – maybe I could borrow some from Octavio when he got back. I discovered that there was a built-in wardrobe. No coat hangers, so unpacking my clothes would have to wait. I stacked my books against the wall and squashed my suitcase into the cupboard.

Taking advantage of my solitude, I had a long indulgent shower. The cleanliness of the bathroom lifted my spirits; it was the first time in months I didn't feel the need to wear thongs in the shower. But the musky scent of Octavio's deodorant reminded me that I was standing in the shower of an attractive man whom I hardly knew.

I looked around for his shampoo, as I had left my own at the hotel. But I thought twice when I saw it. It was in a small and expensive-looking silver bottle. This supported my supposition, I thought happily. And then I couldn't resist seeing what other products he had in his bathroom cabinet.

I didn't find anything really dramatic. But looking at myself in a mirror illuminated by natural light was not an uplifting experience.

❦

As I locked the door of my first Mexican apartment, I no longer felt like a tourist. Now I was on the inside – living with a real Mexican in a Mexican neighbourhood, one that neither drunken backpackers nor the middle-aged matching-tracksuits brigade would know anything about.

Slowly I wandered down the road, through the plaza with the dancing fountain. Maybe I could find a supermarket.

But then cooking was out of the question – no stove, no fridge. The only contents of Octavio's kitchen were a big Pink Floyd poster and a barely functioning sink. I wondered what he ate?

This thought was interrupted by the smell of frying meat and tortillas. I looked up from my feet to discover that the next three blocks had transformed themselves into a vast restaurant. The footpath had been invaded by a multitude of frenzied cooks, frying, stirring and shouting at passersby, '*¡Güera! ¡Güera! ¡Tacos de bistek, suadero, longaniza, lengua, pastor!* What would you like?'

I tried to ignore the taco man. His stall was particularly gory to someone accustomed to western-style butchers. Various unsavoury animal parts – such as snouts and digestive oddments – were being thrown into a bubbling pool of pig fat. Well at least you had some idea of what animal you were eating. Panchito had told me that some taco stalls cut corners by using the meat of stray dogs. 'You know you're eating dog when the price of the tacos is less than the meat,' he had warned. And this was more than just an urban myth; Buck had confirmed that various taco stalls had been outed in the newspapers as serving dog meat.

After it was fried, the meat was then squashed into tortillas. A line of hungry men from the construction site across the road stood waiting, playfully brawling. The taco man said something to me which I didn't understand, and they all started laughing.

'I don't understand,' I told him. 'Can you repeat that?'

And then he repeated it very slowly. 'Free for white girls. What shall I get you?'

'Thank you, but I'm okay. Maybe next time . . .' hoping I would never have to take him up on that offer.

The next stall was occupied by a group of rotund middle-aged women wearing ruffled aprons over generous breasts. They were stirring industrial-sized pots exuding extraordinary spicy aromas. This was *comida corrida*, the Mexican equivalent of fast food, where they serve you one already-prepared dish with soup, bread, salad or rice, followed by dessert – all for about three bucks. It was a wiser choice than tacos, but it was just too big. At my previous *comida corrida* experience, I hadn't been able to finish the main meal and the cook had been crestfallen. 'What's wrong? Don't you like it?'

'Yes, but it's just very big . . .' I tried to explain as she angrily took away my plate. I wasn't going to repeat that experience.

Next was a torta stall. Unlike the Spanish torta, this is not an omelette but a sandwich. It's a grilled bread roll filled with meat, chilli, re-fried beans, cheese and avocado. I sat down at the counter and asked the young man with the pointy white chef's hat for a torta with chicken breast. 'So, you like Mexican tortas, *güera*?' He smiled at me; and then turned and grinned at his colleague with the big teeth, who was already throwing the chicken onto the grill.

'Yes, I like them a lot,' I replied. They looked at each other and grinned. I always seemed to have problems buying tortas. The last time I'd tried to buy a torta, I had confused the words *abogado* and *aguacate* and had asked the man if he could please put some extra lawyers on my sandwich. He had stared at me strangely, until I pointed to the avocado. He looked at the avocado and then at me, dissolving into convulsions of laughter. What could I possibly have said this time?

'Have you tried tortas with sausage and egg?' the big-teethed guy asked, still smiling.

'No, I don't really like sausage and egg,' I said to him.

'Oh, but have you tried them?' he persisted.

'Well . . . no.' His face began to go a pinkish colour.

'Because, *güera*,' he confided, handing me the torta, 'here, we have some very good sausages!'

'Okay, well maybe I'll try one tomorrow,' I replied.

'Okay,' he told me, 'I'll be waiting for you tomorrow.' What exactly had I missed, as I headed toward the park with my torta. It was as if the whole purpose of my being here was to provide entertainment to the locals.

To think of all that time at university – memorising the irregular verb tables, studying the differences between the indicative and subjunctive – and I still had serious problems when it came to buying a sandwich.

Spanish had never been my best subject. In fact I had dropped it in my second year, when I realised it was dragging down my average and that no matter how many hours I put in, or how many Latino-looking men I tried to befriend, I never managed to shine. I had got to know the Colombian nut seller at Glebe markets and a whole Ecuadorian cleaning team at Broadway Shopping Centre. I had even dated a gorgeous but dangerously disturbed Chilean student – but in the end I had always been too nervous to speak to them in Spanish.

꠹

Later that night, while I was searching for an outfit clean enough to wear on my first day at work, Octavio swung through the door. I stayed in my room, to give him his 'coming home' space. But he walked straight in. 'Hey, I need a drink,' he said, looking tired. 'Do you want to come?'

I did. But first I had to solve my immediate garment problem. 'Do you have an iron, Octavio?' He looked puzzled.

'My clothes are ironed at my mother's house.'

'Oh. Don't worry then.'

We walked across the road to the *mezcalaria* and took a seat outside on the pavement.

'So what sort of family lunch requires a hard drink to recover from?' was my first question.

'Well, you know, all the usual. My hair's too long; I'm almost thirty; I should be married by now; what am I doing in the music industry . . . Sometimes I wonder why I even came back to Mexico.'

It hadn't occurred to me that this quirky musician-type came from such a conservative family. He went on to tell me about the problems he had with his father, who was devastated that he had not become a diplomat. I wondered if his sexual orientation was also an issue.

'Anyway, what's your family like?'

I explained that I came from a rather non-conservative family: my parents worked in the media and my father had achieved some notoriety as the editor of an infamous underground magazine in London. He still enjoyed the occasional controversial media appearance damning consumerism and American foreign policy. Myself and my younger sister Angelica had grown up in a house on a hilltop in the Blue Mountains outside Sydney where kangaroos hopped in the garden.

Our conversation moved on from families to food. I told him about my street stall experience.

'What? You mean you ate from one of those stalls on the street?' He was genuinely stunned. 'Do you know how dangerous that is? The meat is left out all day in the sun . . . It's crawling with salmonella and sewage. Really, no one actually eats on the street . . .'

'And all those people I saw today, queuing up on the street?'

'No, ah – how can I say this? . . . Educated people do not eat on the street.'

'Well, where do you eat?'

That perplexed look again, 'Me? Oh, at my mother's house. Her cook is really good.'

Then he looked slightly embarrassed, and there was an uncomfortable silence.

I remembered what I had wanted to ask him. 'Hey, the guys from the torta stall were laughing at me today and I don't understand why.'

'Well, what did you say?'

'Nothing. Just that I liked Mexican tortas . . .'

But before I had finished the sentence, he had choked on his shot of mezcal and was trying to control his laughter.

'What?' I demanded.

Then Octavio taught me a vital aspect of the Mexican sense of humour, which would aid me enormously in my quest to understand and communicate with Mexican people. This is known as the *albur* or 'double meaning'. The idea is to linguistically trick the unsuspecting victim into agreeing to have sex. Many everyday objects turned out to have double meaning: sausage, eggs and chicken breast . . . Well those ones are obvious, but some are less apparent. For example *torta* is a pseudonym for 'bottom'.

Now, my earlier conversation made perfect sense. I had told the taco men that I loved Mexican bottoms, and that I was a lesbian (I didn't like 'sausage and eggs'). But I would come back tomorrow and try out heterosexual sex.

❦ 3 ❦

The First Wives' Breakfast Club

July is summer in Mexico. But at 5.30 am as I leave my apartment, the three thin jumpers I was wearing in place of a coat were not enough. Pitch black outside. It could have been the middle of the night if it wasn't for all the cars on the road and the dark figures rushing around on the footpath. They were streetsweepers and traders setting up little stalls. Walking alone in the dark I felt edgy. But then who would have the dynamism to set up a kidnapping so early in the morning? I began to worry more about the day ahead of me. This would be my first teaching job and I didn't know what to expect. Over the past few weeks I had been attending some afternoon training sessions at the company headquarters in Zona Rosa, an area within walking distance from my flat. Although I had gained an in-depth knowledge of the keys to the worldwide success of the franchise, I was still vague about the work I was about to embark on.

By 6 am Insurgentes station was swarming with zombies in suits. I checked the subway map. To get to Polanco I would need to change from the pink line to the orange line at Tacubaya station.

Coming out from the Polanco metro station, I watched a tiny old woman wrapped up in blankets sitting on a stool near the exit. '¡Tamales calientitos!' she called. From a steaming metal pot she distributed little bundles wrapped in corn husks. The tamale, made with steamed corn dough, is the pre-Colombian equivalent of the sandwich; they are portable and you can put anything inside them. Once taken by Aztec and Mayan warriors into battle, they now serve as a quick breakfast solution for time-pressed office workers.

The metro shoeshiner had also just arrived. He was setting up the red umbrella above the shoeshine seat. I asked him if he knew where Calle Horacio was. He pointed straight ahead and muttered something I didn't understand. It didn't matter. I was half an hour early and I knew from looking at the map in the metro station that it was around here somewhere.

I turned left at a corner into Calle Homero. This area was much cleaner than my neighbourhood of La Roma. There was no rubbish on the street, no street stalls. It could have been any upmarket district in the world, except for the uniformed security guards standing to attention outside the three-storey gates. The next cross street was Calle Horacio. As I turned onto this street the elaborate houses became office blocks and department stores.

I found the number 354. The door was open underneath the big red 'Fifth Avenue English School' sign. As I entered the building I wondered if I was walking into a bank or an English school. The interior decor was based on corporate aesthetics: synthetic blue carpets and hard-edged furniture. The message this seemed to project was that learning English will give you the opportunity to work in a bank.

'*Buenos días,*' I offered, interrupting the receptionist, who was peering into a hand mirror, applying lilac-coloured eye shadow.

'Ah, jes, jou are the new teacher,' she smiled at me, pointing behind her to the jumbo-sized week planner on the wall. 'Jour first class today is a Social Club.'

As I had learnt in my training sessions, a 'social club' is simply a matter of making the students speak with each other in English.

'Jou already have two students waiting,' she said as she led me down the hall and showed me into a small room with dark purple and lime-green walls.

Two heavily made-up women were sitting on the yellow couches. I felt intimidated by their stiletto shoes and power suits until they jumped up to hug and kiss me on the cheek: 'Finally we have a teacher – we are very happy that jou are here.'

'Nice to meet jou.'

We sat down and introduced ourselves. Their names were Elvira and Marisol. Another woman arrived, Verónica, who wore her hair in a bob. A much older woman crept in and sat down. Her name was Concepción, and she was followed by Reina and Silvia. The smell of chemically floral lipstick, cosmetics, perfume, deodorant and hairspray was overpowering. Most seemed to be in their forties, although Concepción could have been sixty and Reina must have been in her early thirties.

'Where are all the men?' I asked the students.

They exchanged knowing looks and then Reina explained: 'Jou see, de men here in Mehico are very lazy. They don't like to get up so early in de morning.' They all laughed.

'I'm Lucy and I'm from Australia.' They smiled at me vacantly. I gave my usual spiel, 'You know: kangaroo, Russell Crowe, crocodile hunter, Kylie Minogue . . .'

'Ah jes,' Elvira finally replied. 'I saw on Discovery channel about the snakes and the spiders – most dangerous in the world. I never go there.'

The other students nodded in agreement. I explained that deaths related to the wildlife were actually quite rare. They remained doubtful.

Most of my students had administrative jobs in big corporations. Silvia was an accountant; Marisol was a computer engineer for Carlos Slim's telecommunications company, Telmex; Elvira was in marketing and Concepción was a personal assistant.

Although they worked in nearby office blocks, not one of them actually lived in Mexico City. They commuted from 'Estado de Mexico', the state that surrounds Mexico City but is technically a separate state with a separate government. It was just too expensive to live in the city, they explained. To avoid the traffic they left for work at four in the morning – arriving at 6 am. This would give them time to either get their hair done (some hairdressers in Mexico are open at 6 am), go to English class or sleep in their cars until work started at nine. The days of the Mexican long lunch followed by a siesta had ended in the 1980s with globalisation.

Why were they learning English? For most it was vital for their job – either to communicate with international clients or to communicate with the owners of their company, who were more often than not *gringos*. But Elvira said she was learning English because she hoped to go and live in the United States.

Veronica snapped, 'Why you want to go there? Don't you know they are all racists . . .'

Marisol agreed, 'Yes . . . Better to go to Canada . . . they are not so crazy like the gringos.'

Elvira defended herself, 'But the gringos are not all racists – my uncles and their children live there, and they are very happy. They have a big house – two levels.'

'Just because jour uncles have a nice house, that doesn't mean de gringos are not racists,' snorted Marisol.

Elvira replied in Spanish and before I knew it they were all shouting at each other in Spanish across the room. I had to change the subject. 'So ah . . . does anyone here have a pet?'

They stopped shouting at each other in Spanish and turned their attention to me. Verónica was the first to answer. 'Well, I had a dog – a beautiful schnauzer miniature. But my husband sell it.'

'Oooh,' we all said sympathetically. 'Why did he do that?'

'Why? Well, you know . . .' Then she turned to me and asked, 'How you say *pendejo* in English?'

I recognised this word. The taxi drivers used it when someone cut in front of them. 'Well there's a number of ways we can say that: arsehole, dickhead, moron, idiot, bastard . . .'

'Jes, my husband is *all* of these things.'

'Jes, my husband too,' Reina called out. 'But he won't be my husband any more. In two weeks we have the divorce!'

'Well I had the divorce five years ago and it was the best decision of all my life,' said Marisol.

'Jes, me too,' said Silvia. 'I had my divorce last year, and I feel free for the first time in all my life.'

At least they had stopped shouting at each other. I tried again, 'So who does have a pet? Reina – do you have a pet?'

'Jes, I have two cats and a dog – but my husband already took the dog . . . because he is – how do you say? ARSEHOLE. Sorry! Ah jes, and the cats will stay with me.'

'Yes,' agreed Elvira. 'My ex-husband was so greedy – he took everything, even the car . . . The only thing he leave me was the childrens.'

The floodgates had opened and there was no going back. It turned out that all of the women in the room were either divorced or hated their husbands. So I sat and listened. Verónica talked about her ex-husband's rampant womanising; Silvia told us how her husband had spent the money saved for their children's education on prostitutes; Marisol described how her ex-husband would arrive home drunk every night and fall asleep on the bathroom floor; and Elvira recalled her ex-husband's violent abuse. And now Reina had just discovered that her husband was the father of not one, but two, of his 23-year-old secretary's children.

However, there was one offence far more infuriating than all of the above. This was the refusal of their husbands to help around the house. Reina was an accountant for a large company and worked twelve hours a day in an office two hours away from her house. Yet her husband expected her to miraculously have dinner on the table when he got home from work, to maintain a spotless household and to rear their four children single-handedly.

'So I get home from work – so tired, jou know, after being in de traffic for three hours – and de childrens are crying and Paco is lying on de sofa watching de soccer. He hears dat I arrive and he tells me, "Hey, what are jou doing? Why jou are taking so long with de dinner?"'

At this, the whole class moaned in recognition. 'Jes, me too!', 'Same for me!' they shouted. Marisol said the problem came down to a difference in expectations – while the women envisioned a mutually supportive partnership, their husbands regarded marriage as little more than the acquisition of an unpaid servant.

This was the unfortunate generation – the one in which it became acceptable and necessary for women to get jobs, and yet it had not become socially acceptable for men to do the washing up.

Two hours later, when the class was over, the room was flooded with a sense of relief. As the students said goodbye and rushed off to work, they seemed cheerful and more relaxed. They agreed to come back next Monday, and Marisol offered to bring breakfast. The First Wives' Breakfast Club had begun.

I, on the other hand, needed a stiff drink. I felt as if I'd been married to a lazy womanising misogynist for twenty years.

⚜

Coming out from the metro and walking back along Calle Orizaba, I found myself once again surrounded by irresistible aromas. Weighing up what Octavio had said about food on the street, I suspected his objection derived from snobbery rather than experience. Anyway, Mexican bacteria would strengthen my immune system.

Before long I heard my name, '*¡Güera!*' and turned around to find my torta friends grinning at me from behind the counter. 'Shall I prepare you a torta with sausage and eggs?'

I had been planning to go back to these guys and to tell them something like, 'Sorry, but I don't like cocktail sausages'. But, on coming face to face, I could feel my cheeks turning pink. '*No, gracias*,' I mumbled, and walked quickly past them, bracing myself for the inevitable burst of giggles. No tortas today then.

This time I was hungry enough to face the *comida corrida* women. I stopped to investigate the contents of their steaming clay pots. The rotund women were shouting out what was on offer, '*¡Mole verde! ¡Mole poblano! ¡Chile relleno! ¡Tacos dorados!* What shall we serve you?' *Mole* is like a Mexican interpretation of curry made with spices, chillies and peanuts.

I sat down on the stool. '*¿Que le damos, güerita?*' they asked me and I ordered *mole poblano*. This is a sweet type of *mole* made with cocoa.

Within seconds a bowl of soup and a container of hot tortillas were plonked in front of me. But they had forgotten to give me a spoon. Damn. How do you say *spoon*? How could I forget the word for something so ordinary? I noticed the man next to me was eating his soup with a rolled-up tortilla, so I attempted to do the same, but my tortilla broke in half and fell into the soup.

'*Perdón*,' I said, bracing myself for a miming act. But then it came to me – *cuchara*.

'¿*Me das un cuchara?*' I asked, feeling proud of myself for remembering – after all that's quite a difficult word for such a simple tool.

But she squinted her eyes and inquired '¿*Qué?*'

My heart sank. I repeated my request. '*Aaah . . . una cuchara*,' she said slowly, which is what I thought I had said. She turned and winked at her grey-haired companion, who put her hand over her mouth and began to giggle. Could the word *spoon* have a double meaning? I wondered.

Then she handed me a spoon. 'Here you are – *UN cuchara*,' she chuckled, emphasising the article, *un*. Okay, I got it – I'd put a male article in front of a female noun. A spoon is quite obviously a woman – how could you possibly think otherwise?

It didn't seem fair. All morning I'd been listening to my students as they stumbled along with their new words. They had made plenty of mistakes which I found hilarious, yet I'd managed to hide my amusement.

A few minutes later, the larger of the two women took away my empty soup bowl and replaced it with a plate of rice and black beans. 'Did–you–like–the–soup?' she asked me, pausing after each syllable as if I were brain-damaged. Yes I did, thank you.

She smiled at me and went back to stirring the giant pots and shouting at the passersby. But she continued to glance at me as she chattered to her companion. And, over the sound of the clanking plates and the gossiping customers, the words '*la gringa* . . . too skinny . . . and so white . . . alone . . . very strange' floated in my direction.

My presence at their stall seemed to be quite an anomaly to these women. It probably wasn't often that a funny-looking person with white skin, who couldn't talk properly, came to their stall and ordered *mole poblano*. How could I blame them for getting the best out of it? '*Gracias, güerita,*' she responded when I paid her for the meal.

Walking home along Calle Orizaba, I was struck by an overpowering sense of my own isolation. When I first arrived in Mexico I had revelled in my solitude, the fact that nobody around me knew who I was or anything about me. I had found it liberating and exciting – it was a chance for self-reinvention. For the first time in my life I had felt completely independent and in control. But this adrenalin-induced confidence seemed to have worn off, and I was feeling for the first time since my arrival here an awareness of my true vulnerability.

Despite chatting to people all day, I felt lonely. I longed for someone to complain to; someone who would listen to me whine – about being constantly referred to as 'white girl', about my frustration at never being completely sure what was going on or what people were saying to me, and about the uncannily slow pace at which I seemed to be learning Spanish. I wandered into the boutique dress shop across the road. This would give me time to calm down before going home – just in case Octavio happened to be there. I walked over to the shoe section because I did need to buy shoes. The sales assistant was wearing a short black mini-skirt and a glittery pink t-shirt. Her legs caught my attention and I realised I hadn't seen women's legs since I had arrived. Women in Mexico City were always fully covered. Come to think of it, all of the skirts and dresses I had brought with me were still scrunched up in a dark corner of my bag. Here it felt more appropriate to dress down – very down.

As the assistant approached me, I felt a surge of adrenalin – I was about to practise my Spanish. Would I say something weird, and create an awkward silence? Or would it be one of those rare occasions where I managed to get across a comprehensible message? But my hopeful '*¡Hola!*' was only met by, 'Hi! You speak in English, right?' She spoke in an American teen-movie accent. Well yes, I admitted. She continued, 'Because I need to practise my English . . . You know, I have this exam next week for go to the university. So anyway can I help you? Would you like to buy some shoes?'

I was beginning to notice two dominant Mexican reactions to foreigners trying to speak Spanish – they either find it hilarious, or insist that you speak to them in English. But of course, as I had learnt the other night at the exhibition opening, if they already know English, don't speak to them in English. Because that is cultural imperialism.

Returning to the empty apartment, I took stock of my situation. The afternoon sunlight shone through the living-room window.

Sitting down on a fruit box beside the cactus, I did the sums. The reality hit me that my job at Fifth Avenue would not be enough to make ends meet. I would be earning 6000 pesos (about 500 dollars a month), which would be just enough to cover my rent. I had noticed another language school near the Insurgentes metro station and decided that I would walk in and try my luck.

When I did, the balding man behind the reception desk looked surprised to see me. 'Hi!' he greeted me enthusiastically. 'You are wanting classes of Spanish?'

I began to explain that I was actually looking for a job. But before I had reached into my bag for my CV, he stood up and shook my hand. 'Yes, very good,' he said. 'Welcome to Easy Lingua College. My name is Manuel, I am the director. You can start tomorrow at three o'clock.'

He gave me a tour of the school: two grim-looking classrooms, no textbooks, no materials. I would have to invent the entire syllabus. But it would just be one two-hour class a few afternoons per week – an extra 400 pesos for food and transport.

He introduced me to the Spanish teacher, who was sitting at the desk at the front of one of the classrooms writing notes. He had long wavy hair that fell over his ears, and dark yellow skin. Manuel spoke to him in English.

'This is Lucy. She is the new teacher of English. This is Edgar, he is the teacher of Spanish.'

Edgar looked up at me through round Trotsky-type spectacles. 'Nice – to – meet – you,' he muttered. 'Ah, do you speak any Spanish? Because my English is terrible.' I explained that my Spanish was far worse than his English, and we exchanged looks of deep understanding. Then Manuel pulled me away to finish the tour. He told me he would appreciate it if I would speak only in English while I was at the school, so that he and the staff could improve their English.

As I walked out the door, I heard someone calling my name. It was the Spanish teacher, Edgar. He asked me if I wanted to practise my Spanish. This was a novel suggestion. 'Yes,' I agreed.

Needless to say, Edgar was also desperate to practise his English. He suggested that we have an *intercambio*, a language exchange in which we would get together and speak for one hour in English and one hour in Spanish.

꧁

A few days later, Edgar and I met up after class and walked down the road to a café. We found a seat in a courtyard that was barely big enough for one table.

I had walked past this building frequently, but had never ventured inside. Like many of the old buildings in Colonia Roma, parts of the stone had crumbled away and one side of it appeared to be sinking into the earth. La Roma had been one of the areas most affected by the earthquake of 1985. There has never been an official death toll, but some estimate that over 40 000 citizens were lost.

Even now large parts of the city haven't been rebuilt. Many people are still homeless after more than two decades. Much infrastructure still hasn't been repaired. Before the earthquake, the tap water was safe to drink; now everyone has to buy expensive bottled water.

Edgar, who was four years old in 1985, had then lived in the south of the city, which was not affected by the earthquake. However, his family soon realised the severity of the situation when they saw their favourite TV host, Felix Sordo, crushed to death while reading the morning news after an enormous metal antenna fell on the studio. And Octavio, over our first drink, had earlier told me of his memories – of piles of bodies lined up on a baseball field, covered with blocks of ice to form a makeshift morgue.

So La Roma must evoke memories for the locals; in fact I had heard that many of the survivors never returned. From the stone courtyard where we sat, French windows revealed a warren of rooms lined with the dust-covered shelves of archaic books. Chandeliers with candles hung from the ceiling and added to the atmosphere of magical realism which pervades the fiction of Latin America.

The walls of the courtyard were covered with flowering vines; a scruffy green parrot perched above us in a bamboo cage. I was relieved to see Edgar finally putting down his red backpack full of books. It had been tightly strapped to his upper back all the way from Easy Lingua College. As we sat down, a curly-haired waiter arrived with a large thermos of black coffee and two shots of rum.

Today Edgar was wearing faded denim jeans that came up to his waist and a flannelette shirt which was neatly tucked into his jeans. We argued for about twenty minutes about whether we should start with English hour or Spanish hour. Eventually I gave up and we began in Spanish.

I started off nervously, stuttering along and hyperventilating each time I couldn't remember a word. In these moments it was tempting to revert to English; but each time I did this, Edgar would block his ears until I switched back to Spanish. And, after a while, I found Edgar to be so intriguing that I managed to forget that I was communicating in a foreign language. He spoke so softly that you needed to stop breathing in order to hear him. And there was something about the yellowness of his skin, his almond-shaped eyes and the slowness of his movements that made me feel like I was sitting in front of an elderly Chinese sage.

Edgar was in the final stages of writing his thesis on the 'applied pedagogics of teaching Latin'. Now he was hoping to do a Masters degree in Asian studies at El Colegio de México, an elite university which had been established by Spanish intellectuals who had fled to Mexico to escape Franco.

But, in order to get a scholarship, he would have to prove he was fluent in English, which he wasn't. In fact he despised English. It had been forced on him his whole life and he had rebelled, finding solace in ancient languages such as Latin, Sanskrit and Aramaic. He was also reasonably fluent in Hindi. But now the prophecies of his parents and teachers were coming true: in order to pursue his true passions he would have to bite the bullet and learn English.

Edgar's father came from a poor indigenous village and at a young age was sent to work as a gardener for a family of German engineers who lived in Mexico City. They put him through school and supported him through his degree in dentistry. Understandably Edgar's parents lacked any comprehension of their son's passion for the dead languages from faraway countries and were still trying in vain to convince him to go back and finish his initial degree in accounting.

When we switched to English, Edgar was possessed by a sudden shyness. To get him talking again, I dived head-first into the strange political situation. What was going on? How could there be two presidents? Who was corrupt?

But Edgar advised me that if I wanted to understand what was going on politically, I would have to read some books about Mexican political history and we would discuss it next time. It wasn't until the waiter began to light the candles on our table that we realised we had been there for far longer than two hours. We gave each other written assignments. His was to write about his family and mine was to write a summary of the Mexican news.

Edgar walked with me back to the flat and waited as I scavenged around in my bag for the keys. We said goodbye and agreed to meet up each week at the same place for our language exchange. As I closed the door behind me I couldn't help smiling to myself. I had found a possible compromise for my predicament: I had come to Mexico with the intention of learning Spanish, yet my survival here depended on speaking English a large proportion of the time. Someone in the world existed to whom I could speak Spanish without having a nervous breakdown. This of course was only possible because he had the same neurosis as me, but it was a definite step in the right direction.

❧

For the rest of the week I didn't set eyes on Octavio. He was asleep when I left for work in the mornings and I would hear him arrive home late at night as I drifted to sleep.

In the meantime, I made an effort to be the perfect flatmate and repress my chaotic nature. Aiming to keep signs of my existence to a minimum, after every shower I would remove each of my hairs from the drain and then quickly mop the floor. I kept all my possessions, except for my toothbrush and toothpaste, in the cupboard in my bedroom and made my bed, which was actually just a mattress, every morning. Rarely would I use the kitchen – only for the occasional glass of water – in which case I would immediately wash and dry the glass and put it back in the cupboard.

Now it was Saturday morning, and I hadn't heard anyone leave the house. I put my ear to my door – silence. No kitchen noises. Opening my door slightly, I could see from where I stood that Octavio's door was ajar. But then again I couldn't remember hearing him come home last night. Just in case, I threw on some clothes and grabbed my toiletries bag, which still contained a few pieces of useable make-up. Under no circumstances could I allow myself to be seen before a shower. This decree stemmed from a deep-seated need to hide my earthly imperfections from my god-like flatmate.

It was only five steps down the hall to the bathroom – the chances of being sighted were slim.

I made a run for it. I looked around before turning the handle of the bathroom door. To my horror, it was locked. He'd made it to the bathroom before me! I should have got up earlier.

Running back to my room I thought about the consequences of all this. Now it would depend on whether he had brought his clothes with him to the bathroom, or whether he would leave the bathroom in a towel and get dressed in his room. The second option seemed the most probable. In that case, there was still hope of me getting to the bathroom without being seen. It was all a matter of timing. I would have to make a dash to the bathroom at the exact moment that he was getting dressed in his room.

Staying by the door, I waited. There was the sound of the door opening. Footsteps. And then silence. Slowly I turned the handle of my door so that it didn't make a noise and opened it slightly. The coast was clear – he must be safely in his room by now. Taking a deep breath, I made a run for it.

But just as my hand reached for the handle of the bathroom door, I heard 'Hey, Lucy!' I turned around to find that he was standing in the kitchen with a white towel wrapped tightly around his waist. 'I thought you had run away,' he said with a smile. Droplets of water fell down from his dark wet hair onto his golden chest and glistened in the sun.

'Ha, ha, ha . . . No . . . Well, I'm still here.' I cringed.

But then he asked, 'Shall we go for a coffee? I mean, if you're not busy?'

❦ 4 ❦

Almost a Revolution

I stared down at the white tablecloth and the rows of shining cutlery. Octavio and I sat next to each other on black leather sofas which looked out through the glass walls over a garden of neatly cut hedges and large trees. Smaller citrus trees in round terracotta pots were positioned at regular intervals throughout the restaurant and on each of the tables was a glass vase of arum lilies, the flower that Diego Rivera made into a Mexican icon.

A flock of waiters hovered around us in crisply ironed white shirts and stiff black bow ties. Why were there so many of them if there were only two of us in the restaurant? Now, it was my turn to order. I had decided on the *chilaquiles* – a typical Mexican breakfast of fried tortillas in chilli and tomato salsa and served with sour cream and cheese.

I only had to say two words – *chilaquiles verdes*. I ordered food every day; it shouldn't be a big deal. But Octavio's presence was increasing my usual level of Spanish-speaking stress.

Here goes. '*Unos chilaquiles por favor,*' I said, aiming to sound as natural as possible.

But the waiter turned to Octavio and, with that expression of utter confusion so familiar to me, he asked, 'What did she say?'

I restrained myself from throwing one of the puffy bread rolls from the basket in front of me directly at the waiter's head. But the moment he left, I turned to Octavio. 'Why didn't he understand me?' I had to ask, hoping that mortification wasn't evident in my tone.

'Because you didn't say it loudly enough.'

'Oh.'

We were in the restaurant attached to the Casa Lamm, an eminent cultural centre and art school just down the road from our apartment. The place was stunning. But despite the soothing sound of the small jets of water flowing over the stream of pebbles that surrounded the building, I knew I would feel more comfortable sitting on a plastic crate and eating a torta.

Then, as if having read my mind, Octavio turned to me and asked, 'So, are you still eating on the street?'

'Yep, every day.'

Now I had the perfect street-food-routine going. In the mornings a tamale from the old woman outside Polanco metro station. After work a sandwich and a plastic cup of fresh fruit from the old man who set up his own kitchen each day in the back of his van. Later on I would find something to eat in one of the hundreds of stalls along the streets of La Roma.

Octavio shook his head with an amused smile. So I explained that eating on the street was a novelty for me. In Australia everything was so controlled – so regimented that even busking in the street required a licence. Here in Mexico, the streets were multi-functional. They served as so much more than just channels to get you from one place to another. They were places to eat, to cook, to sell, to shop, to get together, to perform. But Octavio interrupted me and, in a tone that was designed to highlight my naive idealism, he explained that commercial activity in public spaces was illegal here also and that street vendors were a form of organised crime – they only existed by paying bribes to the police. This had the effect of putting legal vendors out of business, as they could not compete with their non-taxed rivals, who got free electricity and paid no rent.

'But what other choices are there in a country with no social security for the unemployed?' I asked. 'Surely selling sandwiches is a more ethical choice than drug trafficking or kidnapping?'

'Well, there would be more legal employment opportunities available if people like you didn't exploit the informal economy.'

'Well, at least I don't eat at my mother's house every day,' was all I could say to that. To which he began to defend himself with, 'It's just more convenient for me; you know I work such long hours . . .' But his obvious embarrassment was satisfying.

We decided to buy some groceries for the house since Octavio's mother had given us a fridge. After paying the bill, which (thank goodness) went directly to Octavio, we drove over to the local market. Neither of us could face going to a Mega-Mart on a Saturday morning.

Nearly every colonia has a local market known as *tianguis*. The word comes from Náhuatl, the language spoken by the Aztecs. They sell everything – mainly groceries; but also things like plants, flowers, piñatas and fancy-dress costumes. We began with the fruit and vegetable section, trying to maintain a conversation while being shouted at by the stall owners, '*Güero* – mangos, tomatoes, avocados! Best price!'

It comforted me to see that Octavio was also referred to as 'white guy'. He was physically different from most people in the marketplace – his skin was lighter and he towered above streams of other market-goers, making him impossible to lose. At one point, I caught him arguing with a fruit man. 'He thought I was a gringo, so he tried to charge me more,' he said.

We walked quickly through the meat section. Carcasses hung from the roof above puddles of blood and fur on the white tiled floor. Men with big knives and big smiles stood ready to extract the desired body part. We entered the homewares section. Octavio pointed out a mat woven from palm leaves, and suggested we buy it for our living room. I agreed. And then he said something interesting.

'You know, me and my ex-girlfriend could never agree on what to buy for the house.' It hit me like a brick. Octavio wasn't gay. For some reason I had already begun to suspect that this was the case, but now it was official.

'Yeah, we had such different tastes,' he continued.

Octavio and I don't have that problem, I thought smugly. Then I reminded myself that even though Octavio was attracted to women, and we were doing the shopping together for our flat, we were not actually in a relationship.

I listened as Octavio talked about the messy break-up he'd had with his Canadian girlfriend when he had decided to come to live in Mexico. He still thought about her but, despite his mother's desperate attempts to set him up with distant cousins, he hadn't had any luck with women since his return. However, his current potential love interest was a voluptuous French cellist, who had been recording some tracks with his band, and he was planning to ask her out to dinner. The words 'voluptuous French cellist' were enough to confirm to me that he was in a different league altogether and I vowed never to think about him in any sort of romantic context again. Such thoughts could lead to the breakdown of our harmonious flatmate relationship, and could result in not only heartbreak but homelessness.

Then we got to the witchcraft stalls, which sold things like spells and potions in bottles, clay figurines of various saints, baby Jesus, and buckets of dried chicken feet and rabbit paws. I noticed that one of the little bottles had a label on it which read 'love spell'.

'Hey, Octavio,' I whispered, 'this could help with your date next week.'

'Are you suggesting that my charms alone are not sufficient?' he replied.

'Well, it has been six months,' I said. At which he picked up a large watermelon and threatened to use it as a weapon of attack.

As we left the market, Octavio admitted that after years of living in cold, well-organised countries such as Canada and Switzerland, he could see what I meant about the anarchic charm of shopping in Mexico. Octavio, like me, I realised, was in the process of discovering this country. He hadn't lived here since he was a child and seemed to be making an effort to re-connect with his roots, which was very much reflected in our shopping. As well as buying groceries, such as typical Mexican cheeses, tortillas and avocados, we had purchased the traditional palm leaf mat and a bunch of arum lilies.

After unpacking the shopping, Octavio had to leave for a family lunch at his grandmother's weekend country house, which was a few hours south of the city. He would be gone for the weekend. He had invited me earlier that day. 'Come on. They all speak English and there's a big swimming pool – it's really beautiful up there.' He was probably just being nice, because he assumed I didn't have anything to do. Thanking him for the invitation, I told him I had some other plans.

But as soon as he left, it dawned on me that I had absolutely nothing to do or anyone to do it with for that matter. Buck had gone on one of his Vipassana retreats and Edgar . . . well, he was still just my language exchange friend. Sitting down on our new handwoven mat, I stared out the window for a few moments, before deciding to go down the road to the public phone and call my parents. But just as I left the building, it began to pour – I ran back up the stairs and watched the rain from the window.

It had been raining every day lately, starting in the late afternoon. It generally only lasted a few hours. Today it seemed heavier than usual. I watched the gutter fill up with water that flowed rapidly down the street. The afternoon light disappeared and I sat back and listened as the rain beat down harder and harder against the glass windows. Then the thunder rumbled – and suddenly there was complete darkness. No electricity. Looking out the window, I realised it wasn't just in my flat; the whole street was out.

Fumbling around in the kitchen for some matches, I lit the candles on the mantelpiece. Lightning flashed outside and the floor vibrated with the sound of the thunder. The orange glow of the candle flickered and caused the shadows of the maguey cactus to dance around the room. I wondered what Octavio was doing.

He seemed so devoted to his family. A 29-year-old bachelor musician enthusiastically going to spend the weekend with his grandmother and his other older relatives would be an unusual scenario in Australia. When I thought about my own grandmother, I felt a twinge of regret. I had made the decision to leave Australia knowing that it was unlikely I would see her again.

Three years before, at 78, she had been active and engaged – zipping round in her little red Peugeot to dispense cakes and lend a hand to family members and her many friends. On a day I would never forget, she had suffered a massive stroke and was now paralysed, except for her right arm. She could eat and speak, and her brain damage was minimal. Now she was being looked after in her home by our family and hired nurses, but she was not expected to go on for much longer.

I was her first grandchild and she had played a big part in my childhood. Pushing these thoughts from my mind, I resolved to call her tomorrow.

❧

The day, I discovered, is a far more pleasant time to be alone in a big city than the night. On this Sunday morning, with time to pull myself together, the air was crisp and the wide shady streets of La Roma were dotted with slow-moving families. I was determined to use this day to work on my Spanish and try to understand who exactly had won the election. Edgar had recommended that I read a paper called *La Jornada* because 'all the others are government propaganda'. But when I had asked Octavio's advice about newspapers, and mentioned that I had been recommended *La Jornada* he had raised his eyebrows. 'Oh, that's not exactly news – that's opinion. The paper fails to make a distinction between the two.' He recommended *El Universal*.

So I bought both newspapers and, armed with a dictionary and a pink highlighter, I found myself a place on a park bench next to the statue of David and began to trawl through them. The front cover of *La Jornada* featured an aerial shot of the Zócalo taken during one of last week's democracy marches. The Zócalo appeared to have been transformed into a solid square of yellow. Two million people were said to have participated in the demonstration.

Reading Mexican newspapers is an entirely different experience from reading Australian newspapers. Mexican newspapers are about twenty times thicker and over 90 per cent of the news is national. As I skimmed through the articles – about the drug wars, the gruesome kidnappings, the wars between farmers over territory, the teachers that were blocking highways in Oaxaca, the terrorist activities of the socialist guerrillas – I got the impression that this alleged electoral fraud was just part of the general mayhem which permeates the country.

A few hours later I had a two-page list of new Spanish words and a basic understanding of how it was that Mexico had two presidents at the same time. Obrador, the candidate of the left party, the PRD, was claiming that electoral fraud had taken place and that he was the legitimate president. He had formed a civil resistance movement, which he called the 'legitimate government' and they were responsible for organising the huge demonstrations that had been taking place in the Zócalo over the past week. Now the 'legitimate government' had announced that as well as occupying the Zócalo, they would block Paseo de la Reforma, Mexico City's famous 12-kilometre-long boulevard, until there was a total recount of the votes and a formal investigation into the fraud.

According to the articles in *La Jornada*, evidence of fraud had been found in various districts. Mathematicians were drawing attention to irregularities in the vote counting and to the improbability of the sudden reversal in the outcome that had occurred during the early hours of the morning and given Calderón a huge margin. After repeated consultations with my dictionary, I managed to write all this down in Spanish.

§

Five-thirty Monday morning. The worst hour of the week. I switched off the alarm and rolled down from the mattress onto the hard wooden floor, still inside my blankets. I stared out the window into the blackness, fighting the temptation to close my eyes.

Looking at the clock again, ten minutes had passed. I threw on my clothes which I had laid out on the floor by the mattress, and ran into the bathroom. Pulling my hair off my face and cleaning my teeth, I ran out the door and down five flights of stairs. If I had good luck with the metro, I could still make it on time.

But when I got to the big metal door that leads out of my building, it refused to open. This door unlocks from the inside, but the key wouldn't move in either direction. I was constantly having trouble with opening doors in Mexico, but I had always managed to figure it out in the end with enough different angles of oscillation. I tried pushing against the door and pulling it forward and turning the key at every different angle. It wouldn't budge. I began to shake the door wildly and wiggle the key in every possible direction. Nothing. Perhaps someone else would try to leave the building soon. I stopped to listen. Complete silence.

Hoping in vain that it would wake up a nice neighbour who would know what to do, I tried again, this time making a lot of noise. But the door didn't move and no one came to my rescue. The only possible way out of this was to wake up Octavio. His door was closed – what if he wasn't alone? I had heard him come in quite late last night. I knocked. No response, so I opened the door slowly. He lay face down, snoring lightly with his feet sticking out the end of the bed. He really was very tall.

'Octavio,' I said, tapping him on the shoulder, 'I'm really sorry to wake you, but I need your help.'

He rolled over and slowly opened one eye. '¿Qué hora es?' he asked. His voice seemed deeper at this time of the morning.

'You don't want to know.' I explained the problem.

He closed his eyes for a moment and took a deep breath. Then he got out of bed. He was naked except for a pair of red boxer shorts, but then he located a pair of jeans on the floor. He reached, with his eyes still half-closed, for a tool box on top of the wardrobe.

As we trotted town the stairs towards the door, I continued to apologise. He fiddled with the pointy metal devices from his toolbox for a few minutes and then the door opened miraculously. I thanked him profusely.

'Don't worry,' he mumbled, still in Spanish. 'It happens all the time.' Then he leaned over and gave me a hug.

§

Walking quickly towards the metro, I checked the time and realised I had only ten minutes before my class started. So when a taxi approached, I impulsively stretched out my arm. It was one of those old green VW Beetle taxis that looked like it was on its last legs.

'*Hola, güera*,' the driver smiled, displaying a complete set of silver teeth. A plastic figurine of the grim reaper hung from his rear-vision mirror and swung from side to side as we sped off. Immediately I realised my mistake. Still inebriated after the unexpected hug I had received from Octavio, I hadn't checked the numberplate getting in. Edgar had explained how to distinguish pirate taxis from official taxis – simply, official taxis have a letter 'L' before the sequence of numbers, whereas pirate taxis just have a normal numberplate.

Anyone who needs a bit of extra money can decide to paint their car like an official taxi. However, not every pirate taxi is a criminal taxi – they may have genuine taxi aspirations, but simply not be able to afford to buy a real taxi. One student had told me that the pirate taxis have a union or mafia, who pay the police a generous fee once a month to ensure their immunity. And now that there are so many of them operating in the city, they have political leverage.

Looking across at the back of the driver's head, I wondered if he was the robbing-at-gunpoint type. Just last week, I had heard at least five taxi kidnap stories from my students – most of them involving a gun-to-head visit to a faraway ATM. In each of these stories, a third party had been involved. The taxi would stop and a stranger would get in next to you and hold a gun to your head. I prepared myself to jump out if needed; but the heavy traffic ensured that this journey, if slow, was safe.

It was twenty past seven. The manager of the school usually didn't arrive until eight. I ran up the stairs and down the hall and into the classroom. But only two members of the First Wives' Breakfast Club, Verónica and Marisol, were waiting. Before I could apologise for being late, Verónica jumped in, 'Jou were stuck in de traffic too, right? Us the same – and the other students are still there,' she fumed. 'Jou know why there is so much today?' She didn't wait for my answer. 'Because Obrador – can jou believe he is blocking the roads?'

Yes, of course. I remembered that the blockade was going to begin today.

Then Marisol started. 'I always knew this man is dangerous,' referring to Obrador. 'Now look what he is doing to de city – as if it isn't already . . . How you say *jodida*?'

'Fucked up,' I translated for her.

'Yes, fucked up.'

The week before, I had asked them whether they thought electoral fraud had taken place, thinking it would be an interesting conversation topic. But they had stared back at me expressionless, until Silvia finally remarked: 'Well, it's all de same, you know – it just depends on if you prefer de rats to de pigs.' Everyone nodded in agreement and then Marisol pointed out that 'de same principle can be applied to de mens in general', which had led us back nicely to their favourite topic. Now, after spending even more hours of their lives in the traffic, they had become rather less apathetic in their political views.

As I made my way home from work, the events that had taken place earlier that morning re-played in my mind: Octavio emerging out of bed in red boxer shorts, the few words he had mumbled in Spanish and then that bare-chested hug that had occurred unexpectedly on the way out. In Mexico, a hug and a kiss to say goodbye and hello is the norm, even among business colleagues; but there was something about this bare-chested half-asleep hug that seemed somewhat more intimate than your usual hug between flatmates. Then I remembered the voluptuous French cellist and I stopped myself right there.

But I felt I should do something to say thank you to Octavio for helping me out. I understood more than anyone how serious an offence it is to wake someone up early.

I settled for a box of chocolates. The next problem was where to leave it. In his room would be too invasive, so I tied it to the outside of the door handle, accompanied by a thankyou note: *Dear Octavio, Thank you for waking up so disgustingly early to help me unlock the door. Love Lucy.*

But, just as I was falling asleep, I had an uneasy thought: was the thankyou gesture disproportionate to the act? Would it be possible for him to read any other motive behind this thankyou gesture? I jumped out of bed and destroyed the note I'd attached. Then I wrote a new note, this time without the words *dear* and *love*.

Now that there were no possible indicators of affection, I could sleep soundly.

The next day a small piece of paper had been slipped under my door. It was neatly folded into the shape of a sailing boat and it contained the words: *Gracias por los chocolates, Octavio.*

§

As the week went on, the traffic got progressively worse and the number of students who turned up for their classes dropped dramatically. The remaining students became more and more disgruntled. I could understand their anger. Their already difficult lives were being made worse than they had to be. Businesses in the area had begun to suffer and jobs were being lost. Now the traffic had reached a point where people would virtually have to wake up in the middle of the night in order to get to work on time.

For those who took the metro, the situation was even worse. The increased traffic had resulted in twice as many people using the metro. Now I had to wake up at four thirty instead of five thirty in order to be able to squeeze into the train. The metro was so packed that Silvia broke her leg when she was forced to disembark out the window of the train, being physically unable to leave through the door. She stopped coming to classes. The only students who were not angry were two illiterate chauffeurs whose chauffeur company had recently been taken over by Americans. They found they needed to learn English to communicate with their new bosses. To the annoyance of the rest of the students, they began to turn up to class wearing yellow Obrador t-shirts.

Marco had a long handlebar moustache and was missing one of his front teeth. He had lived in Texas for ten years, but had worked on a farm picking fruit with other Mexicans. The few words he did know – like: 'Hi, how ya doin'?' – he uttered with a perfect Texan accent. But that was as far as he got. Carlos, or Charlie as he liked to be called, was 74 years old. He was a small old man with white hair and peculiarly large ears. He had been driving people around the city for 50 years and was very excited about learning English.

They would arrive every day at nine o'clock on the dot, Marco grinning nervously and Charlie clutching several sharpened pencils and a notebook, smiling and breathing deeply as if something magical was about to happen. 'Hell-o-teach-er-Lu-cy,' he would beam.

'Hello, Charlie. How are you?'

Then he would turn to Coco the receptionist and whisper in Spanish, 'What did she say?' And Coco would respond in Spanish, 'She said "How are jou today?"'

Then he would say to Coco, 'Tell her I'm very good, thank you.'

And Coco would turn to me and say, 'Charlie is bery good.'

Then Marco would shake my hand firmly and say, 'Hi, how ya doin'?' And all three of us would walk into the classroom and begin Lesson One: The Alphabet, beginning with 'A'. In today's lesson, however, this routine was broken when Marco suddenly interrupted and asked, 'How say: "*¿Obrador es presidente?*"', pointing to Obrador's face on his t-shirt.

'Obrador is the president,' I told them, and the two men repeated this wish, again and again.

The small detail that neither Marco nor Charlie could read or write in their own language seemed to have been overlooked by the new American owner of the chauffeur company who thought it necessary that they learn English. Illiteracy was a big problem in Mexico. You could see how it happened: small children could be seen sweeping the streets before dawn or weaving through the traffic on the main roads selling cigarettes to commuters. Although education is free and compulsory, families simply needed the extra income to get by.

❧

I finished my class at Easy Lingua and waited outside for Edgar, hoping he would remember our appointment. Now that I had done my reading and felt I had at least a very basic understanding of the last hundred years of Mexico's political history, I had been looking forward to this week's *intercambio*. Although I had found the events in Mexico's history more entertaining than most novels, their complexity had left me dumbfounded.

Edgar finally emerged from the classroom, looking unusually excited. 'Hey, let's walk up and check out the blockade.' He too was wearing a yellow Obrador t-shirt. I agreed – Paseo de la Reforma was only a twenty-minute walk from the school.

Democracy was relatively new in Mexico. Up until the elections of 2000, the country had endured 70 years of 'soft dictatorship' at the hands of the Institutional Revolutionary Party (the PRI), which had seized power in 1929, when a firm hand had appealed to most of the people after the series of bloody conflicts that had occurred after the 1910 Mexican Revolution. The PRI had managed to crush any opposition during the next 70 years through non-stop propaganda, nepotism, rigged elections and giving handouts to poor peasant communities. Critics were subdued with well-paid positions in universities and government. If this didn't shut them up, they were made to disappear.

Eventually the government got careless. Thousands of peaceful student protestors had been shot dead by the army in 1968, an event annually commemorated as the Tlatelolco Student Massacre. Then there was its belated and deficient response to the earthquake of 1985 – during which the government initially refused international aid – and this was followed by two debilitating economic crises, in the 1980s and 1990s.

These stuff-ups strengthened the opposition and in the 1988 elections the PRI was forced to become less subtle with its electoral fraud. This was the election sarcastically remembered as the 'night the system crashed'. Halfway through the vote counting, the computers mysteriously switched off and the next day the PRI claimed victory – again.

Then in 2000, to the surprise of the nation, the Coca-Cola cowboy, Vicente Fox – from the right-wing party, the National Action Party (PAN) – won the elections. Mexico was a democracy at last. But now in 2006, Fox's six-year term had come to an end and re-election is not permitted under the Mexican constitution. The new candidate for the PAN was Felipe Calderón. However, what I didn't understand was why Fox – himself a long-standing activist for democracy – would suddenly behave like his predecessors, and flagrantly involve himself in electoral fraud.

Octavio's explanation was beginning to make more sense to me – that this 'fraud' accusation was just a ploy to increase the popularity of the rival left party, the PRD (Democratic Revolution Party), by tapping into dormant revolutionary fervour.

As Edgar and I made our way to Paseo de la Reforma I asked him what he thought Fox's motives could be. He painted a far more sinister picture. He believed that Mexico had never had a democratically elected president. He explained Fox's victory in 2000 as nothing more than an agreement between the PAN and the PRI to preserve the current circles of power and protect business interests. The same applied to the 2006 election. If Obrador's leftist party, the PRD, had been allowed to win, this would have resulted in investigations into the corruption and political murders of ex-presidents. Fox's personal accounts had also come into question, and he may have had good reason to avoid a formal investigation.

The streets were more crowded with cars than usual. It was easier to walk on the road as there was so much traffic that it appeared to be parked. Some drivers had positioned their thumbs permanently on their horns, so that Edgar and I had to scream at each other as we wove between the cars. Others were just swearing at the tops of their voices.

While the rest of the city seemed to have lost the plot, Paseo de la Reforma – the origin of the problem – had been transformed into a big party. As one of the city's grandest and most important avenues, it stretches from the west to the far east of the city. It has ten lanes, which are lined with huge trees and various modern bronze and silver sculptures. It holds the country's stock exchange, the American Embassy, the Federal Justice Office and Los Pinos, the presidential residence.

Now it was looking very much like I imagined Woodstock to have been. In the place of cars, there were masses and masses of people. Each side of the street was lined with canvas tents, which stretched along the road into the distance. Banners with political messages were strung across the street: '*Voto por Voto*', vote by vote, and '*NO al Pinche Fraude*', NO to the bloody fraud.

Despite the seriousness of these claims, the atmosphere on the street was nothing less than festive. A group of dancers, wearing oversized papier-mâché masks in the shape of evil politicians, wiggled their hips to smooth reggae beats. Further down the road, a makeshift boxing ring had been set up and a band of amateur *lucha libre* wrestlers were performing. Edgar and I bought some tamales from a passing trolley before settling down to watch the show. The barefoot peasants next to us roared and clapped wildly as the chunky purple-lycraed body did a backward somersault and defeated his even fatter red-lycraed counterpart.

A few metres onwards, another sort of competition was taking place. Rows of grey-haired men sat opposite each other, staring at chessboards. They seemed oblivious to the loud pounding of the bongo drums that was going on nearby, or the younger almost-nude activists who were dancing wildly to the beat. As the heavens opened up, we ran for cover to the nearest canvas tent.

Inside, a family that looked like they were from the country sat around a plastic table. An elderly woman stood in the corner stirring a large pot over a stove. The smell of the burning wood made me feel as if I were in a small village. The man at the head of the table gestured to us to sit down with them. The elderly woman approached us and, without saying anything, placed in front of each of us a bowl of steaming broth.

Edgar began to exchange a few words with the old man. They were farmers from a faraway village with a strange name. This was their first time in the city. I glanced down at their bare feet and torn clothing and wondered how they could afford to be here.

As the darkness descended and the rain subsided, campfires were lit and the sound of an acoustic guitar resonated. Edgar and I thanked our hosts and continued on our way towards the music.

Beneath the statue of the Ángel de la Independencia, one of Mexico's most important national symbols, indigenous farmers sang as a heavily-pierced neo-punk activist strummed out revolutionary folk songs. 'Take down the wire – this earth belongs to us!' they screamed.

One part of me was cringing at the clichés, but the other part of me wanted to stay here forever. It was hard not to get high on the euphoria of non-violent civil resistance. Impoverished peasants, old leftie academics and adolescent middle-class activists were united by a deep-seated desire to rebel.

As we wandered back towards the metro station, I asked Edgar how it was possible that a group of activists could just take over one of the city's main roads, and why it was that the military weren't getting involved.

Edgar explained that the blockade was not organised by any old bunch of activists, but by the state government itself. Obrador had been the governor of Mexico City for the last three years and the PRD remained in power in the city. Now it made sense. Such a large anti-government festival could only be possible if it had been organised by the government.

❧ 5 ❧

Meeting the Strawberries

It was about 7 am and I was sitting in the fluorescent-lit lime-green classroom, staring out the window and secretly hoping that no students would turn up so I could have a nap. As the city continued to be paralysed, thanks to the blockade organised by Obrador, more and more students were finding it too complicated to make it to their classes.

Earlier I had been informed that I had a new student, but it was ten past already – there was a good chance that she wouldn't show up. I slumped back in the chair but, just as I was about to close my eyes, the door opened behind me and I was hit with an impression of luxurious scent, of elegance and beauty and black designer gym clothes.

'So sorry I'm late – I've just been at the gym and my Pilates teacher went over time by ten minutes . . . Can you believe that?' she said.

She was carrying a supersized Starbuck's coffee. No students bought Starbucks coffee. A large Starbucks cappuccino cost about 40 pesos. This is just 5 pesos less than the minimum daily wage in Mexico at that time – and about a fifth of my daily wage. Forty pesos was also about the same price as your average *comida corrida* – a big meal at a cheap restaurant. The fact that I hadn't had time that morning to buy my usual 7/Eleven cappuccino, which only cost 10 pesos, added to my general disgruntlement.

She sat down in front of me and ran her hands through her shiny jet-black hair which was cut into a 1920s-style bob. She had sapphire blue eyes and flawless pale skin. Her wealth was evident in the discreet jewellery and the perfection of her exercise ensemble. It was a combination of her faultless grooming and her chirpiness at this hour of the morning that seemed to be making me feel irritable. Why the hell was she here anyway? She already spoke English.

But work was work; so mustering up all my energy, I smiled and introduced myself. 'Hello, you must be Ofelia. Lovely to meet you and welcome to Fifth Avenue. My name is Lucy.'

'Yes. Thank you – nice to meet you too,' she said, confidently and with no trace of a Mexican accent.

'So where are you from?' I asked. She couldn't be Mexican. And it wasn't just her fair skin. There was something about her attitude, even her mannerisms, that was different from the other students. But I was wrong.

'I'm Mexican of course,' she snapped. 'How long have you been here? Do you still think all Mexicans are short, plump men with moustaches, missing teeth and sombreros? Or do you think we all look like narcotics traffickers? Would I look more Mexican if I had a tattoo of the Virgin on my shoulder? That's the problem with the popular media,' she went on, 'you only ever see a certain type of Mexican.'

'I'm sorry . . . It's just that you look like you could also . . . be European,' I said.

'It's okay. You see, all of you gringos always think that I am not Mexican; I studied over there and I always had to explain the same thing.'

'Yes I understand,' I said, 'All Mexicans think that I am a gringa . . .'

'Oh, I'm sorry – where are you from?' she asked.

'Australia.' We were even.

I asked her if she had completed the exercises in the workbook that the students are supposed to do before the first lesson. She hadn't. 'That's okay – we can begin the lesson anyway,' I said.

Ofelia was the only student enrolled at Fifth Avenue who was at 'Pinnacle' level. There is very little grammar left to learn at this level – it's all about learning to speak like a native speaker. I opened the folder, which contained the materials for today's lesson on 'exaggerating idioms'. I wasn't exactly sure what 'exaggerating idioms' were – I had never given a 'Pinnacle' lesson before. Following the lesson instructions in front of me, I wrote the words *hot, cheap, clear* and *quiet* on the white board and turned to Ofelia. 'Can you tell me how I can intensify these adjectives?' I asked. 'Yes, yes, I know – boiling hot, dirt cheap, crystal clear, dead quiet. But you know what, Lucy? I don't really care about this stuff – I just want to talk. I haven't spoken English with a native speaker for years and I need to improve my fluency.'

So we began to talk.

Ofelia was only 23 and had just graduated with a degree in business law. Now she was hoping to get a job with an American law firm. For that she would need to speak English perfectly. She had obtained her current fluency after completing two years at a high school in New York.

She rarely made grammatical errors. Only occasionally she would interrupt herself with questions like 'Which sentence sounds more like a native speaker – "I am going *to be* married next month" or "I am going *to get* married next month?"' She spoke so fluently and openly about her life that I soon forgot that I was supposedly the teacher and she the student. She talked about her travel adventures, her love dramas and her scandalous adolescence, and about her current relationship with her fiancé, who was a blossoming documentary filmmaker. Although her parents would have preferred she date a lawyer, they had come to accept him now.

Suddenly an hour had gone by and Ofelia glanced at her watch. 'Oh, I must get going – I almost forgot – I have an appointment at the beauty parlour.'

I walked with her out to reception and waited as she said goodbye to Coco, who looked more serious than usual. Then I noticed that Doña Yoli, the cleaning lady who usually chatted with all the students, simply raised her eyebrows when she said goodbye. When she left, Coco and Doña Yoli swiftly made their way to the window. I followed them.

Standing on either side of the exit of the building were two bulky-chested men. Clad in black suits and dark Ray-Ban glasses, their expressions remained vacant when Ofelia reached them and they began to walk on either side of her. No words were exchanged between the three as they paced towards a black Mercedes, which was waiting a few metres down the road. The man on the left swung open the back door and waited until Ofelia had shifted herself inside. Then the two men followed, one on each side of her, and the Mercedes sped off down the road.

Coco turned to Doña Yoli. '¡*Pinche fresa!*' she spat. Translated literally, this phrase means 'bloody strawberry'.

Doña Yoli shook her head in disapproval.

'What do you mean by strawberry?' I asked.

'*Fresa?* Oh, don't jou know what *fresa* means?'

'No.'

She paused for a few moments. 'Fresas are Mexican people who are different,' she elucidated.

'In what way?' I asked. 'Do you mean that they are very rich?'

'Jes. But it's more dan dat. Dey speak different, dey act different and . . . well, dey *look* different . . .' she stopped again. 'They look like you, like foreign peoples . . . not like Mexicans.'

'So you mean white?' I asked.

'Yes. Most of de times de fresas are white.'

'So am I a fresa then?'

'No – de fresas have a different attitude . . . But I can't explain. Ask another person,' she advised.

Ofelia was certainly different from most other Mexicans I'd met. In some ways I had found her much easier to relate to than the other students, whose lives seemed to revolve entirely around meeting the social obligations of their family.

Ofelia's approach to family was more characteristic of the Western world. She lived in a flat by herself whereas most Mexicans tended to live at home until marriage, and even beyond. And she talked more about her friends than her family. She had a social life and participated in cultural activities like going to art galleries and the theatre. She was well read and had an opinion about every topic that came up. She strongly believed that the North American Free Trade Agreement was to blame for the increasing insecurity of jobs in Mexico and was passionately opposed to the excessive amount of hair gel worn by most Mexican men.

Like many middle-class Australians or Europeans, Ofelia had gone on a gap year after finishing her schooling. She had backpacked around Europe with a group of friends; then she had completed a six-month volunteer program in Zimbabwe. I did wonder why she had to go to Africa when there was so much work to be done here; but then why had I gone to Costa Rica for volunteer work during my gap year when there was so much to be done in indigenous communities in Australia?

Ofelia had seemed so familiar to me she could have been one of my friends at home. That was until I saw her get into the back of a chauffeur-driven Mercedes-Benz accompanied by bodyguards.

§

'Hey, Octavio, are you a *fresa*?' I asked as we walked down the vegetable aisles of our local *tianguis*. We were now in the habit of going every Saturday, since it was the only time we were both home.

'No.'

'Why not? You're white, and you come from a rich family.'

'Yes, that's true. But the term has negative connotations – *fresas* are arrogant. I am of the upper class, if that's what you're getting at . . . Hey, those mangos look beautiful . . .'

Upper class? I couldn't believe he just said that. I never heard of anyone in Australia referring to themselves, or anyone else, as 'upper class' – it just wasn't done. But Octavio seemed comfortable enough with the idea.

Later on, as we were loading the shopping into the car, Octavio suggested that we stop by his mother's house on the way back. The idea made me slightly uncomfortable but because I couldn't think of an excuse not to, I agreed.

Octavio's mother turned out to live in Polanco, the elite neighbourhood where I went to work every morning at Fifth Avenue. I recognised Calle Campos Eliseos by the recently mowed grass and neatly placed palm trees which ran along the median strip between the lanes. We turned right into the forecourt of a towering modern building and stopped the car at the entrance to its car park. Octavio handed his car keys over to a small man in a suit and we made our way across the white marble reception towards the lift. He pressed a button which read 'Penthouse'.

His mother was in her exercise clothes when we arrived. Her chiselled abdominals shone through the white lycra. She was a blonde beauty – tall and slim, with high cheekbones. 'Hola, mi amor,' she said as she embraced her son.

Then she turned her attention to me. 'And look at you! How lovely it is to meet you.' She kissed me on the cheek. 'Octavio has told me all about you – Australia, wow, how exotic you are! And you really *do* look like Kylie Minogue.' I blushed. No one had said that to me since I was twelve.

She grabbed my hand and began showing me around the house. 'This is the Pilates room,' I glanced at the mirrored walls and equipment. 'This is the meditation room.' Empty and white with some cushions placed on the floor. Upstairs was the guest room. 'If Octy ever annoys you, you can come and sleep here.'

We walked out onto a balcony landscaped with potted trees. The air was crisp today, like mountain air. Looking out over the city towards the surrounding mountains, I remembered that we were in a valley 2500 metres above sea level. Usually, a thick layer of smog covers the city. But today it had been magically lifted and for once I could see Mexico City clearly encompassed. Before and around me, 21 000 000 people, almost the whole population of my own country, were working, eating, sleeping, dying and being born.

'Do you know your volcanoes yet?' Octavio's mother asked. 'Ajusco to the south. And to the east, Iztaccíhuatl and Popocatépetl.' They giggled at my repeated and failed attempts at pronunciation. '. . . Po-po-ca-tép-etl.'

Then she led us into the living room and directed us to her cream linen sofas. I looked around this pleasing room, at the vibrant expressionist paintings that dominated the space. 'Please, sit down. Octavio, darling, can you go and make some coffee?'

When he left the room, she whispered 'Oh, I do hope he's behaving himself with you. I know he can be a real pain to live with. Do call me if you have any problems with him . . . Oh, the other thing – before I forget . . . I know you've probably cottoned on that this is a rather precarious city. Octavio tells me you use the underground, and you walk around all alone – let me just say how adventurous you are, darling, really! But let me be frank – you are vulnerable here.'

Octavio returned with the coffees. 'Mum, please – she's not a child.'

'Yes, yes . . .' she continued, 'Octy is the same. He knows he could have the apartment underneath this one with full security, but he doesn't want it. I do understand – you kids want to be independent and trendy, and live like poor bohemians in Colonia Roma . . . I was the same at your age . . .' Octavio said something under his breath in Spanish and they began to argue.

In the car on the way home Octavio apologised for his mother's safety lecture.

'Don't apologise. It's very kind of her to worry about me,' I told him.

'Mexican mothers like to worry about everyone,' he said.

I was tempted to ask him what her racial origins were, but I had learned my lesson. There were such things as blond Mexicans. 'Wow, her English is flawless.'

'Of course it is – she went to Oxford University.'

I asked him what she did now. He explained that she was involved in various charity organisations as well as being a serious art collector.

೩

My social life was picking up; I was now invited into another private home.

When I met up with Edgar for our next exchange, he asked me whether I wanted to go back to his house and meet his family. It had become clear to me that meeting the family was a necessary component of establishing a friendship with a Mexican, so I agreed.

Two metros and a bus later we arrived in the cobbled streets of the colonial suburb of Coyoacán. This was the town in which Frida Kahlo and Diego Rivera had lived and worked for many years. When León Trotsky turned up in Mexico, hotly pursued by Russia's secret police, he settled in the neighbourhood and continued his anti-Stalin activities, until he was stabbed to death at his desk with an ice pick. Both houses are now popular tourist attractions, Frida's sublime Blue House, intimate with her colour and creativity and Trotsky's, sparse and dark with the odour of death. The bohemian, intellectual atmosphere of that time lives on here through radical graffiti, bookshops, cultural centres and street cafés, providing one of the many layers of history dusting over the stucco buildings that the Franciscan friars and Jesuits erected in the sixteenth century.

On our way there we talked about what was going on with the blockade. The Electoral Commission would not permit a recount of the votes as that was illegal under the Mexican constitution. However, they had agreed to a partial re-count, in which they would check 12 000 booths. The blockade had gone on for over two weeks now and resentment towards it was growing among the city's inhabitants. Edgar didn't think it was likely that Obrador could hold out much longer.

After being disgorged from the tattered minibus I followed Edgar's bright red backpack through a labyrinth of cobblestone alleyways to a gate which led into an overgrown garden. We walked along a stone path to a large wooden door. When we entered the house, a man with a long white moustache was sitting on a couch, watching the news. He stood up immediately and shook my hand. Edgar introduced me to his grandfather. '*Mucho gusto*,' he said smiling; then he apologised that Edgar's parents were away visiting relatives. He had the same oriental-looking eyes as Edgar. Then he sat back down again and continued watching the news.

We moved into the kitchen, where Edgar's grandmother stood before the stove cooking some sort of broth. She wore a long navy-blue dress and had a red shawl wrapped around her shoulders. His younger sister was sitting at the kitchen table doing her homework. She looked up and smiled, but she didn't say anything. Edgar explained that she was very shy and never talked to anyone.

His grandmother directed us to sit down at the table. She brought each of us a bowl of soup. Then she called her husband to come and sit down, before arriving at the table herself. The soup was made with corn, chilli, chicken and avocado. It had a calming effect on me and I began to feel brave enough to join in the conversation. I asked them how long they had lived here.

Their house had originally belonged to Edgar's great-grandparents. Starting off as just a one-bedroom house, it had grown organically as the family grew. Everything in it seemed to come from another time. The same faded floral chintz covered the cushions, the sofas and the table. A slight musky smell filled the air, which I thought just added to its cosiness.

I asked them if Coyoacán had changed much over the years. The grandparents nodded in unison. They recalled how, in their earlier days, Coyoacán had been a small farming village. There was a wide river which ran through the town, where they used to bathe and wash their clothes. Then slowly, slowly the town had been engulfed by Mexico City and the river had been transformed into a contaminated stream. They talked slowly and clearly, like Edgar, taking time to breathe deeply between sentences. I could understand nearly every word they said. It was generally far easier for me to communicate with older people in Mexico City than the younger generations. Younger Mexicans tended to speak with so much regional slang that it often sounded as if they were speaking another language.

After dinner, we walked down the road to a little café called El Jarocho so we could complete the English half of the exchange. We sat outside on the pavement on plastic milk crates. The place was packed, famous for its hot chocolate.

I told Edgar about the encounters with wealthy Mexicans that I had been having recently and my shock at my flatmate's blatant remark that he was upper class.

But Edgar told me that if Octavio did come from a family of high-profile diplomats, then he was probably right to say that he was of the upper class.

'In Mexico,' he explained, 'we have a ruling class and often the members of this class are direct descendants of the Spanish, who in colonial times were referred to as *criollos*. In Latin American history, the social classes are typically divided along racial lines.' I had already come to understand that most Mexicans like Edgar, and nearly every other Mexican I'd met, were *mestizos,* descendants of both indigenous and European parents. Indigenous Mexicans, who are referred to as *Indios*, made up slightly more than 10 per cent of the population, and suffered far higher instances of poverty than the *mestizos*. Indigenous Mexicans had a strong presence on the city's streets. Often in traditional dress, you could find them behind food stalls, selling tamales or quesadillas or handwoven baskets. They were politically active, often staging protests in the Centro condemning the violent paramilitary operations that took place in their communities.

But you never saw fair-skinned people like Ofelia, Octavio, or President Vicente Fox on the streets. Perhaps that was because they were always behind the tinted windows of a chauffeur-driven Mercedes. Five hundred years after colonisation, it seemed as if the *criollos* still held on to a large share of the money and power.

꙰

The exquisite Ofelia turned up at her set time the following week. She greeted me as if we were old friends. Today she was carrying two super-sized Starbucks cappuccinos. She handed one of them to me and I rejoiced. Mexico does not have much of a coffee culture – there are few cappuccino machines and even fewer baristas. It is only under these circumstances that I will confess to having enjoyed drinking Starbucks coffee. In Sydney one of my achievements had been to pass the barista exam.

Ofelia sat down and got straight to business. 'I have lots of news for you today,' she declared. 'And a big dilemma too.'

Her first announcement was that a date had been fixed for her wedding – it would be held in three months' time.

'That's wonderful,' I said.

'Yes, but now I'm very worried.'

'Why?' I asked. 'You told me last week that you were perfect for each other.'

'Yes, we are. But I have a big problem.' She went on to explain that her fiancé thought she was a virgin.

'Why on earth would he be under that impression? And do you think he would really care? I mean, surely he knows that you've travelled around the world as a single woman?' I couldn't believe someone as worldly and outgoing as Ofelia could have such an old-fashioned sort of predicament.

She explained that during their two years of engagement, the subject just hadn't come up in conversation – and that he had been adamant about waiting until marriage.

'Well, is *he* a virgin?' I asked.

'I don't know. As I said, I imagine he is. We've just never talked about it.'

I made an effort to hide my complete incomprehension of this situation and we went on to chat about ways in which she could broach the subject with her fiancé. Then she asked me about my love life. I told her I was reluctantly infatuated with my flatmate. Reluctantly, because I was almost certain that the feeling wasn't mutual, and I loved our peaceful, supportive flatmate relationship. Yet there were moments, often as I was falling asleep to the sound of the flamenco guitar coming from his bedroom, when I longed to be closer to him. Ofelia found this situation fascinating and bombarded me with questions. It felt good to get it off my chest. I was beginning to miss having my girlfriends around and I could feel myself becoming rather earnest – spending my Saturday nights with a dictionary.

When the hour was up, Ofelia mentioned that she had a cousin, Rosalba, who lived down the road and needed private English classes. I jumped at the opportunity – Fifth Avenue was almost a week behind in paying me and, every time I called the main office to inquire, I would be put on hold for what seemed like hours before a squeaky voice finally informed me that they had been 'experiencing problems with the bank' and that 'the payment should come through tomorrow'. Coco, the receptionist, was in the same situation; she explained that this happened all the time and I just had to be patient.

I had been managing to get by on the wage from my other job at Easy Lingua; but that was only two classes twice a week and it was not enough to cover the rent that was due this coming Friday. So I called Rosalba later on that day – she wanted one class a week and was offering to pay me 300 pesos per hour. This was almost my daily wage at Fifth Avenue, so I agreed and we arranged to meet at her flat the following day.

The entrance to Rosalba's apartment block was guarded by two uniformed security guards who only allowed me to pass after my successful completion of a written question-naire regarding the purpose of my visit. A young woman with long glossy blonde hair and a round face answered the door. She smiled warmly and introduced herself as she led me inside. The flat was spacious and full of light, with minimal furniture. She and her husband had just got back from their honeymoon in Corsica, and were in the process of decorating their new house, she explained.

Before sitting down at her desk, Rosalba removed various piles of furniture catalogues. 'I'm so sorry about the lack of furniture. It will be far more comfortable next week, I promise. Tomorrow we are popping over to New York to do some shopping for the house. You must have noticed – there are many good brands that you just can't find here, especially in homewares.'

I hadn't noticed. Although I had noticed on my way over, while walking along Avenida Presidente Masaryk, that the high-end label boutiques – such as Prada, Chanel,

Gucci and Louis Vuitton, and a Ferrari agency – had set up shop.

Like Ofelia, Rosalba had a command of English that was close to perfect. But, in order to work in her chosen profession – immigration law – her English needed to be flawless. She too mainly wanted to talk, but she also requested that I give her writing assignments and correct them each week.

As we chatted, a girl carrying a bucket and a rag entered the room. She had large, dark almond-shaped eyes and wore her hair in two plaits.

Without a glance in our direction, she got to work cleaning the windows.

'Hey sorry, I forgot to ask. Do you want a coffee?'

'Yes. Thank you.'

She turned to the girl. 'Dominga, can you get us some coffee?'

Without saying anything, the girl put down the bucket and rag and walked into the kitchen.

'She's sulking today because my husband told her off for eating all the food in the fridge,' she explained. 'Of course, she can eat whatever she likes, but it's a bit much when you come home and the fridge is empty. My husband doesn't think we should keep her, but I'm quite attached to her.'

She went on to tell me that Dominga was the daughter of her family's maid – Rosalba had 'inherited' her. The two of them had grown up together in the same household, and were exactly the same age.

I was struggling to understand what sort of a relationship the two women had. How could you grow up with someone in the same house and then suddenly become their boss? I told Rosalba that in Australia it wasn't common for people to have live-in maids.

'Well, I could do the work myself,' she explained. 'But then Dominga wouldn't have a job.' Evidently Rosalba saw their relationship as benefactor–recipient. I wondered how Dominga saw it.

I asked Rosalba if it would be possible for Dominga to save up enough money, working as a maid, so that her own children could go to school and have other employment opportunities.

'Well, yes it would be possible. But saving is not in their culture,' she explained. 'Dominga sends most of her wage back to her community, where the money is spent mainly on festivals for their patron saints.'

Later I was to read in Octavio Paz's *The Labyrinth of Solitude* about the high percentage of money spent on festivities in the poor villages. He theorised that the brief explosive ecstasy of the festivals made up for the hopelessness of their poverty the rest of the year. Realising the situation was complex, I still found it disturbing. It was the fact that one woman was white and the other one was indigenous that made me feel particularly uneasy.

§

That weekend, Octavio invited me to the premiere of a documentary made by one of his childhood friends. It was to be held in a hotel in the Colonia Condessa. This was a neighbourhood for prosperous young creative people. Like La Roma, the area was rich with Italianate and French architecture of the late 1920s and 30s. The hotel was in a street containing lively cafés and bars, surrounded by a park proud with statues and fountains. But, unlike La Roma, this neighbourhood showed no signs of decay.

We arrived late at the hotel, which was lit artfully to feature its art deco grandeur, and were led to the door of the screening room where an excited buzz of young *fresas* were greeting each other. There were two spare seats at the back of the room.

The film was about an indigenous community which had inherited the Spanish tradition of bullfighting – their town was poor and dusty, and didn't seem to amount to much, except for a very large bullfighting ring. The cameraman intimately followed the life of a teenage matador with a serious drinking problem – he would enter the arena slurring his words as he shouted at the audience, before being mauled by the bull. Combined with the bloody bullfighting scenes, there was also heavy domestic violence and I wondered how the cameraman could continue filming as a woman was being beaten in front of his eyes. Near the end of the film, the matador, who had been so badly gored in his last drunken bullfight that he was almost dead, promised his wife he would never step foot in the arena again.

The film ended and the audience burst into applause. Octavio caught sight of his friend, the director, who was sitting in the front row. He was wearing a white silk shirt with the first three buttons left undone to reveal a hairless muscular chest. He walked towards us and the two men greeted each other intimately. Octavio introduced us in English. 'This is Lucy, my Australian flatmate. And this is Silvio, one of my oldest friends.'

'A pleasure to meet you,' he said.

Then we were led into a room with a long table that was lavishly decorated and bore ice buckets of champagne. I looked around the room. Everyone was so elegantly dressed – the men in suits, and the women in cocktail dresses and high heels. As I was about to sit down at the table, someone tapped me on the shoulder. I looked around to see a familiar face – it was Ofelia, looking like a movie star. 'Lucy! Wow, what are you doing here?'

Then Octavio turned around and the two of them greeted each other affectionately. 'How do you guys know each other?' Ofelia and I laughed.

Silvio came up behind her and placed his hand around her waist: 'Have you met my fiancée?'

Immediately I regretted having been so open with her the other day – and realised that the feeling was probably mutual.

We all sat down at the table, champagne was poured and a toast was made to Silvio's film. Ofelia grinned at me across the table as Silvio rattled off polite questions about Australia. Initially I felt slightly patronised that they were speaking to me in English. But then I realised that it wasn't for my sake at all. Even among themselves, their conversations were flowing naturally in and out of English and Spanish.

After the champagne, dinner was served and an array of wines offered. Silvio handed me a new glass. 'Do try this Sicilian wine, it's one of my favourites at the moment.'

On the way back in the car, I couldn't help asking Octavio one question. Was it normal in Mexico for men to expect their wives to be virgins when they were married?

'Yes . . .'

'Even in *your* social class?'

'Yes, more in my social class. But I think that's changing.'

'Would *you* expect that?'

He laughed out loud: 'I wouldn't marry a virgin. How boring!' Well that was good news. 'In fact I've never even been with a Mexican girl,' he added, turning to me and smiling. And that too was interesting information.

❧

The next Monday, I received a mysterious call from the head office of Fifth Avenue. The secretary informed me that the director of the company wanted to see me in his office that afternoon, but didn't tell me why. I hoped it would be regarding the delayed payment – my rent was now three days overdue and, although Octavio had told me not to worry, I was feeling extremely uncomfortable about the situation.

After work, I made my way to Zona Rosa, to the office where I had come for the first interview for Fifth Avenue. When I arrived, the receptionist led me down a long hall of offices to the last room. It contained a large desk, behind which sat a huge man wearing an expensive-looking black suit.

'Plis sit down.' He gestured to me that I sit down on the chair opposite him. The over-sized gold Rolex watch he had wrapped around his wrist, together with his chubby fingers and round cheeks, made him resemble a child dressed up in his father's suit.

'Welcome,' he said. 'I imagine jou already know dat my name is Nestor Montes and I am de director of dis company.'

'Yes. Nice to meet you.'

'So tell me – how do jou like Mehico?' He indulged in small talk for a few minutes before looking me straight in the eye and saying, 'I guess jou are wondering why I ask jou to come hir today? Well I would like to tell jou about Fifth Avenue's new proyect.'

He went on to explain that the company had been selected by one of Mexico's most prestigious private universities to supplant their existing English Language department. He stressed that this was wonderful news for the company because, if it were successful, it could mean a Fifth Avenue in every private university in Mexico.

He paused for a while and looked at me. There was an uncomfortable silence. 'Now, I hir dat jou are bery popular wid de estudents. For dis reason I would like to inbite jou to be part of dis proyect. What do jou tink?'

'Sounds good,' I said. I liked the idea of working in a university. I had loved my undergraduate years with the same intensity as I had hated school.

'Great. We lif dis Sunday.'

'What? Leave where?'

'De university is in Querétaro – jou know dis place? Four hours north of hir, bery beautiful. De foreign peoples love it.'

'But I have a flat here – I can't just leave . . .'

'Jes, but over dere we pay for jour house,' he cut in.

'I have another job here . . .'

'How much dey pay jou? I pay jou double . . .'

'But I . . . you still haven't paid me for the last fortnight.' Now seemed like a good time to bring that up.

He stared back at me, as if shocked by my audacity, and then said slowly, 'Jes, we have bin experiencing some problems wid de banks recently. Jou will receive jour money tomorrow.'

Then he stood up suddenly. 'Wait a moment plis,' he told me. He walked out of the room and appeared again a few moments later. 'Hir,' he said, handing me a thick wad of bills. 'I lend jou 2000 pesos until de payment arrive.'

This was good news. I would now have enough money to pay the rent.

Then he got back down to business. 'Look, I am offering jou a wonderful opportunity. Are jou accepting or no?'

Originally I had been planning on living somewhere other than Mexico City – I had only settled down here because I hadn't had the time or money to explore other options. After all, the city is dangerous, dirty and difficult – most people who live here don't actually want to. Now I had the option to escape.

But the idea of abruptly leaving it behind was disturbing. I had barely established my rickety comfort zone and I was so happy with my flat in La Roma. I had some acquaintances . . . some friends now. I would hate to lose contact with Edgar. And Octavio . . . I couldn't just move out without any notice.

I told Nestor that I could not accept the position he was offering me. 'Look, I really appreciate the offer. But I have just established a life here . . .'

He scowled at me for a few moments without saying anything, making him seem even more like a chubby, sulking child. And then he said, 'Well, I expect dat jou come for minimum tree weeks while we get it going. Den jou may return.'

I felt I had to agree, but it was with a sense of unease.

❧ 6 ❧

Sleeping with the Boss

Sitting in the back seat of a big black van that said 'Fifth Avenue' I felt quite important. For once in my life I was a member of a team with a specific role. First there was the chubby Nestor Montes in the driver's seat – the Executive Director, who was made even more important by the fact that he had sizeable shares in the company.

Second in command was Imelda Rivera, in the front next to Nestor. She had been assigned the position of Director at the new school and would be my official boss while I was in Querétaro. 'Are you excited?' was the first question she had asked me when I got into the car. 'Yeah, me too. This is gonna be so much fun,' she said with the standard Mexican–American accent. I couldn't tell if her enthusiasm was genuine or if she was putting it on to impress Nestor. She was a skinny woman with dark, fuzzy hair and a large mouth.

Then, taking up the two seats next to me, was the oversized Sancho. He was the official lazy computer guy. I had seen him before at the school, lying flat underneath the desks, staring up into the computers. Today he had a terrible cold and was sweating profusely all over.

Later I was to discover that once upon a time he had been a rising *lucha libre* star, but had been forced to resign due to an injury and since then had never recovered from the loss of this dream of *lucha* stardom. And you could tell he would have been a magnificent *lucha libre* wrestler. Everything about him was massive. Just his nose was the size of one of my hands. He had bulging eyes – big enough to play tennis with.

Then there was me, the 'Native English Teacher' – without whom they wouldn't have a school.

Manuel, the director of Easy Lingua, had seemed indifferent when I told him I would be away for the next three weeks. 'No problem, I will take the class for you.' He had previously admitted that he loved taking the English classes and I suspected that he had only really hired me for marketing purposes. The words 'Native English Teacher' had appeared on the sign on the street immediately after my first interview with him at the school. My new private student, Rosalba, had also been relaxed about my upcoming absence. She had been planning to 'pop over to Paris for a few weeks' anyway.

It had been easier than I thought to tie up the loose ends and now we were on the open highway. I felt relieved to finally escape the pollution-stained concrete metropolis. The scenery was rolling green pastures dotted with sheep, but I really just wanted to sleep – it was still only 7 am.

A surprise visit in the early hours of the morning had thwarted my plan for a solid sleep before our journey. I had gone to bed sensibly early, knowing that I would need to be in tip-top shape for the venture ahead. But I had woken up suddenly when I heard the front door open and footsteps coming down the hall. I felt my heart beating faster; a surge of adrenalin transported me into a fully alert state.

Could it be Octavio? I hadn't been expecting him to come home that night. Earlier that day at the markets he had boasted that it had been going well with the French cellist and she had invited him to her flat for dinner.

Curiosity got the better of me. 'Octavio?' I called out.

A tall, gangly figure appeared at the door. 'What are you doing still awake?' he asked. 'It's three o'clock in the morning.'

I sat up in my bed. 'You woke me up. What are you doing back? I thought this was your big night.'

He sat down at the foot of my mattress and removed his black leather jacket. He looked tired. 'Well it wasn't really worth staying,' he said, yawning.

'Why not? What happened?'

He stared down at the floor: 'I don't know . . . I mean, she was really hot when she was playing the cello but somehow . . . naked in bed . . . it was all lost.'

This comment had the double effect of causing me to feel a kind of shameful satisfaction, but at the same time strangely sympathetic towards the French cellist.

'So her breasts weren't as perky as you had imagined them to be then?'

'No, that's not what I meant. It's just that there was no chemistry, that's all. It was uncomfortable and I didn't feel like waking up with her in the morning. Anyhow, it's of no importance. She's going back to France next week.'

'Oh.'

'Anyway, I should let you go back to sleep.'

'Okay. Well, bye . . .'

'That's right – I won't see you for a while.' He leant over to hug me. 'I'll miss you,' he said.

'Yeah me too.'

Then he walked into his room. I listened as he got out his guitar and began to play a classical Spanish melody . . .

After that I couldn't go back to sleep. Lying awake, I tried to interpret my flatmate's sudden affection for me after his disappointing one-night stand. What was the true nature of that hug? Was it a hug of appreciation of my friendship? Or could it possibly have been an I-made-a-mistake-with-the-other-woman-and-I-would-rather-be-with-you sort of a hug?

I stared out the car window – more sheep – while next to me Sancho was snoring. Now I would have to live with this uncertainty for the next three weeks. I needed a plan to safeguard my sanity: I decided to give myself two days only to wait by the phone – if he failed to call within that time, I would move on and accept that what I had sensed was nothing more than a projection of my own misplaced desire.

Someone was tapping me on the shoulder. It was Imelda. She was asking me a question – had I tried *barbacoa*? No. I had never eaten it, but I had heard about it so often that I felt like I had tried it. Since starting work at Fifth Avenue, I had discovered that food was an endless and stimulating conversation topic for Mexican students – and *barbacoa* was probably the dish they talked about with the most enthusiasm and love. I already knew very well that *barbacoa* is made by wrapping a whole sheep in the leaves of a maguey cactus and then burying it underground, where it is left to cook slowly over twenty hours. As with almost everything in Mexico, it is then consumed in the form of a taco.

The fact that I had never tried the dish made the other team members very excited. 'Well you know what?' said Imelda. 'We're in *barbacoa* country . . .'

Then Nestor cut in, 'And I know de best *barbacoa* restaurant between here and Querétaro, and possibly de best in all Mexico.'

Sancho's bulging eyes widened. 'Yes, you must try it. The meat is so tender, and yet the taste is so concentrated – you just can't imagine,' he told me in Spanish. He didn't speak English, although he could understand it.

'Jes. And don't forget that it has a sort of smoky taste,' added Nestor, 'with a touch of maguey. Oh and the salsa, it's such a contrast – made with chilli cascabel . . .'

'Don't tell her about the salsa,' Imelda interrupted. 'Remember the gringos don't like chilli. You don't have to eat the chilli – don't worry,' she consoled.

'But I like . . .'

'Oh and the ribs,' said Sancho, 'the taste of the fat in the ribs. Oh and it's so juicy – the most juicy meat you will taste in your life.'

Having spent most of my life a vegetarian, the idea of wet, fatty sheep wasn't doing it for me, but I tried my hardest to share their enthusiasm. 'Great – how far is the restaurant?'

An hour down the track we took a right turn and found ourselves in a whole street of *barbacoa* restaurants. As we descended from the van, we were attacked by a horde of shouting men waving red cloths in our faces: 'Come in, come in! Come and try the *barbacoa* – the best in Mexico. Tender, juicy – come and try it!'

Nestor turned to us and whispered in English, so the men couldn't hear him. 'Don't listen nutting to dis men – I know de best place. Just look straight ahead and follow me.'

Nestor began to walk in front with his head high, completely ignoring the onslaught. We followed his advice and, after a few minutes, he turned to us and whispered, 'This is it.'

The meat was on display outside the restaurant in a large glass cabinet. I tried not to examine it too closely as we were led inside to a table.

When the sheep was served up, the first thing Nestor did was to prepare me a taco.

'Give her the rib – it's the nicest part,' called out Sancho.

'That's what I'm doing,' Nestor replied as he placed the meat inside the tortilla and squeezed on some lime.

I made a list of Spanish words for 'delicious' in my head. They all watched as I took hold of the taco. I spooned on some salsa, hoping it would drown the taste of the slimy fat, and took a bite.

'Wow! This really *is* delicious! Incredible – no doubt about it, the best sheep in the world.' They clapped in delight before diving in.

After a good share of tacos, Nestor leant back in his seat to make room for his expanding belly. 'Jou know, when I was young I never had the money for a meal like this.' He went on to tell us that his first job was as a shelf stacker in a large supermarket, where he had worked for twelve hours a day and made just enough money to prevent himself and his mother from starving. He continued to do that until slowly, slowly he moved up in the system.

We all listened as he described his rise from shelf stacker to the part-owner and director of a corporate language school with a national franchise. Nestor's life story was a motivational lecture, in which the message was clear: work hard for me, don't ask questions, be grateful to be exploited, and eventually you will be in the rewarding position of being able to exploit other people. I was beginning to wonder whether I would ever receive my pay cheque from Fifth Avenue. Although my accommodation, food and transport were being paid for, not having money left me feeling trapped and resentful.

When I felt the van coming to a stop I woke up. Finally we were at the hotel. But when I looked up, Nestor was talking through the window to a guard in a security booth. Looming in front of us was a shiny white building with the words 'Tecnológico de Monterrey' written in black letters on it. Inwardly I groaned, hungry for a few hours of extra sleep. The guard interviewed each of us through the car window. When he was satisfied that our intentions were good, he handed each of us a security pass, and instructed us to keep them around our necks at all times.

We parked the van and followed Nestor across the university grounds. The glistening white structures looked as if they had been built overnight out of cardboard for a Hollywood film. It was strangely clean for a university; in fact it was more like a sort of luxury hospital – no political graffiti, no notices on the walls about Marxist lectures. We walked across the meticulously mowed lawn and into the entrance of a building. Nestor led us up the stairs to the third floor and showed us to the three adjoining classrooms we had been allocated. Inside, stacks of cardboard boxes towered above us and a bewildering array of plastic furniture components lay waiting to be assembled.

'Okay, let's get to work,' said Nestor in English, getting into the English school spirit. 'We have one day to set up dis school. Tomorrow arrive de five hundred estudents – and I want everyting to go like clockwork.' With that, he walked out the door and did not appear again until lunchtime.

We got to work unpacking the boxes of books, taking the bubble wrap off the plastic furniture pieces and setting up the computers. At Fifth Avenue, the furniture was the same in every centre. We started with the multicoloured reception desk.

A few hours later, two local girls from the Fifth Avenue franchise in Querétaro arrived to help. One would be the receptionist and the other would be the personal tutor, who acts like a back-up teacher. Their names were Fabiola and Fernanda, but they liked to be called Faby and Fery. Faby wore a tight pink top and Fery wore a tight yellow top. Other than that, they were quite similar looking: both had green eyes, golden yellow skin and silky brunette hair which they wore out over their shoulders.

Faby was more curvaceous and evidently proudly so, judging by the painful tightness of her jeans. I had come to realise that women's behinds are far more appreciated in this part of the world. The sorts of bottoms which would be sniggered at in many Western cultures are celebrated and exalted in Mexico. As a result, women are prone to wearing tighter pants.

As Faby introduced herself, she offered me a choice of several kinds of lip gloss. 'The Vanilla Huckleberry is my favourite too,' said Fery, in response to my selection. Imelda suggested that the three of us work together so that the girls could get into the habit of speaking English before the students came. So, for the long hours which followed, I was subjected to Faby and Fery's conversations about boyfriends, Shakira and diets, while we stuck labels on diskettes, stacked the student books and continued piecing together the furniture.

Nestor reappeared with a pizza and took the opportunity to check on our progress. After that we got on with the hundreds of other tedious and repetitive tasks until a security guard arrived at the door and told us we didn't have permission to be there after 9 pm. Nestor could not keep us there any longer.

We gathered outside the door as we waited for the last of the team to switch off the lights and lock up. Once in the van, the conversation turned to dinner. Why was I not surprised? Tuning out and closing my eyes, I envisioned a small single bed in a dark room with a door that I could close and be alone.

It was obvious when we had reached the town because the van began to move slowly along the narrow, winding cobblestone roads. Then the van stopped, and we all got out and began walking down the street. It had been raining, and the earthy smell of wet stone was strong in the air.

There didn't seem to be a hotel in sight. 'Imelda, where are we going exactly? Are we going to the hotel?'

She turned to me. 'Didn't you hear? Nestor decided to take us all out to dinner – isn't he kind?' she chirped. 'He knows a fantastic quesadilla restaurant around here.'

Again? Another meal together? I had been making polite conversation with these people since six in the morning. Already I had eaten breakfast and lunch with them – wasn't that enough? I didn't feel like I had anything else to say to Nestor Montes. I looked around for someone to complain to.

Faby and Fery were walking on either side of Nestor, and seemed to be chatting enthusiastically about the quesadilla restaurant. Sancho was waddling along behind us, sneezing and blowing his nose. I waited for him to catch up. 'I'm tired,' I said to him in Spanish.

'Yes me too, but this quesadilla restaurant is famous.'

Evidently, no one else shared my discomfort. In silence I ate my quesadilla while Nestor continued to talk about the joys of hard work.

Later, after what seemed like an eternity, we pulled up in front of a large arch-shaped wooden door, over which hung a white sign that read 'Hotel'. Inside, the rooms were arranged around a moss-covered courtyard full of little tables and chairs and old trees. 'This is so much fun, isn't it?' Imelda said, grabbing my hand. 'Come and look at our room – it's so cute.'

Cute was the word. Small, pink and decked out with plastic flowers and crucifixes. Then it dawned on me that she had said OUR room. There was no escape.

When I entered, I realised something even more disturbing: the room contained only a double bed. I glanced around, searching for any other sleepable contraption – a sofa, a fold-out bed – but there was nothing, just a desk and an armchair. I took off my shoes and fell down into the armchair.

Imelda was busy taking off her clothes. She changed into her little pink flannel nightie and was now brushing her hair in front of the mirror. I looked at the bed again.

'Come on, let's get to bed,' she said. 'We had a big day and we have an early start tomorrow.' I cringed. Now my boss was telling me to go to bed. But there was no point in complaining. There was nothing Imelda could do.

Imelda continued to talk as I cleaned my teeth in the bathroom. 'Okay, so class starts at eight; we'll have to get there at seven. So let's wake up at six,' she suggested cheerfully.

'Yep, great,' I replied, lamenting the fact that I would now have to extend my false enthusiasm for work into the bed with me. At that, she rolled over and went to sleep.

Taking a deep breath, I closed my eyes. Wow, that was strong-smelling moisturiser. I could feel the bristles of her hair spike up against my neck. What if I snore? What if I try to cuddle her in my sleep? Putting the pillow in between us, I closed my eyes. Bloody Mexicans! What is wrong with them? Haven't they ever heard of personal space?

I looked at my phone one last time – no missed calls. If he doesn't call tomorrow – that's it, I told myself and closed my eyes.

❧ 7 ❧

Electric Shock with
My Friends?

Imelda was already dressed when the alarm clock went off. She was sitting at the desk writing notes.

'What are you doing?' I heard myself ask.

'Writing a list of all the things we have to do – it will be a very busy day today.'

It was still dark when we arrived at the school. Faby and Fery were already there, sticking glitter onto the welcome sign. Imelda disappeared into her new office and the girls put me to work blowing up balloons. It was cause to celebrate – the university's English department had been taken over by a multinational corporation.

The decorations complete, I retreated to one of the classrooms to prepare myself for the upcoming oral examinations – not as much fun as it sounds. My job was to lure the students into a false sense of security by pretending to engage them in a non-threatening get-to-know-you conversation. Unbeknown to them, I would have a list of questions with increasing grammatical difficulty, which they were required to answer using the correct grammatical structure. Then I would tick the boxes as they responded and accordingly allocate them to their appropriate level. I got to work memorising the questions, in order to make the process as natural as possible.

It was obvious the students had arrived when the fumes of Tommy Hilfiger grooming products wafted into the classroom, and the tunes of Shakira and Britney Spears echoed down the hall in the form of polyphonic ring tones. Walking out into the hall, I found a queue of grumpy-looking teenagers stretching from the reception desk out through the door, along the balcony and down the stairs.

They came in one after the other without a second in between. Most of them were eager to get into the highest possible level as this would mean less time studying at university. But they continued to get stuck on the conditionals and phrasal verbs.

'So what would you do if you found out that the woman you loved was a man?'

'Well, I never see him again.'

'Would you be upset?'

'No, because it doesn't happen.'

'I see. But if it did happen?'

'No, it doesn't happen.'

This particular student was outraged by the outcome of our conversation.

'Why I am in the Intermediate? My level is the Advanced level.'

'Yes, you speak very well, but you need to revise some structures.'

'I don't have time for this,' he interrupted, pulling out his wallet and putting it on the table in front of us. 'Tell me . . .' He looked at me and then down at his wallet, 'What can I do to get into the Advanced level?'

Staring at him blankly, it took a few seconds before I understood what he was getting at. Then he held up a 1000-peso note; I'd never seen one of those before. A surge of adrenalin rushed through my body, and my immediate reaction was to look around to see if anyone could see us. No one. Classroom door closed – no windows.

At that moment I understood more about politics and the world in general than I had ever come close to during my studies. The thought of accepting the bribe was thrilling. That *mil pesos* would solve a lot of my immediate problems – and did I actually care whether this guy managed to learn English or not? Nope. Did I need the money? Yep.

I thought about how this logic could be applied to other situations: Do I care if this narcotics trafficker goes to prison? Could I do with an extra million? Then I thought about how embarrassing it would be to get caught. I pictured the headlines: 'AUSTRALIAN ENGLISH TEACHER ACCEPTS BRIBE FROM UNIVERSITY STUDENT'.

We stared at each other for a few moments before I started to giggle nervously. But I quickly pulled myself together. 'You can study hard, pass your exam – and then you will get into Advanced.'

He stormed out of the room, kicking over a chair on the way out and slamming the door behind him. For the rest of the week I regretted my decision.

§

The next day, Nestor introduced two new team members who had travelled down from Mexico City earlier that morning. One of them was another teacher – a Cuban– American from Miami. He was a small man with a shiny head whose name was Ace González. The other new team member was Ricardo. He was a manager from one of the centres in Mexico City and had been sent over to help Imelda, who had become quite hysterical under the pressure of it all.

Immediately I felt myself drawn to Ricardo. He had gentle cedar-coloured eyes and an oddly whimsical way of moving. He walked rhythmically, by putting his toes on the ground before his heels and holding his head high in the air. I observed him from the classroom as he walked around the centre, calmly delegating jobs and making everyone feel important and cared for.

Today was the day the classes began. Ace and I decided to take it in turns – I would give a class while he continued with the oral exams, and then we would swap around. This is karma I thought as I faced 40 uninterested teenagers, not that much younger than myself, and attempted to teach them some English. This was payback for all my school years, in which I had never considered that teachers might be human beings. Some of the students gave me a sort of half-hearted attention out of sympathy, but the majority were busy conversing with their mobile phones or applying eye make-up.

I was forced to resort to the humiliation method – punishing those students who were not paying attention by bringing them to the front of the class and forcing them to perform a song or dance routine. Harnessing the collective hysteria this produced, I won support from the rest of the class.

Then it was back to the oral exams. As I waited for the next student to arrive, I stood at the door and observed Ace's lesson. He started by instructing the students to ask him questions. One student asked him if he liked Mexican women. 'Well, the thing with Mexican girls . . .' he replied smirking – this was obviously his favourite question – 'is you gotta go out with 'em before you can sleep with 'em. It's the other way round with American girls – you gotta sleep with 'em first, and then you can go out with 'em.'

Some of the students chuckled, but one girl raised her hand. 'Sorry, I no understand.'

'I am saying that Mexican girls are nicer than American girls,' he replied, winking at the other students who did understand.

After God knows how many more classes and exams, Ricardo walked into the classroom where I was sitting and made an attractive proposition. 'We ought to go for lunch, don't you think? I have notified the pupils that there shan't be any oral exams or classes for the next hour.' Ricardo's accent was neither Mexican nor American, but his own unique creation. He spoke fluently, but his use of old-fashioned words and phrases revealed that he had learnt the language from a textbook.

Ace came along too, and the three of us left the university grounds for the similarly designed Boulevard Palace Food Court in the shopping centre across the road. Fifth Avenue had agreed to reimburse our meals, but only if we had a receipt, which confined us to eating all our meals at chain restaurants, as informal restaurants didn't give receipts.

Over a 'Ster Lion Stockade Mega Deal Lunch' Ace divulged his true reasons for coming to live in Mexico. Like so many gringos before him, Ace had come to Mexico to hide. He was hiding from his cousins, who were trying to kill him over the money he had lost in a failed real estate business. His account lasted the whole meal, which was perfect as I was too tired to talk after shouting at teenagers all morning. Ricardo and I remained silent, only exchanging the occasional amused glance as we listened to

Ace's story – which was highly entertaining even if parts of it didn't quite seem to add up.

§

Friday night: another Fifth Avenue team dinner. We wandered down the road and settled for one of the restaurants on the main plaza. Nestor was back in Mexico City now that he had got everything running smoothly, but the rest of the team remained intact. Ace sat in between Faby and Fery, with whom he had now become obsessed. They seemed to find him amusing, giggling every time he opened his mouth.

Various people approached our table to try to sell us things – a child selling bubblegum and cigarettes, an old woman selling cut roses, a man with a polaroid camera. When we finished eating, an old man with white, spiky hair came along with some kind of an electrical device – it was a small square box with various electrical cords sprouting from the top. '*Sólo diez pesos, un toque eléctrico, con tus amigos,*' he cried. Did I understand that correctly? Ten pesos for an electric shock with your friends?

I turned to Ricardo, 'Sorry, what did he say?'

'He's selling electric shocks; we can get group electrocutions for only ten pesos,' he explained.

Imelda thought it was a wonderful idea. 'Come on, let's get one!' she squealed. And suddenly we were all holding hands and the white-haired man was attaching a cable to Ace's finger.

The next thing I knew, my whole body was tingling and we were all shaking slightly. I tried to let go. 'No, don't let go! The electricity will stop!' Ricardo and Imelda tightened their grips on my hand.

But I want it to stop! *'¡Más, más, más!'* Why was everyone saying 'more'? I was starting to panic. The electric man turned a knob on the machine – and then we all began to shake vigorously. And more vigorously.

I looked around at my companions at the table. Sancho's tennis-ball eyes looked like they were on the verge of falling out; Imelda's fuzzy dark hair was standing on end, and everyone was smiling. When the electrocution was over, Ace gave 10 pesos to the man, who then walked towards the next table. Everyone in the team was laughing. *'¡Qué divertido!* What fun! What fun!' What the hell is wrong with these people? I asked myself yet again. I later learned that electric shock machines are common devices of amusement in public plazas around Mexico.

On the way back to the hotel, Ace tried to convince us all to go clubbing. No one took any notice of him – we were all too exhausted. Faby and Fery went home, and Ace took off by himself. The rest of the group retreated to their rooms. Sitting on the bench outside and looking up at the stars, I took the opportunity to enjoy a moment of solitude before going to bed.

About ten minutes later, Ricardo emerged from his room and sat down next to me. After laying out tobacco and papers on the table, he began to roll a cigarette. 'Would you like to join me?' he asked. I agreed. I've never been able to call myself a serious smoker, but I did enjoy the occasional atmospheric cigarette. However, as it was lit, I realised it was not a cigarette at all, but a joint.

I laughed. The 'Service Manager' – the respectable corporate-looking man in a suit who was supposed to supervise us – was passing me a joint. 'Well it's not something to make a habit of, but I think we deserve it after such a taxing week.' And that was certainly true.

After a few puffs on the joint I began to laugh. And then, as our brain neurons became pleasantly scrambled by the cannabis, we began to talk. And talk, and talk. And I felt like I was talking to an old friend. He told me about his life – how he had grown up wealthy, had attended a private bilingual school and lived in a large house in an upmarket area. But his family had gone broke after investing all their money in prawn farms, which were later destroyed by a hurricane. Then the family had moved from their grand house with servants into a tiny apartment on the outskirts of the city, and the children were moved to a state school.

At one point during this conversation Ricardo asked me if I spoke Spanish. I told him I was learning. Then he said to me in Spanish, 'Well, if you're learning, then why don't you speak in Spanish?'

I replied in English, 'Because I get nervous and I make a lot of mistakes.'

He responded with the obvious answer, *'Así aprendes, pendeja'* – Well, that's how you learn, idiot. Of course he was right. Since being here, I had made learning Spanish second only to survival on my priorities list. I spent at least three hours a day reading the newspaper in Spanish – writing down all the new words in the back of an exercise book – but hadn't managed to do the obvious, and talk. So I did something radical and began to speak in Spanish – and for the first time it didn't feel like an impromptu oral examination, but like a conversation.

≋

The next day I woke up to find that Imelda was no longer in my bed. She had left a note on the mantelpiece explaining that she had gone back to Mexico City for the weekend to be with her husband. I had been getting to like Imelda more and more, even if she was a bit too bubbly at times. But to have the room to myself was a glorious feeling. I stretched out and went back to sleep.

When I finally did wake up, I found myself face to face with Ricardo as I emerged from my room. 'Coffee?' he asked. That's exactly what I was thinking. We walked down the road towards the town square. This was the first time I had seen the town in the daylight and I was overcome by the beauty of the strong earthy colours of the stone buildings – terracotta, crimson and yellow – with their enormous arched cedar doors.

We sat down at the nearest café and ordered a coffee. Neither of us felt like talking much, but it was a comfortable, peaceful silence. We bought a newspaper from a passing child vendor and began reading the different sections. Ricardo helped me with words and phrases I couldn't pick out, and provided me with some political background on the various national conflicts.

After coffee, he and I spent the day exploring. We found that Querétaro was your typical romantic little colonial Spanish town. It contains an uncountable number of historic churches and cathedrals, and leafy plazas with fountains and statues of national heroes. All of this against a backdrop of bright-green cloud-covered hills. Its inhabitants seemed less neurotic than those of Mexico City – there was widespread use of garbage bins and no shouting on the street; no honking of horns and the small police presence looked more human, unlike the militarised robo-cops of Mexico City. The downside of this beauty was the less appealing tourists-with-money scene that came with it. We soon gave up on the kitsch sombrero-selling 'art galleries' and headed for the museums.

We found our way to a park called Cerro de las Campanas – the Mountain of Bells – which contained a museum. Here we discovered that this cutesy little tourist town was drenched in historical significance. It was founded in 1531 by Conín, an indigenous chief who had converted to Catholicism as a result of a deal with the Spanish. It was here that the Mexican independence movement was born after a group of rebels had been arrested in 1810 for conspiring against Spain. This triggered the Mexican War of Independence.

The Mexican anthem was sung for the first time in this town. Ricardo recited some of the lyrics in a stirring baritone. 'War, war! Take the national pennants and soak them in waves of blood . . . War, war! In the mountains, in the valley, the cannons thunder in horrid unison.' Definitely an Aztec influence there I thought, but Ricardo explained that the ferocious nature of the lyrics was inspired by the North American invasion that had occurred a few years before and had resulted in half the country being annexed.

In 1864, long after independence, royalist forces returned when the Austrian Archduke Fernando Maximilian of Habsburg was installed by Napoleon III as the Emperor of Mexico. But a few years later Maximilian found himself besieged here in Querétaro by liberal republican forces and, after his defeat in 1867, he was shot dead by a firing squad in the very park where we stood. This event is the subject of a series of paintings by Manet, entitled *The Execution of Maximilian*.

After their defeat, many of the French soldiers chose to stick around rather than return to France. This explains the French-style street lights, the excellent bakeries and the turquoise eyes of the locals. Then the revolution of

1910, which followed Independence, gave rise to a new constitution, which just so happened to be drafted in this very spot in 1917. This park seemed to have played a role in all the most important events in Mexican history.

§

The next day, I went into the computer room to switch on the machines before the students arrived and decided to take the opportunity to check my emails. There was an email from my mother. At seeing the first sentence, my whole body tensed up and I wanted to scream – *Nan died yesterday morning.*

Unable to read the rest of it, I ran outside and into the bathroom, and watched myself in the mirror as tears began pouring down my cheeks.

I had known that this would happen while I was away. Before I left Australia, I had said goodbye to Nan, fully aware that it would be the last time I would see her. So why did I feel so shocked? Why did I feel as if I'd just received a blow to the head?

I had been sure that I was fully prepared for this moment. After all, she had come very close to dying twice in the last few years. When she had had her first massive stroke, it was touch and go. Then, a few years after that, she'd suffered a major heart attack and we had all said our goodbyes, one by one around her bed in her palliative care room. But then, a few days later, she was asked to leave palliative care; still alive, she went home, where she valiantly continued with her one-handed cake baking, knitting and artwork, assisted by her nurses. So now I felt like I had faced up to, and suffered, her death twice already and that that was enough – that this had happened didn't seem fair.

Never in my life have I felt so lonely. But at the same time I was desperate to be alone. The last thing I wanted was to walk back into the centre and stand up in front of a pack of sulky teenagers. As I walked through the door I came into direct contact with Ricardo's gentle eyes. He placed his hand on my shoulder and I felt his warmth permeate through my body. He asked me what was wrong and I told him. 'Go back to the hotel – I'll cover your classes.'

He passed me my jacket and my bag from behind the reception desk. Without looking at anyone else, I walked out the door, down the stairs and took a taxi straight to the hotel.

Being her first grandchild, I had spent a lot of time with Nan when I was growing up. To me she had represented normality: her house was a world where everything made sense and was predictable. There were certain times for eating, waking up, going to bed and having a bath. This was in stark contrast to my parents' household, where you never quite knew when anything was going to happen.

My grandmother would always give me her full atten-tion – when I talked to her about my problems at school, she treated them as if they were serious grown-up problems, and always gave me good advice.

Our relationship strengthened during my adolescence, which my radical baby boomer parents had found challenging. When my parents overheard one of my phone conversations, in which the word 'ecstasy' was mentioned, they had gone into a state of hysteria and threatened to send me to a boarding school in the desert. The fact that my father in the 1970s had written glowingly about recreational drugs was of course irrelevant. Not long afterwards, my sister and I were moved to an elite Church of England private school in the city, only because there were no boarding schools in the desert.

My suburban-dwelling grandmother, on the other hand, had listened with an open mind when I explained to her that drugs weren't really that bad – she even admitted that she would quite like to try marijuana one day. Later, during the five agonising years that followed her stroke, when she was paralysed except for her right arm and head, a certain type of cookie was kept in the freezer for those moments when the morphine wasn't enough.

For the first time since being away, I longed to be at home with my family, with my mother. I walked down the road to the internet café to read the rest of the email. This helped me to relax a lot more. It was a peaceful death – her children and her twin brother were all by her side, holding her hand. My grandmother had never liked funerals – so instead they were organising a celebration of her life, where they would release 83 orange helium balloons, one for every year of her life. I felt happy that she wasn't suffering anymore.

At the end of her email my mother confirmed that the family would come to visit me in Mexico as soon as my sister Angelica had finished her final high school exams. This news was comforting, yet unsettling. My parents are wonderful, but they are a handful. I knew they would be scrutinising my life closely . . . Were my clothes ironed and clean? Was I too thin? Did I need an appointment with a dental hygienist?

❧

Before I had time to think about what I was getting myself into, Ricardo and I had become a couple. Whether it was a secondary effect of the electric shocks, or just a longing for intimacy that I had at that time, I will never know. But it got to the point where I found myself unable to resist being close to him – and the feeling was mutual.

The transition of our relationship – from being colleagues to friends to partners – was rapid, and yet so smooth and so natural that I hardly noticed it was happening. Its full implications only truly dawned on me when we were together on the bus heading back to Mexico City. There we were – together in the darkness, curled up in silence, as if we had known each other for years.

I had told Ricardo about Octavio – that he was my flatmate, and that we got along well, but we rarely saw each other. It didn't seem relevant to go into details about my ongoing infatuation with him, especially now that it was confirmed that any kind of intimacy I had felt between us must have been imagined. When I thought about him, I felt a tightness in my chest. But it was time to let go and move on. Perhaps having a boyfriend would pave the way for an uncomplicated friendship with Octavio.

It was almost midnight when Ricardo and I arrived at the bus terminal in the far north of the city. As we came out of the terminal into the surrounding industrial suburbia, I began to wonder why we had decided to return. Cement shanty towns were sprawled around the factories. There was a faint smell of smoke in the night air and the sky was a murky yellow colour.

We walked towards the stairs that led to the metro station. Suddenly, Ricardo grabbed my hand and began to walk so fast I almost tripped over. To our right, in the shadows, a group of young men stood in a circle around a man in a suit. Their hands were casually wrapped around their revolvers, which were still in their pockets as they closed in on the man in the middle. From the platform I could see that the older man's shoulders were shaking as he handed over his belongings.

Ricardo accompanied me on the metro and walked me to my apartment. We hugged before he went on his way. It felt odd parting from him after having spent nearly every moment of the previous weeks together. I wasn't quite sure what my feelings were – only that I felt safe and happy in his presence. As I turned the key in the door, I could hear the sound of classical guitar.

Octavio greeted me at the door. He was wearing the red boxer shorts again and a white t-shirt: 'Hey, I missed you,' he said. And my heart lurched into my throat.

❦ 8 ❦

The Virgin

'You're up late,' I said as I walked back into the living room after dumping my backpack in my bedroom. It was almost three in the morning.

'Just got back from a gig.'

And I could tell it had gone well by the way he was grinning and bouncing around the room with his guitar. I slumped down on a cushion on the floor and leant against the wall. I was tired after the journey home, but I decided to make an effort to stay awake a few moments more to touch base with my flatmate.

'How was Querétaro?'

'Exhausting. No, I mean, it was good. A beautiful place, but lots of work – long hours.' I couldn't bear to tell Octavio about my grandmother's death. Although we had become close, I still had a sense that I wanted to remain composed around him.

'I see,' Octavio said. 'Hey, can you do me a huge favour?' he asked, walking towards me with a pair of scissors. 'I'm going to my grandmother's house in Cuernavaca tomorrow and she's going to tell me my hair is too long.'

I protested. 'No, sorry – just because I'm female doesn't mean I can cut hair.'

'Come on, it's easy. Just the back bit – I can do the front . . . About an inch off the shoulders – make sure it's even.'

'Can't I do it tomorrow?'

'No, I'm leaving first thing in the morning. You'll be asleep.'

He plonked himself down in between my knees, stretching his enormously long hairy legs out across the floor. If I was at all perturbed by the intimacy of this position, I was more concerned about the task ahead. I began cautiously, removing the tiniest snippets of his hair one at a time.

'New painting?' I inquired noticing that the wall in front of us had been covered by a huge black and white painting on canvas.

'Yeah. Do you like it? I bought it from an artist friend of mine in Oaxaca.'

I did like it. Graceful expressionist brushstrokes revealed a woman in prayer wearing a cape of stars. Standing on an upside-down crescent moon held up by a child angel, she radiated sparkling light from her body. I recognised the image immediately – this painting was an interpretation of what is probably Mexico's most iconic image, the Virgin of Guadalupe.

This image is present almost everywhere you look in Mexico. Coming out of nearly every metro station, you can be sure to find her standing calmly inside a glass cabinet, decked with candles and roses and fairy lights. The majority of pedestrians will stop for a moment to cross themselves as they pass her. Edgar had once told me that these altars are tactically installed by the council to stop people from littering in certain areas. 'No one drops rubbish near the Virgin,' he told me.

Her image dominates Mexican craft and kitsch, and regularly permeates Mexican art. She is most commonly depicted in psychedelic red, yellow and turquoise; she is sold on the street on posters, jewellery, framed prints with light bulbs attached, or in boutique stores appearing in fine porcelain.

'You know the story, right?'

'Um . . . no . . . But stop moving your head.'

Octavio began to tell me the story behind the Virgin Mother of Mexico. It all started with a peasant named Juan Diego, who in the year 1531 was walking from his village to Mexico City. As he was walking over Tepeyac Hill, something unexpected happened: a young girl appeared. As she approached him he realised she was radiating sunlight. She spoke to him in Náhuatl, the language spoken by the Aztecs, and told him she was the Virgin Mother. She appeared to Juan Diego four times, and the fourth time she requested that a church be built in her honour. So, Juan Diego went to the city and he contacted the bishop to tell him what he had seen. But the Spanish bishop didn't believe him and asked him for proof.

Then Juan Diego went back to the same hill. The Virgin appeared to him again and he told her his problem. She told him to collect flowers from the hill and take them back to the bishop. Once he had collected the flowers, the Virgin arranged them in his tilma – a traditional outer garment which Indians wore. When he presented them to the bishop, the image of the Virgin appeared on the *ayate* (cloth made from maguey fibre), from which his tilma had been made. The bishop fell to his knees. Together, the two men set to work constructing the church.

When he finished telling this story, Octavio pulled out from underneath his t-shirt a string necklace which had a little square piece of brown felt attached.

'Look, this is him – San Juan.' The picture of the saint was sewn onto the felt with delicate golden threads.

'Wow, that's beautiful.'

'The church is still there, and so is the *ayate* with the image of the Virgin. You have to see it.'

'What do you mean? Who painted this image?'

'No one did. I told you, it appeared on Juan Diego's tilma . . . If you want to truly understand Mexico, you must go and see the church.'

We arranged to go on Saturday afternoon after our shopping, as Sunday would be too crowded. After various excruciating minutes, I finished the hair-cutting operation and Octavio went to the bathroom to examine my work.

'Hey, you did a pretty good job.'

Well that was lucky. I said goodnight and made my way to my bedroom.

But Octavio stopped me in my tracks: 'Okay, well, we probably won't see each other until next week.'

'No.'

At this point, another dubious embrace took place. I broke away before he did. 'Okay, well goodnight,' I muttered as casually as possible, before lurching into my bedroom and closing the door firmly after me.

'Why now?' I felt like shouting after him. But then it occurred to me that he was probably still high on the adrenalin of his gig, and had just got a little over-affectionate.

§

Looking around at the grey expressionless faces packed onto the platform in the underground, I asked myself again why I had chosen to return to this city. Judging from the crowd density at Insurgentes metro station, Obrador's blockade must still be in place. After being spewed off the escalator, it had taken agonising minutes before I had been able to squeeze myself through the packed human flesh on the platform. Now I braced myself for the next challenge: entering and exiting the train.

Coco greeted me at Fifth Avenue reception. 'Jou have many students today,' she beamed. The distinctive smell of deep fried tortillas wafted down the hall as I headed for the classroom. Inside, all the members of the First Wives' Breakfast Club were sitting around the table.

'Hello! It's true – dey said you were coming back, but I didn't believe dem.' Veronica jumped up to hug me before I could get through the door.

'Yeah – why jou come back here when jou could stay in Querétaro?' asked Silvia, smiling. She was still on crutches from her accident on the metro. As I made my way around the table to hug each of them, I could feel my cheeks absorbing large quantities of strong-smelling lipstick.

'Here – have some *chilaquiles*. Elvira made them,' ordered Reina as she grabbed my hand and pulled me down into the empty chair next to her.

'Yes, and I made some chocolate *atole*,' added Marisol, handing me a mug full of the sweet maize drink.

'So, how is everyone?' I asked, happy to see them all together again.

Verónica was the first to respond. 'I am excellent,' she beamed. Her tight red power-suit with enlarged shoulder pads seemed to reflect her mood. The other students looked dumbfounded – this was the first time we had heard her say anything positive. 'Jou know why? I met dis wonderful man – and he is helping me to make my ex-husband suffer.'

'Wow, that's great. Your ex-husband must be so jealous,' I said, assuming she had found a lover.

'Jealous?' She looked puzzled 'No. Paulo doesn't know anything about Taiyari. If he knew, then the spells wouldn't work.'

'Oh.'

It turned out that Taiyari was a native Huichol shaman who specialised in revenge. Her weekly consultations with him seemed to be paying off – her ex-husband had now been fired from his job and his latest concubine had returned to the United States with her new diamond engagement ring. Reina scribbled down the shaman's number – she was desperately searching for a way to inflict harm on her husband, who, after having two children with his secretary, was refusing to sign the divorce papers so Reina could be free of him.

❧

Ricardo called that night when I got home from work. I told him, in my most indifferent tone of voice that I would be busy for the rest of the week. It felt terrible being cold to him but, after much contemplation, I had decided that I had become involved with him far too quickly. It was unnerving the way we had acquired the familiarity of an old married couple within just two weeks – and now in the light of Octavio's ambiguous behaviour towards me, I was starting to question what it was that I really wanted.

My resolve was to avoid seeing both men until things became clearer – and I assumed they would.

'No problem. Just call me when you have time,' Ricardo said in his deep, gentle voice. He sounded completely unfussed. I hung up, satisfied with my efforts to keep in line with my plan.

However, this plan was totally undermined the next day. I was woken up by severe stomach cramps – so severe that I felt as if I was being carved up from the inside – initially I decided to ignore them and got ready for work. But a few minutes after I left for the metro station, I began to vomit uncontrollably. Making my way to a park bench, I lay down, relieved that there was virtually no one around at this hour to observe my display.

I would have to walk back home and call work. But when I stood up, I felt so dizzy that I instantly collapsed back down onto the stone bench. Reaching into my handbag for my mobile phone, I called Octavio. No answer. He'd probably only gone to sleep a few hours ago. So I dialled Ricardo's number.

What seemed like a few minutes later, he pulled up in front of the park.

'Did you eat something from the street?' Ricardo inquired as he bundled me into the back of his car.

'Yes.' Of course I had. I always did.

'Well, in that case, you are sure to have *La venganza de Moctezuma* – Moctezuma's Revenge.' This was the nickname given to food poisoning in Mexico, he explained.

'I'll take you back to my flat. That way I can check on you every hour, as my work is just around the corner,' he said. I called Fifth Avenue Polanco to let them know that I wouldn't be coming in.

Back in Querétaro, I had been relieved to discover that unlike most bachelors in Mexico, Ricardo did not live with his mother. Instead he lived by himself in a studio apartment not far south of Colonia Roma.

It was a masculine space. Square, with a high ceiling that had been painted black. An old metal shield which hung above the bed was the only attempt at decoration. The flat contained only one window, which looked directly across to a smog-stained cement wall. But the space was made gentle by the strong presence of music. Four different species of guitar leant against the wall: an electric, a bass, an acoustic and a smaller acoustic, which Ricardo explained was called a 'Jarana', a traditional Mexican instrument from Veracruz. Piles of CDs of almost every genre lay stacked against the wall: 70s progressive rock, jazz fusion, symphonic, metal; but it was classical music that dominated, with a clear preference for medieval lute pieces and Italian baroque.

The room had a cosy, familiar smell and a large, comfortable bed, in which I installed myself immediately. Ricardo went to the shops and turned up a few moments later carrying bottles of mineral water and various boxes of tablets that were supposed to help.

I hardly left that bed for the blurry days that followed. My body ached and my stomach turned itself inside out but at least, with Ricardo's regular visits, I had ample opportunity to moan about the situation.

At night Ricardo sat on the bed and played the Jarana. First, he played a folk song from Oaxaca, which he sung in the local language, Zapoteca. He explained that it was about an ugly man who was in love with a beautiful woman. The melody was so touching and his voice so charged with emotion that I was fighting to hold back the tears. Then he played an amusing song about the marriage between a hen and a rooster, which he accompanied with an animated dance routine.

Two days later I recovered as quickly as I had fallen sick, waking up with an enormous hunger. Ricardo cooked a chicken stew full of fresh herbs and spices. That night he drove me back to my flat and I went to work the next day, feeling strong and revitalised. From that point on, there was no going back. Ricardo was so kind, and so deeply sensitive I could no longer resist his comforting and peaceful presence. And, now after vomiting on his kitchen floor, I felt certain that he knew the inner me.

❧

It wasn't until Saturday morning that Octavio and I saw each other again.

'So how was your week?' he inquired as he cleaned his teeth in front of the bathroom mirror.

'Good.' He hadn't seemed to notice my two nights of absence from the flat during the week and I didn't see any reason to bring it up. And of course there would have been the added embarrassment of having to admit that I had got sick from eating on the street, which Octavio had warned me about all along.

We set off to the markets on our shopping trip, where we had coffee and quesadillas, then continued on our pre-arranged pilgrimage to visit the Virgin.

In the time of Saint Juan Diego, Tepeyac Hill was part of a grassy meadow in the countryside. Now, that same hill is located in a rough neighbourhood in the north of the city. Even though Saturday was supposed to be a quiet day, the crowds were vast. And we were still about a kilometre away from the church. Guadalupe Street, which leads up Tepeyac Hill to the Basílica, is reserved for pedestrians only. A mass of people moved slowly up the slope, weaving around the corn-on-the-cob stands and the Guadalupe paraphernalia stalls. The bulk of the crowd were smaller and darker than the typical Mexico City crowd. Most of the people were in traditional indigenous dress and I could hear snippets of languages that were not Spanish float past us. Some people were walking on their knees. One man was making his way up the hill beneath the weight of a wooden crucifix.

Octavio explained that most of these people were pilgrims, who came on foot from all over the country to pay their respects. 'Fourteen million visitors a year on average,' he told me. 'The second most visited Catholic site after the Vatican.'

Curious faces turned to stare at us as we moved through the crowd. Octavio, with his long lanky body, head of curly hair and brand new t-shirt, looked more alien than I did as he towered over the sea of pilgrims.

Two churches stood on the summit of Tepeyac Hill. The one in front of us was the *Antigua Basílica* (the Old Basilica) – a Franciscan structure of the sixteenth century, with an ornate red and gold domed roof. But this church had been closed for many years, and no longer housed the sacred image of the Virgin. Octavio had explained to me earlier that because the original church was sinking into the ground (such things happen when you build a city on a lake), a new church had been built in the 1970s with the latest non-sinkable technology. This was the modern Basilica, an enormous flattened cylinder made of concrete and dark shades of glass. It looked more like a stadium than a church, and apparently held similar numbers – allowing up to 10 000 worshippers to take part in Mass at the same time.

The Basilica's circular design allows Juan Diego's tilma to be visible from every point inside the building, Octavio explained. From this sacred icon, mounted on a golden pillar and behind a bullet-proof glass frame, the Virgin of Guadalupe stared down at her followers. Her hands were held in prayer and her head tilted to one side. Her motionless pose and colouring seemed similar to other religious paintings of the sixteenth century. But, according to Guadalupe's devotees, this image has shown no signs of decay for almost 500 years – despite being imprinted on *ayate*, the maguey fibre which has a normal shelf life of only twenty years.

The sacred image can be scrutinised more closely from a moving walkway which slides in two different directions; it is slow-moving, to ensure that no one spends too much time in front of her. Octavio prayed and crossed himself as he glided past the image, an act I found somehow unsettling coming from him. I had never seen him so serious and emotional before, and it seemed to directly contradict his rational nature.

Walking back down the hill towards the car, Octavio turned to me suddenly and asked, 'Have you noticed that everyone's looking at me?'

'Yes I know, everyone's looking at us.' Of course they were.

'But you're a foreigner. I'm not – I'm Mexican. Sometimes I feel like a foreigner in my own country.'

It was understandable why he felt like that. Octavio was different from most other Mexicans – physically, economically, culturally. I wondered whether his devotion to the Virgin came more out of a need to feel part of his country than anything else. It made sense that he would cling so passionately to this symbol of his national identity.

In the car on the way home, Octavio invited me to a gig that night in La Condesa.

'It will be fun – Ofelia and Silvio are going . . .'

'Would love to,' I said. But then I remembered I had already agreed to have dinner with Ricardo – whom Octavio still didn't know about. 'But I don't think I can make it . . . I have some other plans tonight.'

'What? Who with?' he inquired.

There was no logical reason I should feel tense telling him about Ricardo. In fact Octavio's behaviour towards me that day had been so casual that the thought of our relationship as anything more than platonic could only have been delusional. Yet I had to really force myself to inform him that, 'I met someone while I was away, and we are having dinner tonight.'

'That was quick,' he said with a half-smile.

'What? No it . . .'

'You be careful of Mexican men,' he interrupted. 'There is a strong culture of machismo here. I wouldn't get too involved if I were you.'

Was that a hint of jealousy in his voice? Or was he just offering me some brotherly advice? I couldn't tell.

'Yes, I've noticed Mexican men can be very patronising,' I agreed.

'Shut up.' Octavio laughed as he reached over to poke me in the ribs, and I decided it was the latter.

⚜

Later that week, Edgar and I met at our usual place beneath the scruffy green parrot in the flowery café courtyard and ordered black coffee and rum.

We started off in Spanish. I began to tell him about my visit to the Basilica, but he interrupted almost immediately. 'So your flatmate took you to see the Vatican's most sacred cash cow? . . . The vessel which takes the coins out of the pockets of Mexico's poor and channels them into the hands of one of the wealthiest institutions in the world.'

He explained that the indigenous people of Mexico had an age-old custom of giving offerings to the gods in order to ensure good conditions for their crops. 'Now, instead, they give all their money to the Virgin,' he said. 'And of course they are blissfully unaware that the money is used to maintain the garden at the Pope's holiday mansion.'

It was refreshing to hear Edgar's cynical Marxist perspective of the Guadalupe myth. We ordered another thermos of black coffee and I asked him why he thought the myth had been so effective in seducing Mexican people.

'Because it was just an appropriation of what the Mexican people had been doing for thousands of years before the conquest,' he explained. Buried beneath the temple of Our Lady of Guadalupe, on Tepeyac Hill, lies the ruins of another temple – a temple of the goddess of earth and fertility. She was known by the name of Tonantzin, meaning 'Our Venerable Mother' in Náhuatl. Another name for her was Coatlicue, Lady of the Serpent Skirt. She was the virgin mother of Huitzilopochtli, the warrior sun god, the one who at birth had murdered his sister and army of half brothers using a turquoise serpent. Pilgrims would come from far away to give offerings and make sacrifices to her – to them she was Mother Earth. Some indigenous communities still refer to the Virgin by these names, Edgar told me.

Another reason for the success of the Virgin myth was its role in bringing together Spanish and native Mexican culture. The Virgin of Guadalupe is said to be the first *mestizo* or mixed race in Mexico, as her physical features show a mix of both Spanish and indigenous blood. As she appeared just ten years after the Spanish conquest, this race had yet to exist. The serpents which made up Coatlicue's skirt were transformed into the rays of light surrounding the Náhuatl-speaking Virgin Mary.

Edgar was on a soapbox now – I had him on a favourite subject. The earliest representations of Tonantzin had taken the form of a vagina, he said – representing birth and fertility. The modern image of the Virgin maintains characteristics of the original: the shape of the image itself resembles the shape of a vulva. Edgar was being serious, but I couldn't help relishing the irony that the Virgin should be represented by a vagina, especially in the Catholic Church with its historical contempt for female sexuality.

'So you see how two mothers came together to create such a powerful image that has shaped the identity of our country – even if there is no such unity politically!'

Edgar completed his lecture and wiped the steam off his spectacles with his handkerchief.

Speaking of which, I had to ask before the end of our *intercambio*, how Obrador's blockade was holding out. There had been very little in the papers about it since I got back from Querétaro.

Edgar told me that many of the tents set up on Reforma and in the Zócalo were now empty. 'There's a limited amount of time people can spend away from their jobs, families and farms,' he explained sadly. Now that Mexican Independence Day was coming up – the day on which Mexico shows off its military might by parading its infantry, marines and cavalry along Reforma and into the Zócalo, where they salute the president – the blockade's survival was looking dubious. What would become of the remaining revolutionary peasants when confronted with Mexico's entire military force?

§

Buck was already drunk when I found him in his hotel room that evening – and he didn't seem to be sharing the euphoria of the moment. I had been at a loss about what to do on the eve of Independence Day. Ricardo had invited me to go to a party at one of his friend's houses and Octavio would be attending a gathering at his mother's penthouse. But I wanted to be in the centre of the action so, when I got a call from the old gringo, I immediately made my way into the Centro.

Every year, on 15 September, Mexican people wander down to their local town square to honour their national heroes. Traditionally the president of Mexico makes his way out onto the balcony of the National Palace, where he proclaims the famous '*Grito de Independencia*' (Cry of Independence) across the Zócalo. But tonight this tradition was to be broken. The outgoing President Fox had decided to perform this ritual in another part of the country, to avoid being vilified by the pro-Obrador crowd.

Standing on the balcony instead was Obrador's political ally, the governor of Mexico City. And on a small stage, set up in the Zócalo, sat Obrador himself. This stage was the last remaining bastion of his blockade, which he had very wisely decided to vacate, in view of tomorrow's military parade.

A hush from the massive crowd as the grey head of the governor appeared on the balcony. He clutched the staff of the Mexican flag, which was angled from the balustrade. 'Hail to popular sovereignty!'

'Hail!' roared the crowd

'*¡Viva Zapata!*' He began the long list of Mexican heroes.

'*¡Viva!*'

'*¡Viva Morelos!*'

'*¡Viva!*'

'*¡Viva Juárez!*'

'*¡Viva!*'

The list went on. '*¡Viva la Revolución!* . . . Hail to the heroes that honoured our country!'

And then finally: '*¡Viva Hidalgo!*'

Miguel Hidalgo, the priest who started the Mexican independence movement, was the first man ever to lead this cry of independence from Spain. '*¡Viva México!*' he had roared 200 years ago as he rode through the towns and rallied the peasants to go into battle against the royalist forces. At that stage Mexico was yet to have its own flag. But Hidalgo was holding a flag that was just as powerful, a flag that contained the image of the Virgin of Guadalupe. '*¡Viva la Virgen de Guadalupe!*' Hidalgo had shouted, and before long he had gathered enough indigenous peasants armed with machetes, slings, knives and axes to challenge the Spanish artillery.

'*¡Viva México!*' cried the governor of Mexico City now across the sea of sombreros and giant Mexican flags flying in the breeze.

'*¡Viva!*' we chanted. The passion in the voices of the tens of thousands of people around me reverberated through my bones, causing me to shout louder and louder.

'*¡Viva la Libertad!*' he bellowed, clutching the Mexican flag.

'*¡Viva!*' we cried, while children blew hysterically into plastic trumpets, and brass bands marched hither and thither.

Pulsating red, white and green lights – the colours of the Mexican flag – illuminated the buildings surrounding the Zócalo. On the National Palace, lights made the shape of an enormous golden eagle perched on a cactus – the Mexican Coat of Arms. Radiant portraits of the faces of the national heroes – Morelos, Juárez, Zapata and Hidalgo – were created from thousands of tiny lights which shone from the buildings surrounding the vast square. There was a moment of silence before the crowd belted out their national anthem; then fireworks went off in every part of the city.

'And they say that we Americans are nationalistic,' Buck rolled his eyes. We made our way out of the Zócalo and sat down at a street stall. We ordered the only dish on the menu, *pozole*, the ancient Aztec stew which every good Mexican mother prepares for Independence Day. It is made from corn, radish, chilli and usually pork, as that is the closest substitute to the human flesh said to be used in the original recipe. A group of men wearing tight white cowboy pants and sombreros danced to a mariachi band as we ate.

𝕾

After a long, hard look at the Guadalupe painting in our living room, I decided that Edgar may have had a point. The Virgin's outline did possess female reproductive qualities – something like the inside of an orchid, perhaps.

When I saw Octavio again the following Saturday morning, I asked him what he thought of this insight. He didn't find it quite as amusing as I did. 'That's ridiculous! She is the Virgin Mother, not a vagina,' he told me.

'Can't she be both?' I pushed.

'Anything can look like a vagina if you want it to.'

'You just don't want it to.'

'I don't care if she does, or she doesn't look like female genitalia. She just isn't.'

And that was the end of that discussion.

∾ 9 ∾

The Wedding

That Saturday night as I lay on the living room floor and conversed with an irregular subjunctive verb table, I was feeling slightly sorry for myself. Beyond the two men in my life, I hadn't yet managed to carve out for myself much of a social calendar.

caber (to fit) – *quepa*
caer (to fall) – *caiga*
decir (to say) – *diga*

And so on. I said the verbs aloud and then put them into sentences, which I repeated to myself again and again. Then it occurred to me that, no matter how much I studied the verbs now, when the time came for me to use them to communicate, I would most certainly forget them anyway. On that note I decided to give up and go to bed.

I was on my way to the bathroom when I heard the key turning in the door. It was unusual for Octavio to be back this early on a Saturday night. He was equally surprised to see me.

'Where's your boyfriend?' he asked.

Ricardo had gone out to a rock concert and hadn't been able to get any extra tickets, I explained.

'Mezcal?' Octavio inquired.

'Yes.'

After pouring two shots of mezcal, he selected a CD from the shelf and placed it into the CD player. The lively rhythm of a Cuban salsa filled the room, and my gloominess began to evaporate.

'Do you dance?' he asked, shuffling towards me, his feet and hips beginning to move in time with the beat.

I didn't know how to answer that question. Dancing was one of my various neuroses – originally brought about when I was kicked out of the Year Two musical *Footloose* due to my lack of physical co-ordination. Other than a small amount of amphetamine-induced bouncing up and down in my teenage years, this trauma had marked the end of any further attempts at dancing.

That was until my first trip to Mexico – when I had seen something which made me realise that dance was too important to remove from your life just because of a lack of talent. In a pokey candlelit bar in Oaxaca, a small grey-haired couple had got up from their table in the corner, taken each other by the hand and transformed themselves into art. I watched mesmerised as they soared around the dance floor – she embodying femininity, he embodying masculinity. Both passion and torment were expressed vividly in their movements. As I watched, I became certain that what I was witnessing was the perfect celebration of love, sexuality and the beauty of the human body. It wasn't until they went to sit down that I realised this couple must have been in their seventies – on the dance floor they had been ageless.

The next day I enrolled in the salsa course offered at the cultural centre where I was taking Spanish classes. My classmates – a small group of international students – picked up the steps immediately, as if it were the most natural thing in the world. But for me, achieving even just the basic forward and backwards step required my full concentration. The instructor had sped through the steps, and by the fourth lesson the choreography was entirely beyond me – my arms and legs clumsily tangled themselves up in the twists and twirls and dips. How it was possible to control one's feet, one's arms, one's hips, while at the same time reading and responding to the corporeal messages of one's partner – and, on top of all of that, keep in time with the rhythm – was a mystery to me. So when the teacher began to show obvious signs of frustration, I had decided to spare myself any further humiliation.

But back in Sydney, the impression left by the geriatric dancing couple remained firmly engraved in my mind. So, when a smiling Austrian named Klaus handed me a leaflet for his beginners' salsa course, I eagerly signed up. Klaus went along very slowly, teaching one step at a time. He had to, since most of the other students seemed to be IT students who weren't accustomed to any kind of physical movement at all. Under these conditions, I managed to complete the course before embarking on my next trip to Mexico.

But I didn't admit any of this to Octavio. I simply told him: 'No, I can't dance.'

'It doesn't matter – I'll teach you.'

'Okay, but don't tell me to listen to the rhythm in my heart,' I warned. 'I'm not from a Latin culture, and I don't have that supposed rhythm in my heart.'

'Neither do I. I learned in Switzerland,' he declared, as he led me into a right-hand turn.

'What?'

'We don't really dance here in Mexico, and salsa is very popular in Switzerland.'

I didn't believe him – dancing was everywhere in Mexico. I voiced my objection.

'Okay. Yes, you're right,' he admitted. 'But not in my social class.'

'Oh, that's right – you're of the upper class. I almost forgot.'

I still hadn't got used to Octavio's blatant references to his class.

'Shut up!' he snapped, as we moved into a cross-body-turn.

How was it possible that Swiss culture had been more accessible to Octavio than that of his fellow Mexicans of a lower social class? I wondered. But then I remembered that Rosalba, my *fresa* private student, had admitted to learning to dance salsa in New York. Class division in Mexico was so strong that rich Mexicans were forced to go to rich countries to learn the dances that were popularised and created by the people in their own country.

'Hey, by the way, I've danced with girls that can't dance and you're not one of them.' Relief permeated through my body – Klaus's salsa course had paid off after all.

'But try not to look so anxious,' he went on, as he secured his left hand around my waist. 'This is supposed to be fun.'

Yes. I should try to have fun while my abilities in co-ordination and gracefulness are being evaluated by one of the most attractive men I have ever met, I thought as he concluded the song by leading us into a closed backwards dip, in which my thighs were secured around one of his thighs. We stayed in that pose a few seconds after the song had come to an end. Then my phone started ringing and I broke away from Octavio's grip to pick it up.

'Hi, Ricky.'

Hearing his voice made me feel strangely anxious. Then Octavio did something which increased my anxiety. He put on his brown leather jacket, picked up the keys from the table and walked out of the flat.

'Hey Octavio – where are you going?' I shouted after him.

'Out,' he answered, before closing the door firmly after him.

'Who are you talking to?' Ricardo asked.

'No one . . . Just my flatmate.'

Ricardo was driving back through La Roma after the concert and wanted to drop by. I panicked. How would Octavio react if he came back to find Ricardo sitting in his living room? The way he had reacted to Ricardo's call suggested that he may not be so hospitable.

Although I had stayed at Ricardo's house plenty of times, I hadn't yet invited him back to my flat. So the two men had not met. Octavio had never invited other women back to the flat and I had got the sense that he expected the same sort of courtesy from me. We seemed to have developed an unspoken agreement.

'I'm pretty tired. I think it's better if we see each other tomorrow,' I said.

'Okay. But you sound apprehensive – are you okay?'

'Apprehensive? No, just tired,' I stuttered.

§

Even before I went to bed I realised that sleep just wasn't going to happen that night. First I was too cold, and then too hot. And in between worrying about whether Octavio would come back, I started thinking about just how absurd this situation was. Never in my life had I fallen for anyone so fast and so intensely as I had with both Ricardo and Octavio. Although I'd had a couple of long-term relationships – it had taken years of friendship before they had finally turned into romances.

So why now had I instantly developed overwhelmingly strong feelings for two men at the same time?

Was I the butt of some sort of cosmic joke? Or was there a more rational explanation? Perhaps it all came down to probability – living in a highly populated area must increase one's chances of meeting potential partners. Or was it psychological? Maybe being out of my comfort zone, away from my friends and family, had caused me to lose control of my emotions and get attached too quickly.

Then there was the question of what the hell I should do. The mature course of action would be to tell Ricardo exactly what the situation was with Octavio – but then he would start objecting to me going home. And really, I wasn't sure what the situation was with Octavio – there was now no doubt that we shared a physical attraction for one another, but did his feelings go any deeper than that? It was still unclear.

Octavio did come home at some point during the night. I heard the door of the flat open and then footsteps into the kitchen. When the living room light shone under my door, I rolled over to face the wall. Then the footsteps moved towards my room. I listened as my bedroom door swung open. But I remained motionless, until finally the door closed and the footsteps moved in the opposite direction.

❧

It was a relief to get to work on Monday and escape my own head. At 7 am the First Wives' Breakfast Club arrived and I immersed myself in their latest husband revenge dramas. Reina had followed Verónica's example and enlisted the help of Taiyari, the Huichol shaman. And Concepción had finally decided to leave her husband after 30 years of unhappy marriage.

Then Ofelia arrived for her class. She was preoccupied with a different marital drama – her impending wedding. As we spoke, twelve tailor-made designer bridesmaid dresses were being flown down from Los Angeles. But one of her cousins had suddenly gained several pounds and there were fears that she might be too large for her designated frock.

In the third hour, the student scheduled for the class called to cancel. I wandered into the reception area and flopped down on the revolving office chair next to Coco, who was busily engaged in examining photos of topless blond men on a website called 'Sexy or no?'. There seemed to be a general consensus among Fifth Avenue staff to do as little work as possible in light of the latest pay situation. Although I had been paid after getting back from Querétaro, the payments were again a month behind.

Luckily, Rosalba had passed on to me some more students who lived in her area, making private classes my main source of income. So now I had come to regard my Fifth Avenue job as simply a means of maintaining my work visa and my life insurance, while offering a place to hang out, with free internet and good company. Having both a formal day job and an informal after-hours' job seemed to be how many Mexicans operated under the current economic circumstances. Doña Yoli, for example, had her own quesadilla stall at the markets on the weekends and Coco operated a pirate video business with her big brother.

'Wow, jou look terrrrible! What happened?' Coco inquired when she turned around to look at me.

She and I had been getting closer lately. Her shyness around me had come to an end when she heard me speak Spanish for the first time. 'Ha! Ha! Ha! – Say dat again!' she cackled. 'Jour accent is so funny!' But when I informed her that I found her accent funny also, she had looked back at me, her glittered eyelashes sticking to her bright purple eyelids as she gasped, 'Are jou serious? Jou mean dat I have an accent?'

'Coco, I have a problem,' I confessed. Now she closed the windows on her computer screen and gave me her full attention. She listened solemnly as I told her the details of my predicament, and then, when I finished, she turned to me and asked, 'So jou told me jou didn't make sex wid jour flatmate, right?'

'Right.'

'Only de Fifth Avenue manager?'

'Right,' I confirmed.

'Well, jou need to make sex with de other one,' she advised. I didn't see how that would help. 'Because dat will help jou decide which one of dem jou like more.'

'But what about Ricardo? I don't think he would . . .'

'Don't tell him, of course!'

That afternoon, during our *intercambio*, Edgar presented me with an entirely different take on the matter. 'You must move out of your flat in La Roma,' he advised me. 'That will give you neutral ground, from which you can make an objective decision.'

'What? No. I love my flat,' I objected.

But I knew he was right. In fact this thought had already occurred to me, but I had pushed it out of my mind. It was an awkward and inconvenient reality, made even more inconvenient by the impending arrival of my parents. It wasn't easy to find a place in this city. I had searched for almost a month before I finally gave in to living with Octavio, because I'd been feeling like this very situation might arise.

So where would I go in the meantime? Back to my room next door to Buck in the hotel in the Centro Histórico? My mother had not been entirely delighted with my decision to go and live in Mexico, so there was a part of me that wanted to convey to her a sense of stability about my life here – to show her I had a good job, a sensible boyfriend (even if I wasn't sure which one it would be at that point), that I lived in a quiet leafy neighbourhood and that life in Mexico City didn't necessarily involve anarchic gangland warfare.

Right now, my childhood house in the Blue Mountains was in the middle of huge bushfires which were making news the world over. My parents had fire brigades camped on their property, fighting for more than a week while water-bombing helicopters constantly roared past only metres above the roof of the house. From her emails and phone calls I could tell that my mother, grieving from my grandmother's death, had reached an extreme stress level.

The last thing I wanted to do was go back to square one before my family arrived. Hi, Mum – welcome to my mouldy hotel room – hope you don't mind sharing the bathroom with the other backpackers – this is what I have achieved in six months.

Although Edgar's advice was undoubtedly more sensible, I feared that Coco's advice might be more achievable.

❦

I arrived home later that day to find a brief but informative note from my flatmate. As I read it, a huge weight lifted from my shoulders: 'Gone to the coast with friends from Canada – back in about two weeks, Octavio.'

Now, with my immediate problem solved, I fell back comfortably into a state of denial. I focused my attention on expanding my private classes, studying Spanish and planning the logistics of the approaching family visit. And I continued to see Ricardo.

It wasn't until a couple of weeks later, just a few days before the arrival of my family, that I received an alarming phone call from Octavio as I was on my way home from work, and I was promptly reminded of my predicament.

'Hey, welcome back,' I said when I heard his familiar voice on the other end of the receiver. He had arrived back that morning but was now at his mother's house.

'I just wanted to check that you hadn't forgotten about the wedding tomorrow night,' he inquired casually.

I had completely forgotten. He had asked me a few months earlier whether I would accompany him to his cousin's wedding – and I had agreed, never imagining that the event would actually materialise.

When I got back to the flat, I examined the invitation stuck to the fridge. Two particularly disquieting words stood out: 'Etiqueta Rigurosa'. Did that mean the guests were expected to be rigorously well-mannered?

I called Octavio and discovered that – to make matters worse – it meant 'rigorously formal attire'.

'Octavio, I think it would be better if you found somebody else to go with you.'

'No, you can't do this now. You agreed months ago and your name's on the list.'

There was a note of desperation in his voice that prevented me from arguing any further. The church service would commence at midday. I went to bed early to avoid seeing Octavio when he came home and set my alarm for 7 am so I would have time to address the problem of my hair.

Since my arrival I hadn't braved a Mexican hair salon. There were several on my street so I walked in to the one that looked the least expensive. When I got there, I glanced around at the extravagant grooming being performed on the other women in the salon and then at the fading pin-ups of pouting girls with fluffy 80s perms. While there had been a noticeable improvement in my conversational Spanish, it soon became evident that I hadn't made any progress in terms of hair vocabulary.

'*Muy sencillo* [very simple],' I instructed my stripy red-and-white-haired stylist.

'*¿Estilo natural* [natural style]?' she asked.

'Yes, natural,' I agreed, relieved that we seemed to be understanding each other after all. But, inevitably, we turned out to have different ideas about what constituted 'natural'.

I emerged from the salon feeling like a Pekingese on the way to a dog show.

Thankfully, Octavio was too preoccupied with his own condition to notice my new pedigree hair. He burst through the door a few minutes after I got home carrying two freshly dry-cleaned suits. 'I couldn't decide which one – so now you are going to tell me.'

He dashed into his room and emerged a few minutes later wearing a black suit. After examining himself in the mirror in the living room, he turned to me.

'Very nice,' I confirmed.

'Yeah? . . . Now what about this one?' He ran back into his bedroom.

'That one is also very nice.'

'Okay – but which one is nicer?'

'That one,' I said, pointing at the one he had on, even though I thought it looked exactly like the first one.

'I look like a complete imbecile with this bow tie.'

'Yes well, don't wear it then.'

'You know what – I won't wear it. I don't care what they say.' He took off the bow tie and threw it onto his bed. 'Okay, let's go!'

'Wait! What the hell am *I* going to wear?' I cried. His nervousness had rubbed off on me and magnified in the process.

'I don't know – something nice.' I went into my room and changed into my only presentable option – a vintage blue 1950s-style knee-length dress.

'No. Too colourful and too short.'

Shit. I should have hired something. I returned to my room, and changed into the black pants that I wore to work and threw my mother's black cashmere shawl around my shoulders. If it was the widow look he wanted, it was the widow look he would get. Then I unearthed the few remnants of make-up that had survived from Australia and rushed into the bathroom.

Octavio burst into the bathroom as I smeared out the last bit of concealer over the dark circles under my eyes. Peering over my shoulder into the mirror, he began to attack his hair with a comb. 'They are all going to tell me my hair is too long,' he groaned.

'It's fine. I just cut it . . .'

'No, you don't understand . . . This is my dad's side of the family.'

Octavio had already me told that his father's side of the family were acutely conservative – and that they saw him as 'that problematic nephew', the one who was 'out of control', and had most probably 'fallen off the rails'. All the men of this family were either lawyers or diplomats, but Octavio was in the music industry. Another cause for concern was that he had yet to be married. And today's event would signify the second last of the cousins being married off – the older generation would be able to sit back and breathe a sigh of relief, if it wasn't for Octavio.

❧

We turned onto the second storey of the Periferico Highway (building a second storey above the southern section of highway had been one of the many public works completed during Obrador's term as governor) and our car came to a halt as we encountered a vast herd of unmoving cars. Octavio slammed his fist on the steering wheel. 'Only in bloody Mexico is there traffic on a Saturday morning – a bunch of morons going to have lunch with their parents-in-law,' he grumbled before glancing at his watch. 'Oh my God, we're going to be late!'

He placed his thumb on the horn and left it there for a few nasty moments before leaning back fatalistically into his seat. Then he turned to me, 'You know, I don't know what I'm going to introduce you as.'

'I'm your flatmate.' It seemed obvious enough to me.

'No. They wouldn't be able to identify with that concept. In fact, don't tell them that we live together.'

'Then introduce me as your white slave,' I said.

'I know what – I'll introduce you as my sex partner . . . Ha! Ha! Ha!' He threw his head back and began to laugh hysterically. 'Imagine the looks on their faces! "Aunty Graciela, Uncle Roberto, allow me to introduce you to – my sex partner from Australia",' he went on. But I was experiencing too much dread to share his amusement at this hypothetical situation.

Our car inched with the traffic along the highway. It seemed to take hours. We were late. Concerned faces glanced in our direction as we crept in and found an empty space on a pew at the back of the church. The guests were in black – black suits, black dresses, black high heels, as if attending a funeral service. Octavio had been right about the blue dress.

In the distance the bride and groom knelt beneath a pulpit, their hands held in prayer. In front of the pulpit a grey-haired man in a white robe was standing under a crucifix and murmuring monotonous words into a micro-phone. The words blurred together as they echoed through the space, transforming into a single somniferous sound.

But dozing off was made impossible by the regularity with which we were required to stand up to sing and then get down on our knees to pray.

'How much longer of this?' I mouthed to Octavio after the first hour.

'About another three hours,' he whispered. He couldn't be serious.

Three hours later, the newly married couple stood up, the rings were swapped and a nervous kiss was exchanged. Bones cracked as we stumbled outside into the daylight. An older man with perfectly parted black hair and a rectangular beard placed a hand on Octavio's shoulder.

'Don't worry – no one noticed that you arrived twenty minutes late,' he snorted at Octavio in Spanish.

Then he turned to me. 'And who is this?' he inquired, in English. 'Another exotic foreign girlfriend, I see,' he said to Octavio under his breath in Spanish.

'This is my friend Lucy from Australia.' He introduced me to his uncle, who then raised his eyebrows at Octavio, as if to say 'An Australian now? What next? An Inuit?'

Then the uncle turned to me and smiled graciously. 'Such a pleasure to meet you, and welcome to Mexico,' he said squeezing my hand.

After presenting our invitation at the door of the reception centre, we were led to our designated table, where we found an assortment of tall white people with high cheekbones and straight teeth. One of them was Octavio's older brother Ramón and his wife Elena. The rest of the clan were cousins and spouses.

'Nice hair, Octavio,' smirked a cousin with very short blond hair as we arrived at the table. Octavio ignored the remark and sat down next to Ramón.

'No tie,' were the first words Ramón uttered to his younger brother. 'You came to our cousin's wedding without a tie . . . Well it's good Dad's not here . . . What would he say?' He was a serious-looking man, cleanly shaven and immaculately dressed. 'So, just travelling through, are you?' he asked me in English.

'Actually, I live here,' I told him.

The smoked salmon arrived and Ramón launched into the 'what-are-you-doing-with-your-life' sort of questions – what had I studied, what my plans were for the future. When I told him I had studied a degree in Arts, and began to explain what that was, a blank look passed over his face.

'I see . . . and where does that get you?' he asked, genuinely puzzled.

'I'm not sure if it will get me anywhere. That wasn't really the point . . .'

'Well, I can see why you and Octavio are friends . . .' he laughed.

Then his wife Elena, a delicate blonde who was sitting across from me, came to the rescue, 'Well, it doesn't really matter what you study if you're going to get married anyway.' She explained that she had met Ramón at law school, and the two were wedded immediately after graduation.

Suddenly the lights dimmed and four pudgy bodies in sequined lycra bodysuits took to the stage. 'Money, money, money' the chorus began. Octavio rolled his eyes, but I was grateful for the distraction from the conversation – even if it came in the form of an ABBA impersonation.

The other distraction was a waitress who arrived every few minutes to offer us more alcohol. 'Two tequila shots, Reserva del Patrón,' ordered Octavio.

'This is the best quality tequila you will ever have,' he explained, grabbing my knee under the table. And it really was beautiful tequila. The conversation going on around me was becoming increasingly difficult to follow, so I sat back and gave my full attention to the performers, who were becoming more and more enjoyable.

It wasn't until I stood up to go to the bathroom that I realised the full extent of my intoxication. 'Octavio – can we go?' I managed to articulate.

'Go . . . You want to go?' he spluttered, knocking his chair over behind him as he stood up.

We said goodbye to our table companions and began to move towards the door. We were making quite good progress when our path was blocked by a middle-aged woman. 'Octavio, darling!'

'Aunty.'

'Now, judging by the state of your hair, I imagine that you are still in the music industry . . . Oh and look – no tie. That's my Octavio,' she joshed. She had short silver hair and pearl earrings.

'And who is this?' I heard her ask.

'This is Lucy, my sex partner from Australia.'

§

I woke up the next day with a violent pounding in my head, which increased in intensity as a series of disturbing realisations occurred to me. The first was that my body was being pressed against the wall by a mass far greater than my own, and two hairy feet stuck out the bottom of the sheets at the end of my mattress.

The second thing I became aware of was the horrible high-pitched noise that was reverberating through the room. Reaching over the large hairy body I found that Ricardo's name was flashing on the screen of my mobile phone. I stared at the screen until it stopped ringing.

'Turn off your bloody phone,' mumbled the large body mass, as it pulled the sheets over its head. This was the twelfth missed call from Ricardo that morning.

Then I realised something even more disturbing. It was Sunday. My family would be flying into Mexico City airport any minute.

❧ 10 ❧

Parental Guidance

Through the crowds at the international arrivals terminal I saw a mountain of half-unzipped luggage. As I got closer, I could see that one of the bags was spewing its contents onto the airport floor, leaving a trail of loose toiletries, underwear and ravaged books. Next to this mound stood what appeared to be a Swedish movie star. Silky white blonde waist-length hair flowed over a vintage floral sundress that clung to her strapping curvaceous figure.

'Jell!' I shouted.

She closed her paperback copy of *The Sun Also Rises* and ran over to give me a hug. My sister Angelica's Nordic colouring and soft features had once caused me to give her the nickname of 'Potato Face' but those days were long gone.

Two other dazed-looking figures were seated on the luggage. 'Oh darling, you're thin,' cried my mother as she caught sight of me.

'Hi, Mum. Sorry I'm late. Have you been waiting long?'

'And you're still wearing those pants,' she said. 'They must be over three years old now.'

My father stood up, clutching onto his laptop bag, which was bursting at the seams with magazines and papers and the book he was currently reading, *The History of Bombing*.

'Hi, Dad.'

'Hi, darling.'

I grabbed hold of one of the wheelie suitcases and led the way towards the pre-paid taxi stand.

My original arrangement had been to go with Ricardo in his car to pick them up, but this morning I hadn't been able to muster the courage to face him. On answering his thirteenth call, I had found myself up against a series of daunting questions. 'Are you okay? Why weren't you answering your phone? I thought you'd been kidnapped . . . Where were you last night? . . . And this morning? You sound strange . . .'

With each question the pounding in my head had increased, until I finally told him, 'I'm sorry. I'll explain everything tonight. Don't worry about the airport.' After all, it was too soon for a confession – I needed time to absorb the situation, and then to find the words to explain it in a way that would evoke sympathy and understanding, although we all know that such words do not exist in the English language. Octavio had then offered me his driving services. 'Where are you going? Why are you in such a rush?' shouted the large creature that was wrapped up in my sheets as if he were a burrito.

'My family are due at the airport in an hour,' I informed him.

'What? . . . I can take you.' He sat up quickly, rubbing his eyes.

'No, don't worry . . . It's all too complicated.'

He stared at me silently for a few seconds: 'You know, I was very drunk.'

'Yes, me too.'

Then he stood up and, taking the sheets with him, waddled along the hall to his room and closed the door behind him. I took the metro.

❧

'You know, I'm worried about your mother,' said Dad. He and I were walking ahead of the other two. 'Dr Lee gave her sleeping pills called Stilnox for all the flying. Apparently they have been involved in sleep crime. I just don't know if it's combining well with the painkillers and antidepressants. She disappeared in Santiago Airport and we had to call security to help us find her.'

'That's terrible,' I said, although this didn't sound like unusual behaviour for my mother. When I was thirteen my parents had miraculously survived a head-on collision with a truck and my mother's spine had been badly injured. Since then she had frequent bouts of severe back pain, which had led to depression, and all this was being treated by Dr Lee with a panoply of pharmaceuticals as well as trips to psychiatrists, and every imaginable therapist. A sense of humour, sometimes black, kept the situation workable.

But she still had the energy to worry about her husband. A week earlier she had told me over the phone, 'I'm really worried about Richard. The bushfires have been over-whelming and he's so stressed, and he's doing too much flying . . . he's always flying off to conferences about the pollution caused by flying. He used to be so much more fun and relaxed when he smoked dope – I think he should take it up again.'

Finally, when we were all packed into a safe taxi van I asked them, 'So how was your stopover at Santiago?' Mexico was one stop on a round-the-world trip, courtesy of an old friend of Dad's – a sixties radical who had grown up to become an irascible publishing tycoon and poet. For years he'd been inviting us to stay at his dream house in the Caribbean. After Mexico the plan was for my parents and sister to visit Cuba and then to travel on to holiday at his island paradise – so they could experience directly the extremes of socialism and capitalism . . . their idea of a humorous itinerary.

'Santiago was really interesting . . .' began my sister, who had just completed her final school exams and written a prize-winning essay on Latin American history. 'We went to the Presidential Palace where Salvador Allende was killed during the *coup* and . . .'

'Yes,' Dad interrupted, 'and everywhere you go you get frisked by these female security guards with red lipstick, skin-tight black pants and these tight black boots . . .'

'Dad!' Angelica cut in. 'Can you stop talking about the dominatrix policewomen – I know they were really exciting for you, but it's the only thing you've talked about since leaving Chile.'

It was dark by the time we pulled up in front of the Hotel Majestic. And it *was* Majestic. After weeks of scouting, this was the hotel I had found that met the criteria of my mother's strict desirable hotel dot points: light, space, high ceilings, colonial architecture, balcony, cleanliness and a view.

The porter who led us to the room finally managed to avert his gaze from Angelica long enough to open the curtains on the French windows. This revealed a bird's-eye view of the vast Zócalo and the flashing psychedelic nativity scenes made up of tiny coloured lights that were strung across the buildings surrounding it. A five-storey Christmas tree, constructed entirely from tiny golden lights connected by cords, stood in the centre. I didn't tell them that various people had fallen to their deaths during the construction of the decorations. 'Where can we get food around here?' was my father's first question after they took all this in. Of course they had had to arrive on a Sunday night – the one night of the week when the normally throbbing Centro Histórico happens to be completely dead. As we wandered along the empty cobblestoned streets, Angelica continued to fill me in on my mother's latest pharmaceutical adventures.

'Last night in the hotel I heard her get up in the middle of the night and the rustling of her pill bag. So, I told her not to take another Stilnox. "I'm not taking another *one*," she said. "I'm taking another *two*".'

'Santiago had a lot more life on the streets, didn't it?' I overhead my mother say to my father as they walked along behind us. Then we heard the sound of gunfire. It seemed to be coming from down the alley. Although I suspected it was probably just firecrackers, I was pleased to see, by the look of fear on their faces, that they were already more impressed by life on the streets.

Food at last. Around an open garage door a small crowd was gathered and some women were cooking fried quesadillas. My family sat down on upturned crates set up on the pavement while I made the order.

'I don't think I should eat this,' said Angelica, glancing down at the deep-fried bundle dotted with red and green salsa. 'I'm feeling a bit sick in the stomach.'

The rest of us wolfed down the quesadillas before making our way back towards the hotel.

'You know what?' Dad asked, when Angelica was out of earshot. 'I think Jell might be pregnant.'

'Why?'

'Well, she's been vomiting.'

'She's probably just got a bit of food poisoning from the plane . . .' I reasoned.

'Still, I think you should talk to her – just in case.'

Leaving them at their hotel, I walked back towards the metro station. It was shaping up to be a fun family holiday – a mother taking medication that was implicated in sleep crime, a father whose stress levels were so dangerous his wife was prescribing marijuana and a possibly pregnant sister. At least it was a distraction from my dysfunctional love life.

When I arrived at Ricardo's dimly-lit apartment at 11 pm, I still had no idea what I was going to say to him. Just be honest, I told myself – it's always easier in the end.

It was clear he was prepared for the worst by the high volume at which he was playing Paganini and the half-empty bottle of whisky which sat open on his desk. But his first words came as a shock. 'Was it your flatmate?'

How the hell did he know? I stared at him dumb-founded for a few moments before I managed to articulate the word 'Yes'.

'I thought so. You always get uncomfortable when you speak about him.' But it was the next question that really threw me: 'Do you have feelings for him?'

One of the first things that had attracted me to Ricardo was the expressiveness of his face. Every emotion he felt played across his handsome features like the weather and it was the unbearable intensity of emotion now conveyed on his face that compelled me to break my honesty pledge.

'No. I was just drunk . . . I'm sorry,' I spluttered.

'Do you still want to be with me?'

'Yes,' I told him. This part was true.

§

The smog was so thick I could only see a few metres ahead as I walked across the Zócalo to the Hotel Majestic. The air tasted like exhaust fumes. It was the most polluted day I could remember since being here. During winter the dirty air stayed trapped in the valley as if it were a Dutch oven.

'I can't bear to think of you breathing this pollution every day,' said my mother as she stood looking over the hazy Zócalo.

'It's not always this bad.' I suggested that they come and see my flat in La Roma, where I knew the pollution would be less severe.

Once again the hotel porters didn't attempt to hide their wonder as Angelica floated down the Moorish tiled staircase, sliding her fingers along the brass banister. Their mouths fell slightly open and their eyes rolled back in disbelief. They stood motionless as she swept past them without a look in their direction. Her transparent blondeness combined with her sartorial extroversion was proving almost too much for the Mexican men to cope with. Angelica had not yet learned the most basic tools for getting by in Mexico City: unless you have an armed bodyguard or two, dress down to the point of invisibility.

We disembarked from the taxi at Calle Orizaba and I led them up the dilapidated yellow staircase and through the door of my first Mexican apartment. I could hear my mother Julie thinking, It's rather stark – where's the sofa?

'Well, it certainly looks very Mexican,' said Angelica, as she looked around at the cactuses and the life-size painting of the Virgin of Guadalupe. 'I mean, you wouldn't want to be living in Mexico in a flat that didn't look Mexican,' she added.

'It's very small . . . And you're sharing this flat with another person? Wow, you do live in very close quarters,' Dad observed as he popped his head into Octavio's room.

I poured my sister a shot of Octavio's best mezcal and left her to cross-examine his bookshelf. My mother had already got to work sorting out my dirty clothes.

'You know, Dad, William Burroughs used to live in the house next door.'

'Really? That's right – he shot his wife in Mexico,' he recalled. 'He was aiming at the martini glass on her head.' He was becoming increasingly excited. 'Can we go and see the house?'

'Here it is – number two hundred and ten.' I pointed to the decrepit-looking building on the left and waited while Dad took eight photos of the door from different angles.

I didn't tell him that I vaguely remembered reading something about the original house having been demolished.

'You know it wasn't just William Burroughs – he came here first to escape the law, but then Jack Kerouac, Neal

Cassady, Allen Ginsberg, Gregory Corso . . . the whole
gang came over. Wow – you really hit the jackpot finding
a place here,' he said as we walked back up the stairs. I
paused before I opened the door – a familiar booming
laughter was coming from inside the flat.

Octavio stood up immediately as we entered the room.
'Hello! You must be Richard – I'm Octavio, Lucy's flatmate.
A pleasure to meet you – and welcome to our home.' The
two shook hands firmly.

'What are you doing here?' I asked Octavio.

'I'm on holidays – the school is closed for Christmas
break.' He glanced at his watch. 'But don't worry – I'm
off to a rehearsal now,' he grinned. Then he turned to my
mother, 'See you at ten o'clock tomorrow at your hotel.'

'What?'

'Octavio is going to take us on a master tour of the
Centro Histórico,' explained Angelica.

'Yes, that would be great,' Dad said and then yelled at
Octavio's retreating figure, 'You know, Lucy took us to
eat in a gutter on our first night here.'

'Yes, I can imagine,' said Octavio. 'She likes that sort
of thing.'

§

The next day, I stopped by the Hotel Majestic after work.
My family seemed quite ecstatic after their master tour
with Octavio.

'It was fascinating,' observed my mother. 'He knows so much history – he talked about human sacrifice with such eloquence that I think I need to take a shower. I feel disturbed.'

'And he took us to the National Palace,' added my father. 'To see the Diego Rivera murals – incredible! A complete visual history of Mexico. And all the other tourists needed to line up and show their passports, but the guards took one look at Octavio and directed us through the door.'

Mum agreed. 'Yes, Octavio's aristocratic bearing has an effect on everyone – no one asks questions. And then he took us for lunch at a historic restaurant on the rooftop of a building, where you could see the whole city. It wasn't even open, but he told them to open and they did.'

'So you're not hungry then?' I asked.

Ricardo was on his way over to the hotel, and we had been planning to take them to lunch. He had insisted on meeting my family. Considering the fragile state of our relationship, I had told him this wasn't really necessary, but he had persisted. 'No I must meet them – they shan't be here for long.'

The hotel phone rang. Ricardo was waiting at reception.

'Tell him to come up,' I told the concierge.

'Ricardo's here,' I announced.

'Who?

'The guy I have been seeing.'

'As opposed to the man that you live with?' confirmed my father.

'Yes. In fact . . . Please don't tell him anything about your tour with Octavio – it's a sensitive topic at the moment.' I was starting to panic.

'So you want us all to lie about what we did today?' Dad asked. While my mother and my sister looked suspicious, he appeared to be both intrigued and amused.

'No, you don't have to lie – just don't mention Octavio's name,' I begged. Surely there was a difference.

Poor Ricardo, I thought – Octavio was a hard act to follow. But when I opened the door, he was standing straight and proud like a mariachi and wearing his best shirt, the white one that he knew I liked. He greeted each member of my family graciously.

'Shall we go and get some lunch?' Ricardo suggested after the introductions.

'I'm afraid they've already eaten,' I explained quickly.

'Oh, well . . . How about we go on a stroll to the Templo Mayor?'

'They have already been there . . . Look, why don't we go and get a beer,' I suggested.

We headed down to the Opera Bar, the notorious cantina where Buck had taken me after we first met. My mother was a big hit there with the elderly male drinkers. Ricardo, despite the tense situation between us, exhibited perfect manners and an endearing warmth. When the family is involved, Mexicans will rise to the occasion – no matter what the circumstances may be.

§

That night I decided to take my family for dinner at the bohemian café which Edgar and I frequented for our *intercambios*. I knew they would be impressed by the walls lined with old books and the ratty chandeliers with candles. In the labyrinth of rooms civilised drinking and sociable activities – such as chess, jazz and animated political discussion – were all taking place in an atmosphere of sophisticated conviviality.

Unfortunately, however, the ambience was not enough to distract my family from the controversial topic of my love life. My mother had tried to inculcate firm rules on etiquette with boyfriends, inspired by guilt over her own youthful behaviour. 'What happened to you that made you want to exact revenge on men?' she asked. 'I mean, when will you be satisfied? Why not get ten boys infatuated and hold a jousting contest?' It was only her second mezcal, but it was creating a chemical cocktail she had never tried before.

'Look, I didn't create this situation on purpose – that's just how it eventuated,' I explained.

Dad, who has had more experience with multiple lovers than my mum, understood me perfectly well. 'Yes,

I know. Every time you decide on one, the other seems more appealing,' he consoled.

'Yes,' I agreed. He was exactly right.

'Well that's pathetic,' snapped Mum.

But Angelica swiftly brought the conversation back to my dilemma. 'Well, Lucy, of course you feel you didn't create this situation on purpose; but it must be some kind of subconscious . . .' she started.

'Don't try to psychoanalyse me,' I cut in. I was beyond the point of caring whether I was sadistic or not – or what perverted reasons I might have had for obtaining two lovers. The psychoanalysis could come later; right now, I just had to make a decision – to choose one or the other.

My mother had a clear preference for Octavio, but I wasn't sure if I agreed with her reasoning. 'Ricardo doesn't deserve to be involved with someone who treats men like handbags – Octavio is better equipped to deal with your games.'

'Ricardo is so warm and gentle,' Angelica said. 'He's like a cuddly polar bear – and you always know exactly what he's thinking.'

'Octavio's got the world by the balls,' said my father.

'Well, yes, Octavio is charming and erudite,' Angelica admitted. 'But frankly, I find that rich-kid over-confidence tedious. You can find that model anywhere in the world. I imagine the son of an important Turkish diplomat would have much the same characteristics . . . I feel sick – where's the bathroom?'

As I made my way back to my flat, after putting my family into a cab to the Centro, I received an unwelcome phone call from Ricardo. 'Are you sleeping at Octavio's house tonight?' he inquired.

'No, I'm sleeping at my house,' I told him, before hanging up the phone. I was at breaking point, and all I really wanted to do was shout at people.

Octavio was sitting on the couch playing the guitar when I came in. 'Where did you sleep last night?'

This charged question, combined with my fatalistic mood and my slight inebriation, set the scene for a satisfyingly melodramatic fight. 'Why? How does it affect you?' I challenged.

'You know exactly how it affects me,' he said, getting up from his seat.

'No, I don't – you've never made it very clear . . .'

'Me? You're the one who never made it clear!' He was shouting now.

'Well, tell me now then – what do you want? Do you want to be with me . . . in a relationship?'

'I don't know . . . I want you to break up with your boyfriend.'

'What? To be with someone who doesn't know what he wants?'

It went on like that for a while – both of us furious, and neither one of us knowing exactly what we wanted.

Finally Octavio walked out of the flat, slamming the door after him, and I went to bed.

§

The next morning I was in a class with Ofelia, who was now in a complete state of panic about her wedding the following week, when I received a hysterical call from my mother. 'Angelica's really sick . . . You have to come over now – the hotel's arranged a doctor, but he doesn't speak any English.'

When I arrived at the hotel, Angelica was sprawled across the bed; her skin had gone pale blue, echoing the colour of her nightdress.

'Could it have been those fried things you gave her in the gutter?' said my mother.

'Mum, she was already sick on the plane.'

There was a knock on the door. 'Quick!' shrieked my mother. 'It must be the doctor.'

A handsome young man with a nervous smile was waiting outside the door. He looked the part – a stethoscope was strung around his neck, and he clutched a large black briefcase. But there was something unsettling about his appearance and his mannerisms.

'Well, here's the patient.' I directed him to the sofa where Angelica was lying.

'God, he looks about fourteen,' whispered Dad. He was right – the white uniform he wore was far too big for him and his awkward movements were characteristic of an adolescent. Angelica looked up; her pale skin was glistening with sweat and the doctor began to blush wildly.

Earlier that week I'd read about an armed robbery of a chemist, during which the staff had been instructed to hand over their white coats before they were locked in a cupboard by the thieves. The intruders worked all day behind the counter serving the customers, occasionally popping their heads into the cupboard to demand advice at the end of a gun. At the close of business they emptied the till, unlocked their captives and went home. I wondered if a similar situation could be taking place right now.

The doctor seemed lost for words, so I began to list her symptoms. But you could tell by the way he was looking at Angelica that participating in a conversation about vomit was the last thing he wanted to be doing with her. His hands shook as he pressed them into her stomach.

'It looks like she has a stomach infection,' he said finally. Then he opened up his briefcase and began to transfer the contents of a plastic bottle into a large syringe.

'What's he doing?' Angelica sat up suddenly on the bed. I asked him what he was doing.

'What am I doing? Oh . . . ah, preparing the antibiotics,' he stuttered.

'What? Antibiotics? Why in a syringe?' she yelped.

'That's how they give them to you here,' I told her.

'Can you ask her to take her pants down,' he asked.

His voice was quivering now. Angelica looked horror-struck.

'Come on, Jell – don't you want to get better?' I cajoled her, although I felt rather glad not to be in her position.

'What the hell is this imbecile doing?' asked Dad, a bit too loudly, as the needle penetrated his daughter's flesh.

He looked even more appalled when the doctor presented him with the bill – US$300.

❦

The next morning at the flat I removed my clothes from the closet and packed them into my suitcase. That was really all I had to move, other than the small pile of books stacked against the wall. All the furniture was Octavio's, including my mattress. My only contribution to the household had been a yellow Otomi bedcover, embroidered with whimsical animals and plants, which I had bought for my room when I received my first pay cheque, and a small jade plant. I left that for Octavio, as well as a bunch of arum lilies, which I placed in a vase on the mantelpiece. Under the vase I put a remorseful note, in which I attempted to justify my sudden departure.

The once harmonious flatmate relationship between Octavio and myself would never be the same again. And yet it had not had the opportunity to change into a new sort of relationship, I thought, with a strong sense of regret.

Ricardo was lovable and loving. But the drama the night before had left me with an overwhelming urge to get away from both of them. Thanks to a scheduled family holiday to the historic desert city of Guanajuato, I would have somewhere to sleep for the next five nights at least and a change of scene from which to contemplate my next move.

I finished writing the note to Octavio and swept the floor of my empty bedroom. Taking one last look at my first Mexican apartment, I then caught the metro back to the Hotel Majestic, where, feeling that I had failed, but not knowing why, I left my suitcase in storage.

§11§

Death Tour

Guanajuato: picture-book picturesque, colonial Mexico. And it was holiday time – not only for my family, but for every family in Mexico. Above the jagged golden peaks dotted with organ pipe cactuses, the sun in the cloudless cobalt-blue sky beat down on the old town; all the buildings were painted in deep-pastel colours: yellows, blues, mauves and pinks. Square stone buildings followed the shape of the valley along narrow cobblestone roads. And every street and alleyway was packed with tourists. I had not taken into account that it was an official public holiday, which was why our journey had been a little challenging.

But, after many hours queuing at the bus station, we had finally boarded our luxury Greyhound and set off on our journey north. Falling into a deep sleep, I hadn't woken up until hours later, when it occurred to me that something was getting pushed repetitively against my legs.

It soon became clear to me that it was the seat in front of us, which was bouncing back and forth violently.

'What's going on?' My mother had woken up with a start for the same reason.

There was a brief moment of silence as we both realised what was going on. 'I thought this was a Catholic country,' said my mother.

'It is,' I said. 'That's why they are doing it here – because they're not allowed to do it at home.'

I too had often been baffled by the extreme levels of physical intimacy that were socially acceptable in a country where virginity was a prized possession and abortion was illegal in all but one state. No public realm was off-limits – park benches and buses or library aisles often doubled as beds. Even a relaxing jog in the park was made awkward by stumbling upon gyrating bodies. It was acceptable as long as it didn't take place in the family home, it seemed. And since most homes were family homes, that left few alternatives. The abundant pay-by-the-hour hotels were an option for anyone with a spare 100 pesos – but, for the rest of them, to the streets it was.

However, tonight's episode was especially incongruous because we were on our way to Guanajuato: a state which frequently made the newspapers for its conservative government's repeated attempts to ban kissing in public, as well as the wearing of short skirts. Any couple who 'kisses with intensity in public' would be sent to prison, announced Guanajuato's Mayor Romero Hicks the other week. But so far he had been unable to muster up the support he needed to pass his bill.

Six hours later, we arrived at the hotel, and I was relieved to discover I had once again successfully fulfilled my mother's foreign accommodation fantasy – our cheapish hotel was 400 years old and built of stone with loads of wrought iron, and from the balcony the view of the brightly coloured town virtually forced you to sit at the solid oak table and dash off a watercolour.

Angelica added to the lovely scenery as she slipped into another of her vintage dresses with a full skirt and a tight waist. Despite a few awkward vomit moments at the bus station, it looked as if the injection given by the underaged doctor had miraculously worked – she was feeling better. Leaving our parents to snore, we made our way down the hill, along the cobblestoned street towards the main road. There were no cars permitted in Guanajuato's historic centre – tunnels for traffic had been built beneath the town so as to preserve its colonial charm. The crowds were so thick that they shuffled along slowly, as if they were grazing.

From a distance, I was almost certain they were all from Mexico City. Perhaps it was the tightness of their jeans and their elaborate hairstyles, or the distinctive way in which they walked. But when we joined the crowd and I began to hear snippets of conversation, I was left with no doubt as to their origin. Mexico City slang saturated every sentence and there was no mistaking that harsh urban inflection. All the people I had been desperate to get away from had followed us to Guanajuato!

We eventually managed to cover the three blocks to the leafy central plaza and find a seat at a café. 'Busy today?' I muttered sympathetically to the overwrought-looking waiter who was holding several plates of eggs.

'It's *chilango* season,' he told me, squinting his eyes with hatred. I grunted in agreement, delighted to find a like-minded human being.

'*Chilango*' is the name given to people from Mexico City, and people who are not from Mexico City tend to hate the people who are. *Chilangos* will tell you that they are hated because they are progressive-minded – unlike the rest of Mexico, which is backward and conservative. But non-*chilangos* will tell you that they hate *chilangos* simply because they find them to be rude and arrogant. Back in Querétaro my *chilango* companions had forced me to do all the restaurant ordering, so the locals wouldn't pick up on their *chilango* drawl and serve us last. Even alleged gringas like myself were considered to be better than *chilangos*.

After we had ordered some enchiladas, Angelica asked how I was planning to deal with my love problem. 'Why don't you just get your own flat and work it out from there?' she asked. It was the obvious solution and I explained that that was my intention, but the realities of Mexico City real estate virtually precluded it. To rent a flat on my own I would need a *fiador* – someone who owned real estate in Mexico City and who would agree to pay my rent for me if I disappeared. I had yet to befriend such a person – apart from Octavio's mother – and I didn't feel right about asking her. Homeless, worried and angry, my anger was primarily directed at myself; how had I allowed my fresh new Mexican life to degenerate before my eyes into a crass soap opera plot? All the mistakes I had made now seemed so obvious: why hadn't I told Ricardo about my feelings for Octavio from the beginning, for example. And yet I couldn't think clearly about what my next step should be.

Our parents were breakfasting on oranges and takeaway coffee when we got back to our picture-postcard room. I decided they were now ready for another dose of Mexican history. Only a short walk from our hotel stood the Alhóndiga de Granaditas Museum, the former granary where Mexico's first-ever attempt at getting rid of its Spanish colonists occurred.

In 1810 the Spanish in this rich silver town got word that a peasant army of independence fighters was heading their way, so they packed into the local granary. They took all their treasure with them and fortified themselves inside, placing some gunmen on the roof and others surrounding the building. Miguel Hidalgo's army, when it arrived, launched an aggressive onslaught, bombarding the building with stones. The oppressed miners and workers of Guanajuato happily joined in. The hero of this event was a deformed silver miner who they called *El Pípila* (the female turkey), referring to his limp. After tying a large flat rock on his back, to protect him from the bullets being shot from above, he ended the battle by setting the door of the granary on fire with a torch. His heroism is remembered in the form of a massive stone monument that stands on one of the hilltops overlooking the city.

Eventually, the Spanish retook the city and the decapitated heads of the four main instigators of the attack – Hidalgo, Allende, Aldama, and Jiménez – were stuck onto hooks at the four corners of the building, where they remained for ten years to serve as a warning to any other Mexicans who may have dared to entertain thoughts of rebellion.

꙰

At sunset I headed to a nearby internet café to tackle the correspondence from the two men in my life and to focus on the more urgent task of finding somewhere to live.

As I opened an email from Octavio I held my breath. But his prose was less aggressive than I had anticipated. My sudden escape from his abode hadn't gone down so well – but that was to be expected. And he said at the end that he understood why I had left, and to call him when I felt up to it.

The email I received from Ricardo was more upbeat. He told me that a friend of a friend was renting out a 'lovely' one-bedroom house in a colonial suburb called San Ángel near Coyoacán. It was furnished and had a rooftop terrace full of plants. He seemed to be implying that we could move in there together. But for me it was still unclear what sort of a relationship we would have.

My family was right – I needed to live independently. I had to find something else. I gave a hopeful once-over to the Mexico City flatmate-search pages, just in case something new had come up. But, as always, the only people looking for flatmates were foreigners and in most cases they were looking for Mexican flatmates so they could practise their Spanish. I wrote a half-hearted application to share a flat in La Roma with a gringo DJ called 'Wave' who was on his way down from California by car. But I hoped it wouldn't come to that. The expat scene was something I was desperate to avoid.

Christmas passed us by; it's a low-key event in Mexico that takes place mainly in private homes. Other more flamboyant holidays such as the Day of the Dead, Independence Day, Virgin of Guadalupe Day and Revolution Day overshadow Christmas in the festive calendar.

Despite the holiday crowds we found many places to escape. By walking up the cobblestoned alleys to the hilltops, we came miraculously into empty flower-filled squares, where masculine statuary memorialised yet another bloody loser-take-all historic event. The blood-soaked history of Mexico was causing my mother to ask far-reaching questions about the culture of my newly adopted country.

Despite this, we all felt we would have failed as tourists if we did not take the classic tour of Guanajuato, which climaxed with a visit to the mummy museum – the town's best-known attraction. It sounded grotesque enough to be interesting but, as we piled onto the dusty minibus, I noticed that our companions were many of the irritating *chilangos* I had been observing around the town.

'I'll translate,' I boasted to my non-Spanish-speaking family. But I regretted this claim as soon as the tour guide opened his mouth. All I caught was 'Hello and welcome to . . .' Then everyone on the bus burst into laughter.

'What did he say?' Jell asked.

'Um, I didn't catch that one.'

He wore dark sporty-looking sunglasses over greasy combed-back hair. He was one of those tour-guide wannabe-comedian types, whose contribution to humour consisted of speaking abnormally fast in the same tone, making it impossible to understand him. We sped off behind him down into an underground tunnel and then back up into the daylight, before we began our ascent of a steep rocky ridge. The first time we stopped was outside an old silver mine. At its entrance a shadowy bar looked out over an old overgrown garden. My mother, who is claustrophobic, walked straight into the bar with her journal and the book she was reading, *Going to Pieces Without Falling Apart*. She ordered a mezcal. The rest of us followed the guide into an opening in the ground.

As we made our way down the steps, the hole seemed to contract around us. It wasn't until we had lost sight of the circle of light indicating the entrance that the tour guide began his lecture on the many landslides which had taken place in the mine and the number of workers who had died trapped in between the rocks. The indigenous people worked as virtual slaves, he told us. Most miners working underground survived for an average of three years.

Next stop was the Museo de la Inquisición. Once again my mother decided to pass her time writing in her journal in the sunny, flower-filled garden outside. She watched in disbelief as a group of small children disembarked from another tour bus, clutching their black 'Inquisition' balloons and ran laughingly into the Museum of Torture, as though they were going to a zoo.

The Spanish colonies had not been exempt from the Catholic Church's reign of terror that took place in Spain in the sixteenth and seventeenth centuries. When we arrived at the front of the queue, a bubbly student from the local university approached us and introduced herself as our 'Inquisition Host'. Her dark hair with blond streaks was pulled back in a high ponytail; her hairstyle told a different story to her work uniform, which was a long black robe tied at the waist with a piece of rope.

'Wow,' my father whispered. 'A dominatrix Inquisition Host! She looks like she enjoys her job.'

'Please try to control yourself, Dad,' muttered my sister.

We followed our Inquisition Host through the arched doorway and into the ancient stone building. It was almost pitch black inside, but the exhibits were illuminated by means of individual red lights. A human skeleton inside an iron cage hung from the ceiling and a guillotine sat in the far right corner. Underneath the blade was a bucket filled with human skulls. Although the cobwebs decorating the cobblestone walls were fake, it was evident that the human remains were not.

Further on we were confronted with a complex array of torture machines and devices: stretching machines, chairs of spikes, beds of nails. One of the more creative devices was a hollow iron statue in the shape of a human body with a detailed outline of a face and hair – the accused heretic was placed inside and stabbed with burning rods through holes in the metal, explained our Inquisition Host, whose job it was to provide us with meticulous descriptions of how the devices were used and exactly what effect they would have on the victim. Many of the exhibits incorporated human skeletons or mummified human remains. It wasn't clear whether they had just been dug up for the display, or if they were the skeletons of the real victims who had died in this way. But the expressions of extreme terror on the faces of the mummies made me think that it was the latter.

Even the walls themselves had been used as devices of torture. Part of the rock in some sections had been knocked out to reveal fossilised mummies crouched in the foetal position – they had been buried alive inside the wall. Thanks to our Inquisition Host, I learnt a new verb: *emparedar* (to kill someone by suffocating them inside a wall) – a practice which must have been such a common occurrence during the Spanish Inquisition that a special word for it became necessary.

With the sun now slanting golden rays down on the valley, we visited an ornate church on a hilltop. It was confusing looking at the Virgin's compassionate face while the contorted grimaces of the church's victims still haunted our imagination. Then there was the final high point. But as our death-tour companions skipped eagerly towards the queue, their cameras poised, my mother decided yet again to go for a coffee with her journal.

We shuffled slowly towards the entrance. A text on the walls explained how the human remains in this museum had been naturally mummified before they were able to decompose. This was because of Guanajuato's dry climate and soil conditions.

We began our single-file stroll through the aisles of desiccated corpses. Paralysed yellow faces stared knowingly through the glass at the cameras. Some had been buried in their best clothes; others were still in their humble nightgowns. Some with hair, some without. One woman had lost her nose but her hands, which were held in prayer, had been preserved in the most lifelike detail.

'Are we in a museum or a morgue?' My sister wondered aloud as we came to the end of the first row of bodies.

'At least these corpses aren't being tortured,' I said.

But they weren't exactly resting in peace either. Most of the bodies were placed upright, posing like action figures. Many had extremely animated facial expressions. One woman was clutching her stomach; her mouth was wide open and her eyes appeared to be popping out of her head. One old man, who was standing upright and fully clothed, appeared to be laughing. But in most cases their faces were contorted in pain. I had always assumed that there was a point when you were dying at which you suddenly become peaceful, regardless of the physical pain you might be in; but here it was evident that this was not the case. The most haunting of all was the baby section. Tiny little bodies in rows, some still in their nappies. One appeared to be screaming for help. This was too much for my sister, who took one look at the shelves of infants and began to push her way past the crowd towards the exit.

'Mum, give me the camera – I want to take a photo of the dead baby,' screeched a chubby Mexican child.

'And why were these desiccated bodies dug up in the first place?' I asked our tour guide as we boarded the bus.

'Because their relatives had failed to pay their yearly "grave tax",' he explained.

The law in Guanajuato once gave people who couldn't afford to buy a permanent place in the ground the option of paying rent instead. So what was to be done when they couldn't pay that either? In 1865 they found an ingenious way of making the corpses pay their own rent – and generate much more. This museum receives over a million visitors a year. So these impoverished corpses are now largely responsible for making up the backbone of Guanajuato's tourist economy.

Back on the bus there was a rare moment of silence between my family members while the rest of our tour group were chirpily comparing corpse photos on their digital cameras. As the bus began to make its descent, the valley of Guanajuato became visible to our right, suffused in a bright orange afternoon light. The driver's beaded crucifix, which hung from his rear-vision mirror, swung violently from side to side as we skidded along the narrow winding road beside the cliff edge. We were moving at an alarmingly fast pace.

'Who's afraid of heights?' Our driver grinned at his passengers through the rear-vision mirror and steered the bus so that the wheels were startlingly close to the edge.

'This guy is a bloody lunatic,' my father cried out, grabbing onto the seat in front of him. But the rest of the passengers on the bus burst into laughter.

Fortunately my mother was now completely oblivious to what was going on. Her Stilnox seemed to have kicked in unexpectedly and she was now resting her head peacefully against the window of the bus.

'These people are insane,' squealed Angelica as we sped around another corner. Yes, they were. After our intimate encounter with the dead, we now had death three centimetres to our right and it was terrifying.

This behaviour was less shocking for me than it might have been when I first arrived. Foreign observers are often baffled by the Mexican attitude towards death. Whether it has its roots in Catholic fatalism or the Aztec exaltation of death, Mexicans today still act like death is a big joke.

You don't need to be in the country long to observe a general contempt for the Western obsession with safety. This makes itself most obvious on the roads – seatbelts, speed limits, and drink-driving laws are for wimps. No exam is required to get your licence in Mexico, just A$40.

And the Mexican tourists had robustly enjoyed the corpse exhibitions that had made my family green around the gills. Perhaps not so surprising considering the graphic photos of beheaded narcotics gang victims displayed on newspaper stands in Mexico every day. The Day of the Dead says it all. It was a subject I wanted to explore further.

❧

As I said goodbye to my family at the airport I felt mixed emotions. The overwhelming emotion was sadness. But at the same time I felt a weight lift from my shoulders. The smog, stomach infections, long queues into museums and lunatic tour guides of Mexico were no longer my responsibility.

I took the metro back to the Centro, where my bags were in storage at the Hotel Majestic. From there it is a short walk to the Hotel Isabel, where I had stayed when

I first arrived in Mexico, and now it was my best option again. I had fond memories of the place, but the thought of returning there was disheartening. After putting so much effort into trying to understand and be part of this country, I would be back where I'd started.

Another miserable thought was that it was Sunday night, which meant work tomorrow at 7 am. With an emptiness in my stomach I pondered all of this as I made my way across the crowded Zócalo towards the Majestic.

I stopped for a moment to answer my phone. It was Ricardo. 'What? Don't be ridiculous. I'll be there soon,' he said when I told him what I was doing.

'Wait . . . Ricky . . . I think we need some time apart . . .'

'Okay. Well, stay at my house tonight,' he interrupted, leaving me unable to finish the speech I had been rehearsing in my head about 'space' being necessary. 'You can sleep on the sofa – and tomorrow I'll help you find a flat.'

I agreed. Even though I knew he didn't have a sofa.

❧ 12 ❧

The Flower and the Song

Ricardo drove me all around the city to find somewhere to live. There was a room rented out to students by an old communist, who used the other room on weekends and kept pornography in the bathroom. Another potential home which was rented by two artists turned out to be a humpy on the roof. And while I grimly searched, I was still staying temporarily in Ricardo's dark den-like apartment. Even though it was den-like, there was something homely about it, and I looked forward to coming back after work to be with Ricardo – he was so solid and affectionate – I felt lucky to have found a best friend so far from home. But there was one feeling I couldn't discuss with him: the niggling sense of regret I felt when I thought about Octavio.

The sun-filled one-bedroom house Ricardo had found when I was in Guanajuato was still available, and was starting to be a tempting option. But the First Wives' Breakfast Club had strong opinions on this situation.

'Jes – jou know, Paco could cook . . . before we were married,' sniggered Reina.

'Ah yes – Mario even told me he like doing de shopping . . . Ha ha ha!' laughed Elvira.

'Everyting changes de second you move in together,' Marisol recalled bitterly. And Veronica agreed. 'Dis is de problem wid de Mexican mens – dey are good at tricking. Dey are romantic – dey sing to jou under de moon and all of dis blah, blah, blah. And den . . . bang! Suddenly jou are deir slave!'

'Yes, the gringos don't know what is romantic, but at least you know what you're getting,' said Elvira, who was now up to her third date with her Texan supervisor.

Even the upper class *fresas* were not immune to this sort of swindle. After her wedding, which had taken place just over Christmas while I had been in Guanajuato with my family, Ofelia had suddenly found that her career choices were being greatly limited. Her sensitive, creative husband Silvio was now telling her that he didn't think it 'appropriate' for her to accept a job that would require her to travel. Never mind that Silvio himself, as a documentary filmmaker, would be away for long periods of time adventuring around the world.

But finding somewhere to live in this vast city was proving impossible. After three weeks of exhausting and fruitless searching I had pinned all my hopes on a share house in San Ángel with three English girls. San Ángel was one of Mexico City's more elegant tourist centres, in the south of the city next to Coyoacán – home to the studio where Frida Kahlo and Diego Rivera lived together, before she allegedly found him in bed with her sister. Every Saturday the leafy central plaza, which had fountains and neatly cut hedges, became an art market; and it was on a Saturday that I had made an appointment to inspect the share house. Ricardo drove me there.

From the outside the place lived up to my expectations: a street lined with ancient stone walls and grand sixteenth-century iron gates, complete with gargoyles, underneath a cloud of purple jacaranda trees.

A thin blonde girl answered the door. She wore skin-tight designer jeans over pointy black boots. 'So you're the Aussie,' she said, completely ignoring Ricardo. We followed her into the house.

Just hearing the word 'Aussie', and especially pronounced as 'Ossie', made me cringe.

'Wow. You know, back in London I didn't really get on with Ossies,' she said as she showed me around. 'There's just too many of them over there. But here I go out and party with them all the time . . .' The house wasn't half as nice as it had looked in the pictures and the room available was the size of a closet – it must have once been the servant's quarters. Hairdryers, mirrors, make-up and clothes were sprawled across the house, and it smelt of competing duty-free perfumes.

A door opened and two other English girls appeared. Like their compatriot, they were wearing skin-tight jeans and pointy boots; and their hair had been ironed straight and shiny, to match their shiny manicures.

'This is Lucy, she's an Ossie.' Following the introduction, our conversation sunk to the lowest common denominator – the standard expat-to-expat cathartic bitching session about the inconveniences of life in Mexico City. After we had covered the lack of retail options, the crude behaviour of the men on the streets and the absence of tofu in supermarkets, one of the girls said, 'Hey, you guys should come out clubbing with us tonight in Polanco – the Ossies I was telling you about will be coming. I think they said they were from Sydney.' At that moment anxiety clutched my stomach, it was almost like one of those dreams where you realise you're in the wrong place – you're at the beach when you're supposed to be in your final exam. I could see myself so easily getting sucked into that comfortable English-speaking world. The degree of my panic made me realise to what extent I had set myself on a mission to become a true part of Mexico, not to be an outsider.

'Yes, it was lovely to meet you,' I muttered before grabbing Ricardo by the hand and darting out of the house.

We headed for the local *tianguis*, where we sat down at a table surrounded by dark red carcasses and bright yellow and purple piñatas which were hanging from the ceiling and ordered two *tlacoyos de frijol*, black beans cooked inside oval-shaped maize dough. It was a relief to be back in Mexico.

'Would you really consider moving in with the Spice Girls?' Ricardo asked.

'No,' I answered simply.

❧

So I consented to go and look at the house Ricardo had found. After all, it was just a ten-minute walk away from San Ángel's central plaza, in an area called Guadalupe Inn.

Ricardo pressed the buzzer on a heavy wrought-iron gate. We were greeted by a cheerful-looking woman who must have been in her late sixties. Ricky introduced me to Carmen, the landlady. He had only met her once before, when he came to inspect the house, but I could tell by the warmth of their greeting that they already liked each other. They had been introduced by the woman at the local quesadilla restaurant, which was frequented by Ricardo since the Fifth Avenue where he worked was just around the corner.

Carmen led us through the gate into an outside area. To one side, a wall covered in pink and red bougainvillea towered above us; on the other was a large stone house with two separate entrances. The first door was to her house. The second was the smaller house she was renting out.

'I had it built for my son . . . but he fell in love with a girl from Finland and then went and moved over there,' she said. She led us up some stairs to the entrance and opened the doors. Inside there was a living room and a kitchen. The thick stone walls were painted white and there was just the right amount of plain wooden furniture. An iron spiral staircase led up to a white bedroom with a window looking out over the snow-capped volcanoes of Xitle and Ajusco.

Xitle had last erupted almost 2000 years ago, burying in molten lava the civilisation of Cuicuilco, the first known civilisation to settle in the valley of Mexico. Although not so good for the Cuicuilcans, the smooth volcanic rock now gives much of the south of the city a moon-like feel. Strange succulent plants, unique to the area, grow in profusion. This layer of solidified lava has the added benefit of blocking seismic waves, meaning that earthquakes are hardly felt in the south of the city. But what I wanted to avoid was another earthquake in my own life. Ricardo was a gentleman, a man of honour; I sensed these things were important qualities. We made each other laugh and we shared interests in politics, music, art, cooking . . . just about everything. I was starting to feel that we could live together easily and be good for each other for as long as it lasted.

§

A glass door to the side opened out onto a rooftop terrace with terracotta pots full of cactuses and red geraniums.

Ricky and I stood there looking out over the rooftops at the volcanoes and breathing in the familiar smell of the geraniums. 'So, what do you think?' he asked.

'I don't need you to sign a lease – it will be a pleasure to have you,' said Carmen. So if it turned out to be a disaster, I could always make my escape.

§

A week later we moved the contents of Ricardo's den into our sunny new house. Un-scrunching the embroidered Otomi bedcover from my suitcase, I laid it out on the bed. We drove around the city searching for the right curtains and bought some blue and orange stripey blankets from the markets to go over the grey sofas.

Then we drove further south to the flower markets at Xochimilco (pronounced Zochimilco). This is the only area of the city that still has the original Aztec set-up of a network of Venetian-style canals. It is what remains of Lake Texcoco, one of the vast lakes surrounding the island where the city Tenochtitlán – the current Centro Histórico – was built. The lakes were drained by the Spanish after the great flood in 1629.

The market is huge: 13 hectares of plant stalls built along *las chinampas*, the fields constructed along the waterways by the Aztecs for agriculture and the cultivation of flowers. In Náhuatl the word Xochimilco means 'garden of flowers'. Flowers had been central to the Aztec view of life in both a practical and spiritual sense; and botanical gardens of aromatic, medicinal and ornamental plants had been an established tradition in the Aztec empire. And nearly all the poetry I had read written in the Náhuatl language was about flowers.

The great Aztec King Moctezuma II had a famous garden, and the Spanish conquistador Bernal Díaz del Castillo had written in his memoir, 'Many varieties of flowers and sweet scented trees planted in order . . . and the variety of small birds that nested in the branches, and the medicinal and useful herbs that grew there. His gardens were a wonderful sight'. This was before they captured Moctezuma and annihilated the entire city of Tenochtitlán. It was also noted that the Aztec nobles would hold bouquets of flowers to their noses when they were forced to address the Spanish, who did not share their same standards of hygiene.

'Flower-and-song' was a compound noun in Náhuatl and it was used as a metaphor for art. The Aztec sages taught that the flower and the song are the only two things in life that are true and eternal – their essence lives on, while everything else dies. In that spirit, we bought red and orange amaryllis flowers, herbs for cooking and pink flowering vines to climb over the pergola.

As we colonised the house together, kneeling on our roof-top garden and transferring our new plants into handpainted blue and white pots, I realised that for the first time since being in Mexico, I felt truly at home.

Although I had loved living in the flat in La Roma, it had always been Octavio's flat and I had felt the need to keep the evidence of my existence to a minimum.

Now that I was living with a real Mexican, I could get serious about my Spanish, which hadn't been going as well as I had hoped it would by now. Although I had no problems communicating for my everyday needs, I still wasn't fluent. The words still seemed to bury themselves away in a mysterious corner of my brain just when I needed them. And I knew the humorous subtleties of the language, such as irony, sarcasm and puns, simply swept straight over my head. But this was going to change very soon, given my new draconian policy: no English outside work hours. This meant nothing in English, not even reading books or writing emails, would be permitted.

Ricardo was passionate about cooking and we would go to the markets to buy the ingredients. He taught me how to make Caldo Tlalpeño – a soup made from avocado, chicken, onion, lime, coriander, baked tortillas, sour cream, chilli cascabel and chilli guajillo. I attempted to make him a Thai green curry – Thai cuisine is virtually unknown in Mexico. But after weeks of gathering the ingredients from obscure Chinese wholesale stores and faraway herb markets, the result barely lived up to expectations.

'That smells intriguing,' observed our landlady Carmen, poking her head into our kitchen window.

'Why don't you come in and try some?' I suggested, but I knew she wouldn't accept.

LUCY NEVILLE

Carmen always respected our privacy, despite our living in such close quarters and her being quite alone. Yet on the frequent occasions when I would lock myself out of the house, she would invite me into her vast home, which smelt of cats and ageing cedar furniture. She was a retired linguist, divorced and with both her children living overseas. We would sit on her sofa and sip tequila until Ricardo arrived home with the key. Our discussions were generally centred on the complex social dynamics of her seven cats; but after a few tequilas she would sometimes release her venom about her ex-husband, who had started another family with a younger woman. 'Men like Ricardo are rare animals,' she would slur. 'You should hold on to him.'

And I did. We had become an old married couple days after we met; as the months passed by we were now even more settled. Both of us worked long hours and made the best of our free time together, sitting in cafés in ancient plazas discussing the finer points of our respective languages and mulling over the madness of Mexican affairs. Now the price of tortillas had gone up by over 60 per cent virtually overnight, partly because America had decided to turn most of its maize harvest into bio-fuel rather than food. The streets were filled with hungry peasants who could no longer afford the staple part of their diet. '*Sin maíz no hay país*,' they chanted. Without maize we have no country.

Ricardo never turned into a *machista*. We distributed the housework evenly between us; also the household bills.

234

But when it came to matters of time, Ricardo didn't seem to think of it in the conventional Western sense.

The major obstacle in the way of me understanding this was an incongruity between adverbs of time in English and Mexican Spanish. The dictionary translation of the word 'now' in Spanish is '*ahora*' but I have rarely heard a Mexican actually use this word. More common is the word '*ahorita*', which the dictionary will tell you means 'right now'. However, in reality I discovered that '*ahorita*' actually means *at some unspecified point in the future*.

'I'm coming home *ahorita*,' Ricardo would tell me.

'Okay, I'll start cooking dinner *ahorita*.'

Half an hour later, dinner would be on the table – but with no sign of Ricardo. So I would dial his number: 'Hi. Where are you? Are you stuck in traffic?'

'No, I'm in my office.'

'Oh. I thought you said you were leaving half an hour ago.'

'Yes, I'm leaving *ahorita*.'

'Okay . . . well when exactly will you get here?'

'I told you – *ahorita*.' At which I would slam down the phone and go for a long walk.

By the time Ricardo did arrive home, he would wish he never had. 'Are you okay? You sounded a bit short on the phone.'

'You told me you were coming home *now*, so I cooked you dinner – and you didn't come,' I would snarl.

'But I'm here,' he would plead, with a look of complete befuddlement.

'Yes I am aware of that!' I would growl. 'But you're about five hours late.'

'Please calm down. I just don't understand why are you getting so angry – would you prefer it if I didn't work?'

Unlike me, Ricardo was happy to live in a state of perpetual uncertainty about when things would happen. His general reasoning was that, since one can never really know how long something is going to take to complete, there was no point in trying to predict it.

'But why do you always want to know *when* things are going to happen?' he would ask. 'That's just impossible to know!'

The opening up of the Mexican economy in the late 1980s may well have destroyed 'Mexican time' in the work place, but you can never really take the 'Mexican time' out of a Mexican.

Ricardo found my writing of to-do lists absurd. 'Surely you'd get more done by just doing things rather than writing about the things you intend to do,' he would say.

§

On weekends we would visit Ricardo's parents and younger brothers, who lived together about ten minutes further south, in the area that was completely covered by the porous volcanic rock thrown up by the volcano Xitle. They had a tiny flat in a sprawl of rundown cement towers that were saved from looking depressing by the backdrop of dark blue mountains. The block of flats where Ricardo's family lived was painted crimson and had its own garden of flowering cactuses and highly scented datura, which you could see from the window in the dining room.

Old red velvet sofas faced a large television. Faded wedding photos hung from the walls and a modest-sized crucifix was attached to the front door. Ricardo's mother, Chavela, came from a once-wealthy conservative Catholic family, but she had long given up trying to enforce these beliefs upon her staunchly atheist husband and her disinterested children. She was a smaller and rounder version of Ricardo. Rarely seen without her large white-rimmed spectacles and red-and-white checked apron, she never sat down for more than two minutes at a time.

Chavela was the youngest child in a family of six. Her father died when she was young, leaving her mother to bring them up alone. So her childhood had been full of work, and she rarely stopped working now. She sped around the house either looking after her family or cooking cakes to sell at the local *tianguis*, so as to supplement their meagre pension. She paid particular attention to me, having raised three boys; she liked having a girl in the house.

'Here, you need more tortillas,' Chavela would say as she placed some more tortillas on my plate. 'Has that soup gone cold?' Before waiting for my answer, she would carry my bowl into the kitchen. 'I'll just put it in the microwave again,' she'd mutter.

'Mum, please sit down,' begged Ricardo.

But she had just noticed that I hadn't eaten much of the *frijoles*. 'Do those *frijoles* need more salt?' she inquired.

'No, they are perfect – thank you,' I assured her.

'Well I'll just get you some more salt – just in case.'

'Mum, stop hassling her and sit down,' Ricardo pleaded.

'I just want to make sure she's happy.'

Ricardo's father Pepe was a slim man with white hair and high cheekbones. He had grown up on a cattle farm and then become an engineer and an entrepreneur. Once prosperous, the family had lost all their money when a cyclone hit their prawn farms. That's when they had moved from a large house with servants to this cramped flat. But Chavela never showed any bitterness.

Pepe, now retired, spent most of his time sketching ideas for inventions, particularly flying machines, in his notebook. He had once built a telescope from scratch, down to polishing the lenses himself. When the children were young, Pepe had created the ultimate toy by attaching an old motorbike to a giant metal spring which he cemented to the ground in their backyard.

Now he religiously watched the Discovery channel in order to keep learning, and, because of me, Australia was his new area of speciality. 'I saw on the Discovery channel that Australia has a problem with rising salination in the soil. Does that affect you?'

He was a passionate autodidact, and this was one of the qualities I found so appealing about Ricardo.

Óscar and Ángel, Ricardo's younger brothers, were in a progressive rock band called Vitruvius Robot. Their parents tolerated their rehearsals, which almost cracked the glassware in the apartment but were put on hold during the break for lunch.

'Do you have hummingbirds in Australia?' asked Ángel, the drummer and youngest of the three brothers.

'No, that has chilli – don't give it to her,' Chavela told Ricardo as he passed me a bowl of red sauce to put on the *flautas* or 'flutes', which were a kind of Mexican cannelloni: chicken wrapped in tubes of deep fried tortillas.

'She likes chilli,' Ricardo informed them proudly.

Pepe raised his eyebrows to show he was impressed: 'Not like the gringos,' he smiled.

Meals were spent trying to strike a balance between eating fast enough to keep Chavela from worrying that I didn't like her food and responding to Pepe's pressing questions about Australia's economic, geographical and ecological situation.

We rarely made it out of the house until late at night – after having arrived at lunchtime. This was another distinctly Mexican characteristic I learnt from living with Ricardo: Mexicans don't like you to leave. The eating part of the visit alone could go on for three hours. The meals were huge: soup, rice, tortillas, *frijoles*, salsas, grilled *nopales* (cactus leaves) and various other lovingly made dishes.

'We better get going now,' Ricardo would say when it was impossible to eat any more.

'But I just baked a cake,' Chavela would say. A maize cake would be taken out of the oven and coffee served.

'It's getting late – we should go,' Ricardo would try again after a while.

'Well you can't leave without having some fruit.'

A bowl of purple '*tunas*' (prickly pears) would arrive at the table, the fruit that grows from nopal cactuses. 'You know the gringos are so stupid – such beautiful fruit, and they don't eat them because they don't know how to remove the spikes. Ha, ha, ha!' Pepe gloated as he removed the prickly skin with a knife and a fork, then added lime, salt and chilli powder.

'Well how about a drop of mezcal? The best mezcal you'll find in Mexico.'

Pepe usually managed to convince us to stay and sip a shot of his cousin's backyard-brewed mezcal while Chavela would get out the family albums and tell me amusing anecdotes about the boys when they were growing up. Ricardo would retreat to the broom-cupboard-sized room where Vitruvius Robot recorded, and his younger brothers would let him listen to their latest tracks.

Mexicans love being together and find it almost impossible to part from each other. I had already become acquainted with this phenomenon in Querétaro, where I had shared a bed with my boss, but it was even more extreme among Ricardo's friends.

'Let's go, Ricardo,' I would whisper in English when

it was almost midnight – we had arrived for a lunchtime barbecue with friends.

'No . . . it would be rude to leave now – let's just have one more beer and then I'll tell them that you feel sick.'

Leaving was always considered offensive; no matter when. Along with the conception-of-time argument, this became another one of our favourite things to bicker about. But really, our fights rarely lasted longer than two hours before we were laughing about how absurd they were.

Sometimes I tried to imagine what things would have been like if I had ended up with Octavio. Both of us being so stubborn and hot-headed, our fights would have been far more destructive.

⚒

Six months after I moved in with Ricardo, the return flight that I had booked to leave Mexico exactly one year after I had arrived, flew to Australia without me on it. There was no reason to leave and many reasons to stay. I still didn't feel I was fluent in Spanish, and I still had so much to learn and understand about Mexico. It was easy to extend my visa since I was working for Fifth Avenue.

⚒

A bamboo fence separated our terrace from Carmen's rooftop, where a mongrel with a large head and short caterpillar legs was running around in a circle with a rag doll trapped between his teeth. When he saw us he dropped the doll and galloped towards us, wagging his tail madly; then he attempted to jump over the fence. He looked like a cross between a golden retriever and a dachshund.

'Poor Camilo is very lonely,' explained Carmen. She told us how she had found him outside the airport a few years ago, but that she had to keep him on the roof because he scared the other animals that lived in the garden at the front of her house.

We soon bonded with our canine neighbour. And, to the delight of Carmen, Ricardo managed to get him down the stairs and we took him on his first walk. Within a week of us being there, a tortoiseshell cat who lived with Carmen, but who had become fed up living with the other cats, decided to move in with us. A few months later, another small white cat followed me home from the metro station and became a permanent fixture on the sofa.

And so, there I was, an Australian living in Mexico City with a dog, two cats, a roof garden and a Mexican.

§ 13 ℀

Distilling Love

Despite having the important-sounding job title of 'Regional Service Manager', Ricardo made barely more money than I did at Fifth Avenue, working double the hours. Worse than that, our employers were once again months behind in paying both our salaries and the reimbursements for our travel expenses. I could always get more private classes; but the more private classes I gave, the more I felt I was living in an English-speaking world in Mexico.

We were managing to cover the rent and the grocery expenses; but if we wanted to do anything else, like go to the movies or buy some new underwear, serious consideration was required. And now the little white cat with the blue eyes that had followed me home had bladder stones and we had no idea how we were going to pay for the operation.

Since we had moved in together I had been telling Ricardo to find another job. 'Ask for a pay rise,' I advised him. 'You've been there for seven years.'

'They'd fire me,' he said plaintively.

'Why are you so apathetic? Just get another job.'

'There aren't any other jobs.'

Eventually I realised he was right. There were no other jobs. This was the reality for middle-class white-collar Mexicans. They worked like slaves for stingy, corrupt corporations, simply because there was no other option.

'I'm trapped here, Lucy,' Coco had told me once. 'I'm bored with dis stupid job. I want to study, but den how could I survive? I want to get out of here. Jou're so lucky . . . when jou get sick of dis place, jou can just pack up and go back to your country.'

And there was nothing like the dear old Australian Industrial Relations Commission to stand up for you here. That is, unless you could afford a lawyer, which was unlikely given that the average salary for 'service professionals' (guys who work in offices) was about A$29 per day!

It was becoming clear to me why most of my students lived in faraway suburbs, hundreds of kilometres out of the city, in houses crawling with overbearing parents-in-law. Needless to say, blue-collar workers were worse off – I had naively considered that getting a job in one of the funky bohemian cafés in Coyoacán would be fun, and a way of spending more time speaking Spanish, until I discovered that they were paid A$8 a day.

Tonight, Ricardo had just arrived back from an inter-state mission to check up on a rogue Fifth Avenue school four hours out of town, and I had been teaching 'Business English' to a group of executives from a chemical company. Too tired to cook or to line up for tacos in the street, we had gone to the nearest Don Taco restaurant chain. Chubby families, with three or four children in each, sat around the plastic tables and gazed up at a soap opera beaming from the massive flat-screen TVs which hung from the four corners of the restaurant.

There was something about the heroine on this particular show that infuriated me. She projected femininity as a form of helplessness. Her little round face with its tiny mouth and big round eyes, which stared innocently into the horizon or wept uncontrollably, popped up every time I turned on the television.

'God, I hate that actor!' I blurted between tacos.

'Yes, she's a terrible actor. But she's really beautiful, don't you think?' said Ricardo.

'Beautiful? She looks like a porcelain doll,' I fumed. 'I hate that sort of over-girly weepy cuteness. You know, I actually met a soap opera actor today,' I boasted. 'One of the stars of *Passion Island*.'

'Really? Where?'

'At Fifth Avenue. Today was his first lesson. His name was Bruno something. Very attractive,' I threw in. 'An Argentine.'

'Yes, many of those actors are,' he replied distastefully. 'Why?'

'I guess because they tend to be tall and blond.'

I looked around the room of the Don Taco chain restaurant. Most people were small in stature, in contrast to the TV actors who entranced them. While the audience had olive-coloured skin and dark hair, the smirking blond faces on the giant screens seemed as though they were from a different race. Whether it was a denial of the pre-Hispanic past or simply because the elites were mainly white, there was a clear preference for white skin in Mexican society. Most of the skincare products you could buy here contained 'whitening properties', unlike the 'tanning' moisturisers widely available in Australia.

'So was he nice?' asked Ricardo.

I recalled my conversation with Bruno. 'Why are you learning English?' I had asked him, trying to ignore the hulking man with dark glasses who sat by his side staring into the distance like a terminator. What I really wanted to know was why the hell he had brought his bodyguard into the classroom with him. Who would bother kidnapping a B-grade Argentine soap opera actor from an English class? The occasional Norteño or Mexican country music star was kidnapped or shot, but that was because they tended to be involved in narcotics trafficking. But not soap opera actors.

Coco walked past the classroom for the third time in ten minutes, making no attempt to suppress the eagerness of her grin. She had a real thing for blonds. Bruno threw her a half smile as he ran his fingers through his glossy hair before turning his attention back to me.

'I want to go to Los Angeles,' he told me in English with a lyrical Italianesque intonation. 'More money over there.'

'Do you like living in Mexico?' I asked.

He did. All except for the food (which had too much chilli) and the lack of exercise facilities here. Back in Buenos Aires Bruno had worked as a personal trainer, so exercise was important to him. In fact exercise was his true passion, and he had only landed a career on *Passion Island* by accident.

'I was here on vacation and I ran out of money, so my friend suggested I could find some work as an extra,' he explained. 'You see, the Americans shoot a lot of films here because it's cheaper. You know *Romeo and Juliet*? Mexico. You know the *Titanic*? Mexico.' The list went on: *Pearl Harbor, Tomorrow Never Dies, Man on Fire*. 'They need Western-looking people to walk around in the background. So I contacted an agent and he got me a role in an ad for shaving cream. Then I got spotted by Televisa and that's how I ended up on *Passion Island*.'

Televisa is a Mexican media company, the largest in the Spanish-speaking world. It owns several television channels known for their breakfast shows hosted by supermodels who end the show square-dancing while wearing cowboy hats. It also owns a soap opera channel called 'The Channel of the Stars'.

'You know, you could do it too,' he told me. 'You're slim and white – that's all you need for acting here.'

I laughed.

'Here – I'll give you the business card of my agent, just in case. If you call him, tell him you're a friend of Bruno's,' he had instructed.

I showed Ricardo the business card.

Adolfo Ramírez
Cotempo Stars
Agency for Modeling and Acting

The embarrassing truth was that acting had been one of my childhood dreams. Every Saturday I had attended drama class and in the school holidays I had forced my parents to send me to full-time acting courses. When I was ten I played Dr Diaforious in Molière's *The Imaginary Invalid*. I wore my father's suit with an enema bag strung around my neck. But this had all changed at about twelve, when suddenly, out of the blue, I gained an over-inflated sense of self-awareness that left me petrified at the idea of any kind of performance. I admitted all this to Ricardo.

'Well, you could conquer your fears while you're here in Mexico,' he suggested. 'Nothing lost by just going in and seeing the agent, and you could make some extra money.'

§

We found Adolfo's agency in a terrace house in a nearby suburb. He led us up a narrow staircase to his office – a large room with a black glass table and black leather chairs. The walls were covered with enlarged photos of young smiling white people. Adolfo didn't look like the people on the walls; he looked more like a guinea pig with a spiky 80s haircut – I found it comforting that he resembled the beloved pets from my childhood.

We engaged in some small talk for a while before he asked me to fill out a rather inconsequential form. Then I stood gawkily in front of a white screen while another man took photos of me from different angles. There was an audition for a push-up bra ad coming up, Adolfo told me. I pretended to be interested, and he promised he would call me. That was it. We said our goodbyes, but, just as we were leaving his front yard, I felt a tap on my shoulder. It was Adolfo. 'Hey, you said you were English, right?' he asked, panting.

'No. Australian,' I corrected.

'Oh,' he frowned. 'What language do you speak over there?'

'English.' His face brightened up at this.

'Is the accent the same?'

'Um . . . no.'

'But can you do an English accent?'

'Ah . . . What do you mean? In English?'

'No, in Spanish. You know, like . . .' He launched into an imitation of a bizarre-sounding sort of Cockney English accent in Spanish.

'Yeah – I guess so,' I said, trying to imitate his intonation.

'Great. Can you wait a second?' He dialled a number on his mobile phone.

'I have Dorothy!' he said. 'She's here with me now . . . Yes, she's English, and she meets the other criteria.'

He hung up the phone and turned to me. 'Can you be at Televisa Studio, San Ángel tomorrow morning at seven?' he asked.

'Yes,' I replied uneasily. I would have to chuck a sickie at Fifth Avenue.

'Great. You are going to play Gaviota's secretary in London,' he explained.

'What? Who's Gaviota?'

He looked at me, dumbfounded. 'You know, on *Distilling Love . . .*'

I turned to Ricardo. I must have misunderstood something, but he too looked vacant.

'You know, the soap opera . . .' Adolfo was getting impatient. 'You can watch it tonight at seven o'clock, okay? Basically, Gaviota goes to London to run the tequila business there, and you are going to be her English secretary – Dorothy. Got it? They will give you your lines tomorrow.'

'Lines?' I asked. He couldn't be serious. Perhaps I should have mentioned that I'd never actually done this before. I had been expecting to play the white-girl-walking-past-in-the-background sort of role.

'Yes, you'll have a few lines. Look, do you want the job

or not . . . ? It will be the final episode, so all of Mexico will be watching,' he added, apparently as an incentive.

No, I didn't. But saying no would be wimping out, so I said yes.

⚘

That night at 7 pm Ricardo and I switched on Televisa's soap opera channel, the Channel of the Stars. There she was – the infuriating woman with the porcelain-doll face, the one who Ricardo and all of Mexico thought was beautiful. I shuddered. The sun was setting over an agave cactus plantation and she was sitting on the ground weeping in a picturesque position. She wore a white frilled blouse, which looked enticingly as if it was about to drop off her shoulders, and a Mexican peasant skirt.

Had I really got myself into this horrible situation? Just because my cat needed its bladder stones removed? Ricardo burst into giggles as an incredibly large man arrived on a horse. He wore a white shirt with his first eight buttons left undone, to reveal a glistening six-pack.

'Rodrigo!' she gasped.

'Gaviota!' he cried.

Ricardo turned to me. 'Make sure you say hi to your "boss" from me tomorrow.' He was having hysterics, so I switched off the television.

⚘

7 am: Televisa Studio San Ángel, a monstrous concrete building at the intersection of two highways. The visitors' entrance was underground in the car park. Here I lined up behind the reception as my agent Adolfo had instructed. Now I just had to tell them the name of the soap opera and they would give me a pass. What was it again? Something to do with *amor* something . . . *Destilando Amor*. That's right: *Distilling Love*.

They gave me my pass and ushered me towards the lifts. When the doors opened I was in a room full of security guards and metal detectors, like at the airport. I placed my handbag onto the conveyor belt and removed my silver bracelet to go through the metal detector. There were two other security stations before I was finally let free into the studio.

Now where? 'Studio 7' said the security pass around my neck. I showed it to a guard and he gestured to a woman with long bleached-blonde curly hair who was walking past.

'Hey, Blanca, this girl's going to Studio seven.'

She stopped and stared at me for a moment. Then she said: 'You must be Dorothy.' She smiled and kissed me on the cheek. 'I'm head of production.'

She must have been in her forties and wore a well-cut suit jacket that revealed a gravity-defying cleavage.

'How adorable – a little English girl. How cute!' she exclaimed, referring to me.

'Actually I'm Australian.'

'Oh!' she looked taken aback. But I quickly explained that we spoke English, not German, and her facial muscles relaxed into a smile again. 'Oh well, my sweetheart, it's basically the same then, isn't it? Now let's get you made up, my love.'

We walked across an internal bridge that led from the offices to the studios. It was painted yellow and led to a vast outdoor terrace, where the grime and chaos of Mexico City had evaporated and everything and everyone was sparkling clean. There were water features and potted foliage and love seats and vine-covered archways, neatly cut hedges and coffee shops, with well-groomed fashionably dressed people scurrying around everywhere. We were in a different universe.

I followed Blanca into a brightly lit room. Lining the walls were giant mirrors surrounded by light bulbs, just like in Hollywood depictions of behind the scenes at the theatre. A swarm of women in white coats were speeding around the room: some held trays of make-up, while others were armed with electric hair-straightening and curling devices.

Blanca issued some instructions to one of the women in a white coat and then vanished. I was directed towards one of the seats, where they began the process of plastering my face with orange and yellow foundation and ironing my hair into bizarre shapes.

I looked around at the other faces in the mirrors. I had seen them all before. The woman next to me must be one of the main characters: a tall blonde with red-and-white streaks through her hair. They were styling her fringe into an outward bowl shape. Maybe she was Gaviota's sister? There was no sign of Gaviota yet – the star of the show, my boss, Gaviota. Sitting opposite me was an older lady – I recognised her bone structure. She played the wise grandmother figure who was always giving the younger generation advice.

By the time this was finally over – almost an hour later – my skin felt so heavy I could hardly move my face and the fake eyelashes made my eyes water every time I blinked. A short man with a goatee and bulging eyes appeared by my side.

'Dorothy?' he asked.

'Yes.'

'Follow me.'

He walked so fast I had to jog to keep up with him. Up some stairs we went, and down a narrow corridor in which all the rooms were numbered like in a hotel.

'Okay, here we are.' He stopped suddenly and used the card that was hanging from his neck to open the door. Room number 26. It was like a shoebox. No windows; just a wardrobe, chair in the corner, a mirror and a tiny bathroom.

'Here are your clothes.' He flung open the wardrobe to reveal a white polo-neck jumper, worryingly small brown pants and some black boots. Then he handed me an envelope, with the word 'Dorothy' scribbled on the front. Inside was a pair of round black-rimmed secretary glasses.

'I'll be back in five minutes to give you your lines.' Then he disappeared out the door and left me alone, to get dressed in my own dressing room. But the feeling of self-importance that the idea of having my own dressing room had evoked in me soon crumbled into an overwhelming sense of despair and regret when, five minutes later, the man with the goatee returned and flung a thick wad of papers into my hand.

'This is the script,' he told me. 'Dorothy appears in four different scenes.'

Calm down, I told myself. Adolfo had told me it would just be 'a few lines'. Surely Dorothy would simply appear in the background most of the time. But, after a quick skim through the papers, I realised that the name Dorothy was disturbingly prominent.

Dorothy: . . .

Gaviota: . . .

Dorothy: . . .

Dr O: . . .

Dorothy: etc.

'Okay, I'll leave you to learn your lines,' he said as he moved towards the door.

'Wait . . . how long have I got?' I asked, hoping he wouldn't notice that my hands were shaking.

But the only answer he could give me was, 'That depends on when they start filming.' And he was out the door again.

Standing completely still, I stared at the terrified-looking orange-skinned drag queen in the mirror. I had to compose myself; there was no escape now. Removing the black-rimmed glasses from the envelope, I put them on.

'It will be okay,' I told the girl in the mirror. 'I'm not me anymore. I'm Dorothy.' And I began to read through the script.

'Doctor Olivarria, Senorita Franco,' was my first line. I addressed the mirror, focusing on rolling my tongue for the double r.

My role consisted mainly of taking calls for Gaviota and then passing the messages on to her. On a few occasions I would walk into the room to hand her important documents, for which I would pass on specific instructions. The most instrumental thing Dorothy did was to tell Gaviota's estranged lover, Rodrigo Montalvo, that she, Gaviota, was not available to take his call, causing Rodrigo to fly all the way over from Mexico to London. (Later in that episode, after Gaviota realises that the reason Rodrigo had failed to call her back was in fact because he had gone to prison in her place, the couple return to Mexico for a grand white wedding in the picturesque colonial town of Jalisco where they had met.)

I said the lines to myself again and again and again – in every different position. Pacing up and down the room, lying on the floor, sitting on the chair and then staring at my new self in the mirror.

The man with the goatee returned some time later. We went through the lines together, him reading the other parts.

'Now that you've learnt your lines, I want you to act like Dorothy. Do you know who Dorothy is?' he asked.

'Well, she's Gaviota's secretary . . .' I started.

'No, no! Shhh!' He placed a finger over my lips. 'Dorothy is a woman with style, confidence and ambition!' He placed his hands on my shoulders. 'You ARE Dorothy! Do you understand me?'

'Yes!' I shouted back, trying to match his enthusiasm.

We went through the lines again. This time, I really tried to be Dorothy.

He stared at me for a few moments: 'Good. But not that good. You are not Dorothy yet. I need you to BELIEVE you are Dorothy.' He paused for a while and then asked, 'How does Dorothy walk?'

I had no idea.

'Show me!' he demanded. He sat down on the seat and waited. I walked up and down the room.

'No!' he exclaimed. 'More style.'

I tried again, this time exaggerating my hip movements.

'No. Watch me.' He got up from the chair and began to prance up and down the room, wiggling his hips from side to side. 'Okay – have you got it?'

This went on for some minutes, until finally he grabbed me by the shoulders and, looking me directly in the eye, whispered, 'Dorothy. You are ready to be Dorothy.' And again he disappeared out of the room.

Collapsing into the chair, I felt my tummy rumbling – it must be well past lunchtime, but then there was no way of knowing. I had left my phone at one of the security stations and I was in a different dimension now – time worked differently here.

A few minutes later the door opened. It was him again, 'Okay you're on.'

I felt dizzy.

'Quick! Follow me!' He charged down the hall. This time I had to run to keep up with him. He opened a metal door and pushed me through.

'DOROTHY.' The name was announced over a loud-speaker. I was ushered into a cardboard office but, once inside, it didn't look like it was made from cardboard – it looked like an expensive London office with crimson walls, framed watercolours of cottage gardens, leather seats and cedar furniture.

And there she was, sitting at the desk, wearing a jumbo-sized pearl necklace and a black business suit which revealed an unbusiness-like cleavage – it was Gaviota, Dorothy's boss. A woman in a white coat was spraying something onto her luscious copper-coloured locks and another was applying powder to her nose.

Her lover, Rodrigo Montalvo, was also busy being pampered by women in white coats. He wasn't on the set yet, but I could see out of the corner of my eye that he was just outside. He must have been getting ready to make a surprise entrance into Gaviota's London office, to try to win her back (she thinks he's in prison back in Mexico).

He was just as big as he looked on television. He was huge – like a prize-winning Angus bull. Since when did humans grow so big? His jaw took up half his face. He would easily be able to eat Gaviota – in one bite he could consume her head.

Blinding lights: we were being circled by monstrous cameras on cranes. I could feel the sweat building up around my neck under the tight polo-neck jumper.

'*Cinco, cuatro* . . .' They were counting down. But what was it I was supposed to do? The man with the goatee had explained that they wouldn't be filming the scenes in sequence, but he hadn't told me what order they would be in.

Someone placed a black folder in my hand. I was standing at the door and Gaviota was behind the desk – that meant I had to walk over to the desk and ask her to revise the guest list for the Tequila Premiums.

'*Tres, dos* . . .' I felt nauseous. What would happen if I vomited on Gaviota?

'*¡Uno . . . Rodando!* [rolling]'

Clutching the folder under my arm, I walked towards the desk.

'*Senorita Franco . . . imprimí la lista de invitados . . .*'
I started.

'*¡Corte!* [cut]'

Gaviota scrunched up her little sparrow nose and clasped her hand to her forehead. Obviously I had stuffed up. But how?

A bald man with a moustache approached and told me how. I had failed to pause when I should have, which blocked Gaviota's upcoming lines.

'Three, two, one . . . Rolling!'

'*Senorita Franco . . .*'

Pause. Then Gaviota, 'Dorothy, if Senior Montalvo calls, don't put him on, not for anything in the world . . . Even if he tells you he's going to commit suicide.'

Okay – now pause again, look sympathetic and then . . . my heart was beating so fast I couldn't hear anything else.

'*Imprimí la lista . . .*' Of what? List of *what*? What list did I print out? . . . Shit – now I've paused for too long!

'*¡Corte!*'

Gaviota rolled her eyes back and looked at the heavens. 'What's wrong, Dorothy?' asked the bald man.

'I'm sorry – I forgot my lines for a moment,' I stuttered.

Suddenly the man with the goatee appeared on the set, and the bald man was talking to him. 'I thought you said she knew her lines,' Mr Bald hissed.

'She does . . . well she did. She was great just a minute ago in the dressing room. She just has stage fright,' Mr Goatee explained.

'We don't have time for this,' muttered Mr Bald as he wiped the sweat from his brow. 'We'll just give her a *chícharo*.'

I understood *chícharo* to mean 'pea'. But how would a pea help? I needed to get out of here. Panicked I glanced at the big metal door – it was like the door of a vault. Even if I got through the door, I would never make it past the three security stations. Besides, the place was like a maze – I could get trapped in this dimension forever. Dizziness swept over me.

Suddenly someone was attaching something to one of my ears and sticky-taping a cord under my jacket. A little man with a small head and round glasses was shaking my hand. He looked like Mr Mole. 'Hello. I'm going to tell you your lines so you don't have to worry now,' he smiled. 'By the way, do you speak English?'

'Yes.'

His eyes lit up.

'I am learning English,' he told me in English.

'Dorothy!'

Kind Mr Mole disappeared and I was being ushered back into Gaviota's cardboard office. But now Mr Mole's voice was in my head: 'Re-lax,' said the voice in English. 'Jou – are – beautiful.'

'Re-lax,' said the voice again and again, like a mantra on a self-help meditation tape.

I took a deep breath. Now I had the lines physically transplanted in my brain, everything would be okay.

'*¡Rodando!*'

'Okay, Dorothy,' said the voice in my head. 'Now walk to Gaviota's desk and say: "*Senorita Franco*".'

I repeated his words. And that's how I was able to survive the rest of the filming – thanks to Mr Mole guiding me every step of the way. And when it wasn't my turn to speak, he would start again with the self-help mantra: 'Re-lax! Jou are beautiful!'

§

It was dark by the time I returned to the real world – from the pristine terraces of the film studio to a highway with no footpath that smelt of diesel and garbage. I flagged down a *pesero* (small bus), it slowed down just enough for me to be able to jump in; then it sped off down the road accompanied by the primordial beats of *reggaetón* blasting from the speakers beside the driver. Blue lights flashed around the pictures of a psychedelic Virgin of Guadalupe stuck lovingly on the dashboard.

As I made my way towards the back of the bus, I could feel the curious eyes of the passengers on me. I was accustomed to being stared at, but not this much. Then I remembered the fake eyelashes and the orange face.

I must have looked like a prostitute. It didn't matter – the day was over, and I had survived it.

§

The next day I walked down to the grocery store on the corner to buy some cheese. I always dreaded going to this shop, but I went there anyway because the cheese was so good. The problem was that the shopkeeper did not maintain the conventions of the normal cheese-buying dialogue.

'*¿Güera, güera, si me muero quien te encuera?*' he would sing when I entered the shop. This part I understood, because I had heard it before many times on the street. It was a common rhyme that people always sang to white girls; roughly translated it means: 'White girl, white girl, if I die who will undress you?'

My standard response was to ignore this and just ask him for some cheese.

But before he gave me the cheese, he would always make some sort of comment that didn't make any sense to me. From his sarcastic expression I knew that it was intended to be funny and, if other customers were in the store, they would always laugh. But all I could do was smile and nod. This time I decided to attempt to memorise exactly what the grocery man said, so I could repeat it to Ricardo.

'*Güera, güera . . .*' he sang.

'Hello. Can I have two kilos of *queso chihuahua* please?'

Grinning, he reached for the knife and cut off a large slab of porous white cheese and chucked it on the weighing machine. Then, as he handed me the parcel, he raised his eyebrows and said something which didn't make any sense. To which I smiled and said, 'Thank you.'

His comment induced a jovial giggle when I later repeated it to Ricardo.

'What?' I asked.

Ricardo attempted to explain but, by the time he had finished his explanation, I had burst into tears.

'What's wrong?' Ricardo gasped.

'I didn't understand.'

'Of course you didn't. Only a *chilango* would have understood that – it's a very old-fashioned expression.'

'But I never understand his jokes, and I should be able to understand things like that by now,' I sobbed.

Ricardo, who was involved in following a slow-cooked mutton recipe, was speechless. He looked so shocked and concerned that I suddenly realised how absurd my reaction was and began to laugh. I was crying because I didn't understand a joke!

What was wrong with me? How was it possible that I had burst into tears because I hadn't understood some peculiar *chilango* joke, I kept asking myself the next day as I disembarked from the metro and made my way to work.

Two older looking men were sitting on a park bench. '*Buenos días, güera*,' they chimed.

Turning around to face them, I replied, '*Buenos días*.'

But the minute I turned my back, they began to laugh. I stopped and turned around. 'Why are you laughing?' I asked them. 'I just said good morning.'

But they stared back at me like frightened rabbits. I wanted to hit them in the face. Instead I let fly with a series of intensely vulgar *chilango* insults that I had learnt from a truck-driver comic (my latest metro reading material), '*¡Chingen a su madre, hijos de los mil chiles!*' Go and fuck your mothers, you sons of a thousand dicks!

Even Coco was shocked when I told her what I had said to them: 'What? I can't believe jou called them that! Just because dey were laughing at jou . . . And of course dey were laughing – dey weren't expecting a *fresa* white girl to say good morning back. Now dey're going to be too scared to say good morning to a white girl ever again!' But I felt I was at cracking point.

♣

That evening I was watering the plants on the terrace. The late afternoon sky was a murky yellow and the volcanoes Xitle and Ajusco had disappeared in the pollution. Thinking about the two old men on the seat in the park, and how shocked they had been at my response, I realised I felt like I was at cracking point all the time now. For over a year, I had been fixated on learning Spanish and becoming part of Mexican culture. How many more years would it take? There is a certain weariness involved in always feeling like an outsider. Not having a full grasp of the idiom created in me a heightened sense of alienation. Plus I was getting up at 5 am to start work and barely making enough money to survive. Sometimes Mexico City felt a bit like a huge pressure cooker, with the pollution trapped inside the valley, the constant stress of always worrying about safety, and scenes of poverty and despair everywhere you looked.

That night I had witnessed a fight between a security guard and a mother of three sick-looking children who, to get by, would have them dress up in animal costumes and juggle between the cars in the traffic. The security man had just caught one of the small children defecating outside the shopfront and the mother was explaining that the kid was sick and there was nowhere else for him to go. Seeing this small piece of a tragedy moved me. Of course, living surrounded by poverty you soon develop a shell – but sometimes it still gets in.

§

And closer to home, why had I reached a stalemate with my Spanish?

Perhaps it was because in reality I hadn't been sticking to my no-English-outside-work-hours rule. By the time I got home from work I was too tired to make any sense in either language anyway. I would collapse on the sofa beneath the cats, and Ricardo and I would communicate with each other in a haphazard sort of Spanglish, in which we would give English verbs Spanish conjugations and Spanish words English phonetics.

But I realised that to get to the next level of Spanish, I needed to switch off the English part of my brain entirely – it can't be there, not even as a back-up, or otherwise it will creep back onto centre stage and take over the show, just like it's been used to doing.

First languages are jealous. They don't like the idea of you picking up another language, and will do everything in their power to thwart your plan. The only way to deal with this is to ignore your first language – to be in an environment where no one else understands or pays any attention to it. I could almost feel myself getting jealous of the students I was teaching – each week they were speaking faster and with fewer grammatical mistakes, and they hadn't travelled to the other side of the world.

Nor was my potential showbiz career bolstering my confidence, even though I had now successfully auditioned for the push-up bra commercial. The audition consisted of me talking about how much my social life had taken off since I discovered this push-up bra. My agent Adolfo was promising me the world. I had earned only A\$25 after my excruciating twelve hours at Televisa Studio, and it was the most stressful day I had ever experienced. So the prospect of a similar day spent wearing nothing but a push-up bra and underpants made me think fondly of my English teaching job. However, one thing I had learned was a deep respect for 'Gaviota' – she was no porcelain doll, but a hard-working professional with iron discipline and the constitution of an Angus bull.

Now it was getting dark and it was my turn to cook dinner. Ricardo would probably be home in an hour, exhausted – my Mexican boyfriend and best friend.

§

The following Sunday afternoon, I met up with Edgar in Coyoàcán for an *intercambio*. Edgar had now passed his English exam and begun his Masters degree, so our *intercambios* had become less frequent. Today, we wandered around Coyoacán's zócalo watching the buskers. There was a bongo drum clan, a group of teenagers playing jazz and a clown making phallic shapes out of balloons. Then we made our way down to the Café Jarocho for the famous 10-peso hot chocolate. We plonked ourselves down on plywood crates on the footpath and touched base.

Edgar was developing the slight intonation of an Indian academic; this was because most of his classes were taught in English by Indian academics. I commended him on his efforts and then launched into a monologue about how I wasn't getting anywhere with my life and my Spanish wasn't improving. Edgar listened to me patiently, as always, and then said, 'Well then, you should go to university too. You could study Academic Spanish – they offer special courses for foreign students.'

He was talking about the UNAM, the Autonomous National University of Mexico. Ten minutes from our house, the walls of its buildings were covered in social realist art and, surrounded by a nature reserve, it was considered to be the most prestigious university in Latin America. Ricardo had previously given me a tour of the faculty of Philosophy and Literature, where he had studied Spanish Literature. It smelt of socialist revolution – long-haired men with furtive eyes handed out flyers about political disappearances, or the military's use of torture in indigenous communities. Dissidents were safe here – since the university is autonomous, police are not allowed to enter the campus.

But the Colombian spies were a different story. It was a well-known fact that there was a constant presence here of Colombian government spies, disguised as Mexican students and keeping track of the leftist student organisations that were believed to have links with Colombian guerrilla groups.

This was university as you would expect it to be in Mexico. There was no doubt it would deepen my grasp of the local culture. Back home, I checked the date of the next intake of students into the Spanish course and two weeks later I was able to enrol.

❧ 14 ❧

Herod's Law

'Oh my God! I can't belief jou met Rodrigo Montalvo and didn't tell me,' Coco squealed when I arrived at Fifth Avenue. She was referring to the actor Eduardo Yañez, heart-throb and lover of Gaviota.

The night before, Adolfo had rung to inform me that 'my' episode of *Destilando Amor* – the final episode – was about to be aired. It had been truly unbearable – watching myself parroting Mr Mole in a monotone, pausing mid-sentence to hear the rest of what he had to say. Then my phone had started ringing.

'Imelda! I didn't think you watched . . .'

'Please . . . *Destilando Amor* is different. Besides, it was the final episode.'

Then virtually everyone who had my phone number in Mexico (except Octavio) was calling. Even the serious Edgar called.

'Edgar! What the hell were you doing watching . . . ?'

'My grandma was watching it – and then she suddenly started shouting, "Oh, good Lord! Isn't that your friend?"'

Coco was now leaning over the reception desk: '*Doctor Olivarria, Senorita Franco, como . . .*' She began parroting my lines, a Mexican attempting to imitate my Australian imitation of an English accent in Latin American Spanish.

'Shut up! How did you go with Jordi last night?' I asked, raising the subject of Coco's latest love interest. He was a very blond young Catalan man and a director at Fifth Avenue. Coco, who had never had much luck in love with her compatriots, had just discovered that she was excessively popular with foreign men, who couldn't resist her exotic silver-brown skin, her round moon-like features and her sinuous curves. And likewise, blond men drove her completely crazy.

She fell back on the revolving chair behind the reception desk and looked up at the ceiling: 'It was incredible. I got home at four in de morning . . .'

Coco was 24, but was still not allowed to go out at night. But now, under the influence of Jordi, she had started to sneak out and go clubbing. She began confiding in me her fantasy that they would run away together, but she was interrupted when Elvira arrived for the First Wives' Breakfast Club.

'Dorothy!' Elvira ran up to me grinning. 'Did you get Eduardo Yañez's autograph?'

On my way back from work I stopped at the main office of Fifth Avenue to complain to the director Nestor Montes about not being paid. It had been two months now. I knew it would be a futile exercise, as Ricardo kept telling me, but I felt like getting it out of my system.

Ricardo was working at the main office today. We exchanged 'good afternoons' as I walked past his office. Although everyone knew we were a couple, it was more comfortable to pretend we weren't while we were at work.

Really I was more worried about Ricardo not being paid. I was getting by on my private classes; but Ricardo was working over ten hours a day, travelling interstate to supervise the new schools that they kept opening up, and meanwhile getting into serious credit card debt paying for petrol and hotel expenses that they were supposed to reimburse but never did. And we still didn't know how we were going to pay for our cat's bladder-stone operation.

Ricardo had taken on some translation work, over which we slaved together at night, trying to convert the almost illiterate prose of an autobiography of a Mexican racing car driver, from Spanish to English.

I knocked on the door of Nestor Montes's office.

'Jes!'

He used his desk to push himself up from his chair, and then waddled over to shake my hand. 'Dorothy!' he gasped. 'Jou know it is such an honour to have a Televisa actress working for our company!' His chubby fingers were still wrapped around my hand.

'Nestor . . . I need to talk to you about my wages . . .'

'Ah jes, we've had some problems wid de banks lately. But de money will come in tomorrow. Anyting else?'

⚘

Although I was already running late for my Spanish class, I decided to make a detour through the faculty of Philosophy and Literature. Here, behind a tiny counter in a crowded graffiti-covered corridor, I had discovered that the best coffee in Mexico City was produced. One barista, with his hair pulled back in a plait and a silver stud through his lip, handed me a political leaflet protesting the torture of indigenous villagers by the Mexican military, while the other barista was making the coffee.

Carrying the cardboard cup across the road, I passed through the gates in the vine-covered stone walls into the Centre for Foreigners, the *Centro de Enseñaza Para Extrañeros* (CEPE).

'Stuck in traffic?' asked Professor Arzaba, with his ironic smile underneath his grey moustache. The rest of the class chuckled. The day before we had been talking about how *chilangos* would be completely stumped if you took the traffic out of the giant metropolis, since being stuck in traffic served as a valid excuse for almost everything. Arzaba was also a professor of French Literature.

'You know why I prefer teaching Spanish to foreign

students?' he had asked on the first day of the course. 'I get paid more.'

But I suspected that it was also because it gave him the opportunity to rant about his theories and observations regarding the Mexican condition. His time living in Paris had given him the vantage point of an outsider but, as a Mexican, he had no qualms about criticising his own culture. So Arzaba's lectures were not only helpful from a language point of view, but also served as a sort of guide to living with Mexicans.

'Today,' he said, 'is the last day of a two-month period – I repeat, a *two-month period* – in which you are able to get your car cleared for environmental roadworthiness, something which all residents are required to do. And today, if you go to any of the eight inspection centres around the city, you will find a queue of cars stretching tens of kilometres down the street.'

Ricardo at this moment was sitting in his car, waiting in one of those queues; I had been speaking to him at various intervals throughout the day, sympathetically checking up on his progress in the queue – which he had had to bribe someone even to be allowed into. But I hadn't realised that he could have gone weeks earlier, when there was no queue.

'Why?' Arzaba went on. 'Why do ninety-nine per cent of us Mexicans choose to wait eight hours in a queue? Because we are incapable of taking action before it's absolutely necessary!'

I glanced over at Mary-Anne from South Carolina. She too lived with her Mexican boyfriend, and we exchanged knowing looks. Needless to say, her boyfriend was stuck in a car near Ricardo's car in the 10-kilometre queue.

About a quarter of our class were Mexican–Americans who had grown up in North America, and wanted to understand Mexican culture and perfect their Spanish. Then there was Tatiana, a stern Russian mathematics professor who was preparing to take a position at the university; there was Nobu, a high-ranking Japanese police officer/martial arts champion, who was here on some government program; and Mary-Anne, an ex-nun who dressed in men's clothing and now lived here with her Mexican ex-monk boyfriend. I later found out he was 50 years older than her. Mexico is a magnet for the oddballs of North America.

Then there was a group of three African Catholic missionaries from Cameroon, who were here to teach Mexicans about 'real Catholicism', as opposed to the 'idol worshipping' that went on in the villages. Their religious views would have been considered conservative even in the Dark Ages and, when any one of them made a comment, the rest of the class would fall completely silent and stare nervously at Professor Arzaba – who would abruptly change the subject.

'Because we all know that the AIDS virus is God's punishment for homosexuality and promiscuity,' Philemon had said when we were discussing a text about Oaxaca's indigenous Zapotec culture.

He seemed to be referring to the happy acceptance of drag queens in the Zapotec community. 'The terrible terrible sins these people are committing in their innocence, where is their spiritual guidance?' he implored.

'Ah yes, so we were talking earlier about the changing use of the gerund in Spanish – has anyone in the class noted any unconventional uses of the gerund?' muttered Professor Arzaba. If they had been white North Americans, no doubt the class would have devoured them; but there seemed to be a general reluctance to get into arguments on cultural imperialism with black Africans.

Coming along to this class with a bunch of other people who felt they didn't belong had the strange effect of making me feel more like I belonged. I was happier in general now – I didn't burst into tears when I couldn't understand a joke, or yell obscenities at befuddled old men. Now I had a means of measuring my progress, and I felt that I was getting somewhere.

And I had discovered other ways of staying sane amid the madness of Mexico City. The key is to escape from its clutches as often as possible. At weekends Ricardo and I had got into the habit of going on picnics in the various secret pine forests in the mountains surrounding the city. I use the word *picnic* in the figurative sense, since picnics are made redundant in Mexico by the fact that wherever you go and no matter how far from civilisation you think you have travelled – you could be at the top of a volcano in the middle of a forest – there is always a group of women standing around a wood fire waiting to cook you beautiful food.

'*Quesadillas, huaraches, tlacoyos, gorditas, sopes*' (all incarnations of the quesadilla) they will sing. And be ready with white cheeses, pumpkin flowers, mushrooms, chorizo or jalapenos to place inside the maize dough, and to grill it, before adding spicy red and green salsas.

One Sunday morning Ricardo and I were reading the newspaper in a café in Coyoacán when we came across a photo of a familiar place. It showed the entrance of a driveway we had driven past and noticed many times. The entrance was on a lonely highway in a misty pine forest called Desierto de los Leones, on the way to one of our favourite picnic spots. A massive curly metal gate was visible through the mist; on either side were pillars several metres high, which were decorated with elaborate wooden carvings of gargoyles, serpents and bloodthirsty demons. We had been so intrigued by its eeriness that we had once stopped the car outside to get a closer look – but had quickly gone on our way when we noticed we were being observed by some high-tech-looking security cameras.

What type of person would live in that house? we had wondered, and had come to the conclusion that it could only have been a witch – an affluent witch. But we were wrong. The caption underneath the photo in the paper read 'Zoo of wild animals discovered in drug lord's mansion'.

A hippopotamus, two lions, two tigers, two panthers and a gorilla had been found on the property when the drug cartel base had been raided by police. It reminded me of something I had once read – the conquistador Bernal Díaz del Castillo's description of the palace of the Aztec king Moctezuma, where he had found 'tigers and two kinds of lions, and animals something like wolves and foxes, and other smaller carnivorous animals'. He went on to describe their diet of human flesh (the leftovers of the sacrifice victims). The animals in the drug lord's zoo looked rather chubby in the photos, and it occurred to me that perhaps they too had practical uses.

How had this particular drug lord managed to operate for so long, and now why was he suddenly arrested? Trying to grasp Mexican politics is like stepping through the looking glass. Nothing is as it seems. And the deeper you go, the more black and white fades into a murky grey.

The Green Party is ultra right-wing and wants to bring back the death penalty. The trade unions are evil – and so powerful that they flaunt how corrupt they are. This was demonstrated when the head of the teachers' union, Elba Esther Gordillo, purchased 59 Hummers for each of her general secretaries. Cardinals get involved in narcotics trafficking and narcotics traffickers execute kidnappers. To shed some light on all this, I had decided to take a Mexican politics class along with my Spanish class.

One night, I was coming home from one of these classes when I stopped to chat to Armando, the owner of a pirate-video stand, which he had set up on the footpath just opposite the metro-bus station. I'd bought a few DVDs from him before and I had since got into the habit of stopping to chat with him for a few minutes while I waited for the pedestrian light to go green. It was dark now and he had already started packing his unsold DVDs into a suitcase. When he saw me approaching, he looked at his watch in an exaggerated gesture, as if to show he was concerned about what time I was arriving home.

'My politics class finishes at nine,' I explained. I usually saw him after my Spanish class, which ended a few hours earlier.

Armando had long copper-coloured hair to his waist, which he tied back in a ponytail, and a long kingly handlebar moustache. There was something noble-looking about Armando – something that led me to think that he hadn't always been selling pirate videos.

'Politics?' he asked, rolling his eyes in disapproval. 'Who do they make you read? Krauze and Monsivais, I suppose?'

I reached into my bag and pulled out my copy of Enrique Krauze's *La Historia Cuenta* (History Tells) to prove that he was right.

'Look, you can sit around your whole life reading these foreign-educated idiots. But all you really need to know about how things work in Mexico is Herod's Law. You know who King Herod was?' he asked.

I nodded.

He rummaged around in his suitcase and pulled out a DVD, with the title *La Ley de Herodes* (Herod's Law). 'Take this,' he said, placing it in my hands.

I tried to give him 20 pesos, but he threw his hands up in the air: 'No, no, no. This is for your education. How could I accept money for your education? Watch it tonight; bring it back tomorrow,' he instructed.

The pedestrian light went green and I thanked Armando. Then I made my way across the road to the metro-bus, the light rail which runs down Insurgentes, the main road in Mexico City.

That night Ricardo and I settled down on the couch to watch the film. We switched on the television. Ricardo paused for a moment to watch the news headlines before putting the DVD in. The reporter was saying that the problems in the American banking system had caused global stockmarkets to fall dramatically.

For the last few weeks there had been bits and pieces in the paper about the economic situation in the United States – the collapse of Lehman Brothers and the government takeover of banks – but now it was really starting to get serious. With its almost complete interdependence with North America, I realised how much this was going to affect Mexico.

Ricardo had seen the movie *Herod's Law* many times, as it was an iconic Mexican film from the late 1990s. Set in the lawlessness of post-revolution Mexico, when the PRI (the Institutional Revolutionary Party) was taking hold of power, idealistic Juan Vargas is appointed as the 'Presidente Municipal' (local governor) of a remote dusty town. However, he soon decides to resign when he becomes aware of the pitfalls of leadership when the corruption comes from the top down. But his boss, the governor of the state, sends him back to the town with a copy of the constitution and a gun and tells him, *'La Ley de Herodes: te chingas o te jodes'*. A more direct translation would be: Herod's Law – you're either fucked or you're screwed, but the phrase has come to be widely understood as 'fuck them over before they screw you' just like King Herod tried to do with Jesus.

In Mexico City there is a general sense that everyone is being fucked over in some way. And when this fucking over starts at the very top, the only thing left to do is to follow the trend and screw over other people, thereby creating a delicate balance of mutual exploitation. How can you obey the law when those who create the law do not? The famous Mexican criminal El Carrizos, who managed to burgle President Luis Echaverria's house, once asked, 'Isn't it okay for a thief to rob a thief?'

Over 30 per cent of electricity in Mexico City is stolen. It's stolen in full public view, simply by attaching a cable to the electricity line. This is how street stalls get their lighting and electricity to cook. Why doesn't anyone try to stop them? Well, the police are kept easily in check by regular bribes and no one else says anything because the Light and Energy Company is corrupt and rips everyone else off anyway. I knew for a fact (because I had insider knowledge) that Fifth Avenue was stealing electricity at three of its schools. I used the same justification when I bought pirate videos, instead of renting them from Blockbuster Video. The company I was working for was exploiting me, so why shouldn't I steal from the film industry? The cost of renting a video is 50 pesos, which was what I was paid for two hours of work.

Piracy generates 9 per cent of the Gross National Product and it's estimated that one third of the workforce in Mexico is informal – so, if you cracked down on people like Armando, it would have serious implications for the economy. There are some sections of the informal economy that specialise in exploiting the middle class. The best at this are the truly amazing parking mafia, the *'viene-vienes'* (come-comes), who have managed to infiltrate virtually every single occupied street in Mexico City.

They look rather like pirates – gold teeth, long hair, scars, tattoos – and they're not supposed to look friendly. *'Viene, viene'* (Come, come) they say as they stand on the kerb and help you park. But sometimes you really need *viene-vienes* – in a city of 21 000 000, professional parkers do serve a purpose. If you can't find a park, instead of driving around for hours, you just chuck your keys to one of these guys and they'll deal with it. They will even supervise your car while you're gone – making sure it doesn't get stolen or towed away by the parking police. But whether you need them or not, you don't have a choice – because, if you don't use their services, you will return to your car to find that your tyres are pinched, your windscreen smashed, or that your car isn't there at all.

Viene-vienes are highly organised. The streets are divided up between the *viene-viene* clans, and the positions are hereditary. Our street was administered by three main *viene-vienes*: Tonyo Grande (Big Tony), the elderly boss, most often seen giving orders with a bottle of brandy in his hand; his son Tonyo, with a mouth full of gold teeth, curly hair down to his shoulders and a collection of psychedelic t-shirts, which he alternated every three days; and Tonyo's wife Jacquelíne, who spent most of her time sitting on the patch of grass outside our home caring for her baby. Sometimes I would arrive home to find the baby alone on the side of the road, happily asleep under a blanket. When Jacquelíne was called in to help with the parking, she simply left her baby on the street. I guess she was confident that no one would bother kidnapping a *viene-viene* baby. She also seemed to be part of some sort of network that re-sold stolen goods. Every so often she would catch me as I was coming home and promote some random device.

'Hey, *güera*, I got these *routers* – I can give 'em to you real cheap.'

'What do you mean – *routers*?'

'Mmm . . . I think it's for a computer . . . Do you have a computer?'

'Yes.'

'Well, I can give them to you for thirty pesos.'

Our relationship with these criminals was completely positive. They trusted us and we trusted them, but I never did buy any routers.

§

The other Mafia organisation that we dealt with on a daily basis was the garbage collectors. Each day a bearded man pushing a trolley would bang on our gate and ask for money. There wasn't any reason why we should have given him any, since this service is paid for by the city government. But we did, because if we didn't, he wouldn't collect our rubbish.

Back in the 1990s, when a new government had come into power in Mexico City, one delegate by the name of Legorreta had been determined to remedy this situation. However, he soon found himself in a catch-22. The deal was that each garbage truck functioned as a family business, with the driver as the CEO. Only the driver was employed by the city government. The other eleven workers that manned the truck, the driver's extended family, were 'honoraries'. As well as the tips, the business made money from recycling, and the resale of syphoned petrol from the truck. Legorreta did not have a big enough budget to include these 'honoraries' in the government payroll, as the garbage haulers' union had suggested. Yet putting a stop to the 'tip' collection would leave thousands of extra people unemployed and a city full of festering rubbish. In the end, he found that it made more sense just to leave things as they always had been. Corruption in Mexico was an important form of social security.

When I arrived at Fifth Avenue School of English the following Monday, Coco was in an unnaturally good mood. It was 7 am and she was shuffling around in the small space behind the reception desk to a cheesy Latino pop song.

'What's wrong with you, Coco? Are you trying to scare away the students?' I still hadn't fully woken up and the garish beats of the music were attacking the stillness of my brain.

She beamed. 'Hey, I'll tell jou a secret. But jou can't tell anyone – not even Ricardo.'

'Promise.'

'I'm going to Barcelona tomorrow with Jordi.'

'What? How long for? Does Fifth Avenue know you're going?'

Coco had no return date – she was simply going to get there and try to get a job, and she hadn't told anyone at Fifth Avenue. 'They would have fired me on the spot if I had told them I was going,' she explained.

'And the money? How did you get the money?' I asked. Saving up for a plane ticket with Mexican pesos is a colossal task.

She smiled. 'There are ways,' she told me.

Then she turned up the volume of the salsa track, and started singing along to the lyrics.

§

And sure enough, the next day I arrived at work to find a line of students waiting outside the door. Coco had not arrived with the key.

Over the following weeks it slowly became clear how Coco and Jordi had been able to get the money. Part of Coco's job had been to sell contracts to students. She had been doing brilliantly at this, except that there had been a discrepancy between what she had sold the students and what she had been recording in the system. For example, if the student had paid for a year-long contract to study at the school, Coco would record their contract on the system as only three months and pocket the extra money.

Jordi had used a slightly more direct method to extract money from the company. Being a director, he had been let in on all of Fifth Avenue's dodgy schemes to avoid paying taxes. So all he had to do was to threaten to disclose this information. He had received a substantial sum of money.

Coco and Jordi, unlike the rest of the staff, had been paid. They had fucked with Fifth Avenue before Fifth Avenue had screwed with them.

❦ 15 ❦

The Dark Virgin

Although they may be criminals, people like Armando and the *viene-vienes* have their own strict codes of conduct and sense of honour. For example, because we had agreed to let them park cars outside our driveway, we had earned from our local *viene-vienes* their boundless loyalty. We knew that our car would always be safe, and Tonyo went out of his way to help us in every way he could. He knew what time I arrived at the metro-bus station after my Spanish class and he also knew that even though it was the rainy season, I never remembered to carry an umbrella. So, on the nights when he wasn't busy, he would meet me at the metro-bus station and walk me home with his umbrella.

As a Mexico City resident, Ricardo's relationship with them was courteous and business-like. I felt safe having them there. I knew they were watching every person and every car that arrived and left our street. And often people like Tonyo, who operate in this underworld, are deeply religious. He never talked about it, but I could tell this from the tattoo on his arm – a skeleton, draped in a black robe and holding a scythe in one hand and a globe in the other. The image resembled what I knew as the Grim Reaper.

When I arrived in Mexico I had been puzzled by the frequent presence of this macabre image, which dangled from the rear-vision mirror of nearly every taxi and bus, and was sold at the markets in the witchcraft stalls among the herbs, candles and Catholic images of Mary and Jesus. But I had since come to understand that in this country the personification of death was known by a different name – La Santa Muerte, the Saint of Death.

In Mexico, this image of the skeleton in the black robe is used to represent a female saint – a virgin in fact, like the Virgin of Guadalupe. Her most popular chapel is in the notorious suburb of Tepito, the centre of the informal economy and a police-free haven for criminals and narcotics traffickers. But she also has various other chapels and shrines throughout the republic and some in Los Angeles, which have a significant number of followers. Her shrines have been popping up more and more in the communities on the border between Mexico and North America, corresponding with the routes of illegal immigration and drug trafficking.

Many people from the *barrios*, the poorer parts of the city, who once would have been in the constituency of the Virgin of Guadalupe, were now turning to the Saint of Death. I had been growing increasingly curious about this phenomenon, and had chosen this topic for my end-of-semester research project for my Spanish class.

'How could you be interested in something so dark?' Ricardo asked. But I wasn't sure if she was dark. I liked the fact that this rogue saint, who was not a concoction of the Catholic Church, was busily winning over hearts and minds. And it fascinated me how death itself could be considered a saint. Lately I had been reading about how in pre-Hispanic cultures images of skeletons often symbolised health and fertility and the gods and goddesses of death also served as deities of fertility. One theory about the origin of La Santa Muerte traces her back to the Aztec devotion to the male god of death, Mictecanuhtli, and to the female god of darkness, Mictecacihuatl.

Although many of her devotees would happily classify their beliefs as Catholic, the Church does not agree that the Grim Reaper is a saint. Some bishops condemn her followers as devil worshippers; but others argue that it's just an unfortunate theological misunderstanding. The Santa Muerte 'cult' is the fastest-growing religious sect in Mexico, with over 2 000 000 followers in Mexico City alone. So many people now attend its services that the cult's promoters are in the process of purchasing land for an even bigger worshipping space, in order to accommodate all the new followers.

Her popularity has also been associated with the growth of narcotics trafficking. Because the Holy Death offers protection, and does not distinguish between good and evil-doing, it is an ideal religion for people who are engaged in criminal activities. And from her followers, the Virgin receives more 'petitions of protection' than any other type of petition. Tattoos of the Virgin are inevitably sprawled across the chests of convicted kidnappers; chapels for her are found in the mansions of the members of drug cartels.

But it's not only criminals who are drawn to her. The Santa Muerte provides a religious outlet for other excluded members of society. Gay and lesbian couples receive a special marriage service at the Saint of Death's chapel and their marriages are given a holy blessing. Prostitutes and drag queens are also openly accepted into the church community. After I compiled my research, I decided that in order to fully do justice to the project, I would have to go and see the Virgin for myself.

I asked Ricardo if he would go with me but he refused. 'Why would you purposely want to put us at risk? How about we go to the art gallery instead?'

Ricardo had experienced numerous unpleasant run-ins with street crime which had left him naturally cautious about which parts of the city to avoid. He had been mugged at gunpoint various times when he had worked at the family shop in the Centro Histórico, and as a child he had escaped by the skin of his teeth from getting bundled into a van outside a music shop. Needless to say, he found Mexico's underworld neither romantic nor interesting.

So, at our next *intercambio*, I asked Edgar if he would go with me. He too was fascinated by the phenomenon of La Santa Muerte. He agreed, but warned me that we may not be able to find the chapel itself, as its entrance was concealed in a private house and its masses took place at midnight (not the best time to make a journey to Tepito). However, there were various shrines to La Santa Muerte in Tepito, and he knew the location of one of the most significant ones.

So, a week later, on a smoggy Saturday morning, I removed my silver bracelet and unearthed my oldest, baggiest pieces of clothing. I slipped two 50-peso notes into the back pocket of my jeans, having been warned that, in the case of any confrontation, it's important to take some money so as not to provoke an angry response.

One of my students had told me that there was a group of gunmen permanently positioned on the top of the buildings surrounding the zone, ready to shoot dead any policeman or military personnel who dared to enter. But Edgar told me that civilians were not subject to such risks and just because criminals happened to live in Tepito, that didn't necessarily mean they 'worked' there. In fact, it was a popular place to shop, given the fabulously low prices achieved through piracy and theft. People from Tepito (Tepiteños) are famous among *chilangos* for their distinctive way of speaking – so heavily encoded with puns and local slang words, it often leaves the outsider mystified.

Edgar and I exchanged nervous glances as we stood clutching the metal handles above us on the metro. Was I really about to walk straight into the most dangerous zone of one of the most dangerous cities in the world, simply because I was curious?

'Why the hell did I agree to go to Tepito with a white girl?' I could hear Edgar thinking, as the beads of sweat formed on his forehead.

When we arrived at Tepito's metro station, we found the normal hustle and bustle of the commercial areas of Mexico City. There were hordes of busy people, some packed up like mules with sacks of merchandise hanging from their bodies. Everyone was trying to make their exit at the same time. Outside the station was just as crowded as the inside – there were so many stalls and shouting vendors that it took us some time before we finally managed to escape and cross the main road. But when we got to the other side, we found ourselves once more in a labyrinth of stalls. The only way forward was through the endless aisles of clothes, computer parts, pornography, mobile phones and other goods. Every imaginable item could be found here in some form. I recognised the ceiling of multicoloured tarpaulins above us from the satellite picture of Tepito I had viewed earlier on the internet. The effect this created – of blocking the view of the surrounding buildings – added to our sense of disorientation.

Edgar knew the name of the street that contained the shrine, but that was all. We took turns asking for directions, and most people pointed vaguely in the same direction. But we were surprised to find that when we finally did emerge from the flea market, we were opposite the street we had been searching for.

We walked across a wide, dusty avenue. Few cars were on the road, and even fewer people could be seen on the surrounding streets.

On the corner, an old man in a three-piece suit was asleep on top of a mountain of garbage. As we advanced down this road, dust from the unpaved footpaths blew into the air and stray dogs scavenged for food. I glanced over at Edgar. Neither of us said anything. It didn't feel right to contradict the strange stillness of the atmosphere.

Then a man who had been perched on the side of the street immediately got to his feet and broke the silence. He put his fingers to his mouth and began to whistle repetitively, his vacant eyes not letting us out of his gaze for a second. Another man, positioned further down the road, stood up and began to stare at us in the same way, whistling to let the next man in the chain know we were coming. But the men didn't do anything except watch us – watch us very closely.

Further along, a lone street vendor had set up shop on the footpath. Two commodities only were sold here: alcohol and cigarettes. We knew we were getting close to the shrine as these were the customary offerings given to

La Santa Muerte. The old woman at the stall smiled at us as she handed over a packet of cigarettes and a small bottle of tequila. 'For the White Girl?' she asked. We nodded. I had read earlier that La Santa Muerte was also becoming known more and more frequently as 'La Nina Blanca' (the White Girl). She was white because she was a skeleton.

Past the stall, a small crowd of people lined up in front of an archway covered entirely with pink and white flowers. We knew we'd found the shrine.

The crowd was respectfully silent. Grandparents, wearing crisply ironed blouses, hushed their restless grandchildren. We could have been at a church service, except for the presence of a few individuals who were quite obviously criminals. We couldn't yet see the shrine from where we were in the queue – only the sea of flowers and candles which surrounded it.

To one side of the shrine was a candle shop. We decided to buy a candle to put on the shrine as most of the people in the queue were holding candles, and there are times in your life when one should be completely kosher, I thought to myself. Earlier I had read that each candle's colour carried with it a meaning: red for love, white for luck and black for protection. We bought a white candle each and went back to the end of the line.

The man before us in the queue wore a black singlet, exposing his enlarged biceps which were covered in tattoos; his wrists and neck were draped in gold chains. We observed him carefully when he arrived at the shrine.

Firstly he lit a black candle and placed it down in front of him beneath the altar. Then he got down on his knees and crossed himself. With his eyes closed, he began to utter a prayer under his breath. Finally, he stood up and lit a cigarette. He took one puff and left the rest on the ashtray as an offering.

Edgar went first. He completed each step of the ritual perfectly, but burst into a rather awkward coughing fit after inhaling from the cigarette.

Then it was my turn. A human skeleton dressed in a white wedding gown stood proud above a sea of glowing candles, most of them black. Holding a scythe in one hand and a globe of the world in the other, her empty eye sockets stared back at me from behind the glass. I was reminded of my visit to La Basílica to see the Virgin of Guadalupe with Octavio – queuing up to look at the image of the Virgin from a moving conveyor belt. There was a sort of stillness induced by the shared awe and admiration of the crowd, both then and now.

Before we left the shrine, we asked the man at the candle shop where the chapel was located. 'There is no chapel,' he told us. 'Just shrines.' There was probably some secret gesture we had to know before we could be given that information.

But we knew that it wasn't far from where we were, so we decided to try to find it. We wandered further along the road. The buildings were old and beautiful, similar to some parts of the Centro Histórico, but completely decrepit with broken windows, graffiti and garbage everywhere. Teenagers with large black pupils sat in the gutter and stared at us as they played with knives. And there were absolutely no policemen to be seen – unheard of for Mexico City.

About every ten metres there was a religious altar – not just for La Santa Muerte. The Virgin Mary, Jesus and Our Lady of Guadalupe could all be found offering spiritual guidance from the inside of a glass cabinet, lovingly adorned with candles and flowers. Tepito was the most intensely religious area of Mexico City I had seen. But here, unlike other altars in Mexico, the glass cabinets were behind metal bars, making them seem like animal cages.

A woman with large black pupils suddenly came up behind us and began to talk. 'Hey, sister – I'm gonna walk behind you for a bit – 'cause they're after me – just until I get to my *area* just hide me, sister – keep walking.' I turned around. 'Be normal! Don't look at me – I'm not here . . .' And then she turned a corner and bolted down an alleyway.

At this moment Edgar turned to me. 'Hey, see that guy over there?' He was referring to a man with vacant eyes who was standing on the corner and not letting us out of his sight. 'That's the same guy we saw before.'

Our movements were being monitored with such impressive efficiency that we both decided to head back towards the metro station.

§

That night I arrived home to find Ricardo sitting on the sofa with the cats, playing the guitar. He stopped playing and glared at me when I walked into the room.

'Are you okay? Why didn't you answer your phone? Why are you home so late?' He hadn't wanted me to go to Tepito.

'It was completely fine,' I told him. 'I don't know what you were so worried about.'

§

But I could feel the heaviness of the place strongly on my body. As I stood under the hot water in the shower the adrenalin slowly began to melt away. I was thinking about what I would write for the conclusion of my research project. I had been to have a look at 'the darkness'. It was real and it was sad. It was the place where there was so little hope for the dispossessed that they put their hope in a saint they created for themselves. The Saint of Death didn't discriminate against anyone. She welcomed drag queens, prostitutes and even narcotics traffickers. They imagined she was Catholic, but she had come back to them from their pre-Hispanic past.

Getting into bed next to Ricardo, I felt lucky.

❧ 16 ❧

Chocolate Skulls

Tonight Ricardo arrived home later than usual. And because I too had arrived late after my politics class, it was inevitably going to be one of those nights when, after staring gloomily into an uninviting fridge, Ricardo and I would decide with guilty pleasure that going for tacos was the only possible dinner option.

The best food in Mexico, I had discovered, is found in unlikely places – wrapped up in small plastic packages in the baskets of passing bicycles, or in trolleys pulled along by shouting people; sometimes it's handed to you through the window of the car while you're in the traffic. Tacos de Chupacabras, one of the most famous taco stalls in Mexico City, is situated under a cement bridge in a dreggy oasis between two highways in Coyoacán. Chupacabras, which means 'suck goats', refers to a mythical creature that resembles a kangaroo with fangs and is said to suck the blood of goats and other farm animals. The first reports of its killings appeared in newspapers in the early 1990s and it's now widely believed that the reports were fabricated by the Mexican government in order to divert attention away from a series of political killings which still remain unsolved.

Although at the time, this tactic had had the desired effect, 'suck-goats' were now a sort of national joke. The taco stall we were going to had named itself after this creature in reference to the 'secret ingredient' it used to make such tasty tacos.

At first, the look of these street tacos seemed grotesque to me, but I was now addicted to their distinctive taste. Professor Arzaba had come up with an explanation as to why the simple recipe of slices of meat inside a tortilla – they cost on average about 6 pesos (60 cents) and are cooked in about two minutes – could be so delicious and so addictive, and why this taste can never be replicated at home or even in a restaurant.

'In the majority of cases,' maintained our professor, 'the taco meat has been left outside, unrefrigerated in the heat of the day. And there is a very specialised French dish, you know, in which the meat is just at the point of going rotten but still edible – this enriches the taste of the meat.'

I liked his theory even though I could find no reference for such a French dish. It fitted with so many aspects of Mexico, where beauty has often been achieved as a result of an accident permitted by the overriding chaos.

When we got to the front of the queue, we ordered six 'tacos of suck-goats' each. The rain began to beat down on the tarpaulin above us. As we waited, we admired the mastery of the taco makers – their faces glowing under the bare light bulbs and their hands moving so fast that their actions became a blur. They cut through the slabs of meat with enormous knives and threw the slices into the tortillas. Within one minute we had our tacos, which were, without doubt, the tastiest tacos imaginable.

Out of the corner of my eye I watched Ricardo as we ate. He seemed withdrawn, and he'd hardly said a word since he had got back from work. This was strange considering we were eating *tacos de Chupacabras*.

'What's wrong?' I asked, shouting to be heard above the sound of the rain and the truck that was speeding across the bridge above us.

'You know they're closing down another three centres,' he told me. He was talking about Fifth Avenue schools. Like many other companies at this time, Fifth Avenue was downsizing as a result of the Wall Street crash. Mexico was in recession. The United States, Mexico's biggest trading partner, was out of pocket and many Mexicans living over there were also out of pocket, causing them to stop sending money to their families back home. This was a big deal, considering these payments made up Mexico's second biggest source of income after petroleum.

'Really? Which centres are they closing now?' I inquired.

'Guanajuato, León and Linda Vista.'

'Ha! They opened two of those centres a few months ago – and they just opened the one in León a week ago. Didn't you just get back from the grand opening?'

Now it would be Ricardo's job to pick up the pieces – to travel to each of these places and impose an agreement with a bunch of enraged students who had just paid huge amounts of money to attend a school that no longer existed and who would not be getting their money back. Nestor Montes would order Ricardo to placate them with some sort of trashy online course or CD-ROM pack.

'That's half of them now,' he muttered. 'Ten out of the twenty schools have closed down in the last month.'

The owners of the school, Ricardo explained, who also owned gyms and tomato farms, were falling further and further into debt as fewer and fewer students were signing up at Fifth Avenue. Many of the current students were losing their jobs and could no longer afford to keep studying English, so the classes were shrinking.

Yet I had found there was a certain doggedness in the attitude of the remaining students. 'You know, Teacher Lucy, here in Mexico we are accustomed to de crises,' explained Oswaldo, who was still working as a computer programmer at the large pharmaceutical company. 'That's why – always, we have a Plan B. If I lose my job, I paint my car like a taxi – always dere is work for taxi drivers. Dat's what I did in the last crisis, and dis one is not nearly as bad as de last one.'

He was referring to the Peso Crisis of 1994, when the Mexican peso had plummeted and interest rates had skyrocketed overnight, forcing millions of Mexicans into un-repayable debt. Ricardo's parents, who before the crisis had been in debt by 300 000 pesos, had suddenly found they owed one million.

Any panic that the First Wives' Breakfast Club may have had about the economic crisis was overwhelmed by the pleasure they got out of the prospect of their ex-husbands being worse hit than themselves.

Verónica had been in particularly high spirits after discovering that the architectural firm her ex-husband had been working for in America had collapsed, leaving him with no option than to come back to Mexico. 'And you know what I tell him if he knocks on my door?' she'd asked the class. Verónica had been lucky enough to keep the house after they were divorced.

'What?' we asked.

'If you need somewhere to stay, you can stay here in de back room. I don't have a problem. And I only ask one thing in return – dat you do de housework!'

'Ha, ha, ha!' The women in the class had let out a triumphant cackle at the thought of their ex-husbands being forced to clean their houses for them in order to survive.

Ricardo, however, was now genuinely worried about losing his job.

'Well, have you started searching for other job possibilities?' I asked.

He didn't say anything, but the look he gave me said, 'Yes, of course. You know that I'm always searching. And if I had found something, I would have told you.'

Now, for the first time, I considered what it would be like if Ricardo did lose his job. In a country where there is no such thing as the dole, this was a terrifying prospect. And, although I could get by on my private classes, I was reliant on my job at Fifth Avenue for my visa.

A thought that had been at the back of my mind for a little while moved forward and demanded consideration. Perhaps Ricardo and I could go back to live in Australia.

❧

It had been almost two years since I had arrived in Mexico, even though I had originally been planning to stay for one year only. And it didn't feel like it, but I had now been living with Ricardo for a year and a half. Since my semi-nervous breakdown following my appearance in the soap opera, I had been gradually finding new ways to make my life here work better. In between Fifth Avenue and my private classes, I had finished off all the Spanish courses at the National University, and taken various cultural night classes such as the one on Mexican political history and an 'indigenous folkloric dance' workshop where I had appeared in the end-of-semester concert dressed as a Mexican peasant girl. Here I had made some close friends – like Mary-Anne, the ex-nun with the 78-year-old boyfriend, and Christina, a Mexican–American batik artist from LA. They were exceptions to my ban on expats – since they operated in the local circles and we spoke to each other mainly in Spanish out of habit.

I'd been learning as much as I could about everything, how things worked here, and learning more and more words, which made my life easier and easier. For example I had finally learned the difference between a *tlacoyo* (oval-shaped maize dough – usually with beans), a *huarache* (massive oval shape with meat), a *gordita* (round and thick), an *itacate* (triangular with white cheese), a *quesadilla* (folded over with cheese), and a *sincronizada* (made with flour tortillas).

In fact I was now so settled into my life here, my relationship with Ricardo had been going so smoothly that the thought of returning home permanently hadn't crossed my mind until now – now that our future here was beginning to look uncertain.

Both Ricardo and I had been planning to do our Masters degrees next year at the National University, but the reality was beginning to hit home that surviving on part-time work in a rapidly contracting economy just wasn't going to be viable.

'Ricardo,' I asked, 'do you want to come and check out Australia?'

‰

We were coming to the end of October and elaborate public offerings had already been laid out around the city in preparation for El Día de los Muertos (The Day of the Dead), one of the most important celebrations of the year in Mexico. The streets smelled of marigolds and banana leaves. The bakeries had started making 'Pan de Muerto' (Bread of the Dead) – sugar-coated buns with long-bone decorations on the top.

On this day, the spirits of the dead are able to return and enjoy earthly sensations like food, music and dancing. A common tradition among indigenous Mexicans is to adorn the graves of their deceased relatives with candles and flowers and lay out the food that the dead had been known to enjoy when they were alive. It is essentially a party for the dead. The first day of November is reserved for dead children only, and the adults come the day after, on the second.

The year before I had been so distracted with my love crises that I had hardly noticed the Day of the Dead. I vaguely remembered the offerings that had been laid out on the streets of La Roma, and that both Octavio and Ricardo had offered to take me to see the shrines at the university; but I had ended up refusing both of them. Whenever I recalled that time, I felt a huge sense of relief that it was over, and a heightened appreciation of the peacefulness of my life now with Ricardo.

It was impossible to deny, however, feeling a touch of regret that my relationship with Octavio, my first Mexican friend, had to come to an end so abruptly. Since I had moved in with Ricardo, I had seen Octavio just once. I needed to return a book of his about Mexican history that I had been reading when I left the flat and to collect a few items which I had left behind in my haste. Ricardo had insisted on driving me there, perhaps not entirely out of charity, and had been waiting downstairs in the car when I ran up the familiar yellow staircase and banged on Octavio's door.

'Hey! Come in, can I get you a coffee or something?' he asked. God, he was tall – I'd almost forgotten.

'Sorry. Ricardo's waiting downstairs, I have to go.'

'Oh, okay.'

Handing him the book, he gave me a plastic bag containing some clothes and the Spanish grammar books I had left behind.

Then we hugged. A hug can encompass so many unspoken feelings.

§

After that I had forced myself to resist calling him at various times after I moved in with Ricardo. Instead, I had occasionally sent him carefully worded emails, to which I had received replies in the same sort of reserved but polite tone. He'd never mentioned anything about his new girlfriend, whom I had heard about from Ofelia. 'What's she like?' I'd inquired.

'I think she's Swedish – a ballet dancer or something. Very beautiful . . .' she told me, and I had immediately regretted asking.

§

On the Saturday before El Día de los Muertos, Ricardo and I set up an offering in our house. I went with Chavela, Ricardo's mother, to La Merced, the huge market next to the Centro Histórico, to buy everything we needed. We got off the metro at the Zócalo and walked east. Chavela talked a lot. She talked about her childhood here in the Centro; her family history; how the Morales had been one of the wealthiest families in Mexico, with their own railway lines and haciendas all over the country. Then she described their dramatic downfall after the revolution of 1910.

I tried to listen to everything she was saying while avoiding a collision with all the thousands of people who were heading in our direction. I had almost forgotten how insanely crowded this area was. Recalling my time living in the Centro Histórico, I had walked all around these streets, searching for flats. Back then, this place had seemed astonishing to me. But now, when people asked me what it was like living in Mexico, I didn't know what to say. Everything just seemed so completely normal – just like life anywhere else – and I couldn't think of anything exotic to tell them. Sometimes when I told people here what my nationality was, it occurred to me how strange it was that I came from Australia – this British penal colony on a huge island somewhere near Asia with hopping animals and a government that gave people money if they didn't have a job, and a populace that was so laid back it had never bothered to have any wars of its own, revolutions or even to become independent from Britain. I wondered what Ricky would make of it.

The crowd density increased again and the shouting began: '*¡Chile ancho! ¡Chile pasilla! ¡Chile mulato!*' We were in the markets. Row upon row of massive buckets overflowed with strong-smelling dried chillies. Then everything smelled of sugar and chocolate – the handmade sweets stalls. In preparation for the Day of the Dead, they were filled with skulls. Most of these were made from white or dark chocolate. But there were also sugar skulls, which were bright pink or white. Some were life-size and some as small as golf balls, with animated facial expressions that were intricately drawn on. I chose two life-sized dark-chocolate skulls.

We walked outside into a sea of golden orange marigolds or 'Flowers of Cempazúchitle' as they are known here. Marigolds were one of the first flowers to have been cultivated by the Aztecs and are said to act as a guiding light for the spirits when they return for El Dia de los Muertos. We bought two huge bunches and some bundles of banana leaves, as well as candles, incense, *papel picado* (coloured paper made especially for the Day of The Dead, with cut-out images of skeletons dancing and partying) and some red mangos and papayas. I cringed when it occurred to me that in a few months from now, I would be doing my shopping in the sterile neon-lit aisles of a Coles/Woolworths supermarket chainstore. Shopping in the colour and light of real markets was just one of so many things about life in this country that I knew I would miss. A week before, Ricardo and I had told his family about our plans to move to Australia at the end of the year. This was something we had been feeling slightly dubious about, considering the closeness of his family. We had explained that it would not be permanent – we would be away for two years at the most and, if things didn't work out for Ricardo over there, we would come straight back.

But the idea had been growing on Ricardo. For him it would be a chance to experience another culture, to perfect his English and to see the world I had come from, just as I had seen his. Chavela had smiled, 'Well, I say get out while you can. Thanks to the gringos, this country's screwed,' she said, giggling at her use of coarse language.

When I separated from Chavela and got home, Ricardo and I covered the desk in the living room with banana leaves and sprinkled it with marigold petals, and hung the *papel picado* on the walls above. Then we laid out the chocolate skulls and the fruit, and lit the candles and the incense. The food left out on the shrine is said to taste different the day after the spirits have come.

We added some photos of the dead – our midnight dinner guests. My mother had sent me some photos of my grandmother; also, just before she died, she had painted some watercolours of flowers, which we laid out. Then we settled down on the couch to sip a shot of mezcal. The house glowed with warmth and colour.

§

Ricardo and I decided to escape the city for the actual night of El Día de los Muertos, 2 November. These sorts of celebrations are always much more beautiful in the small towns. There are some villages around the city that are famous for their extravagant celebrations of the Day of the Dead – like Mixquic, where they throw a massive party in the cemetery and everyone dresses up as skeletons and ghosts, and mariachi bands are called in to play music for the dead.

But these celebrations have become so popular among *chilangos* that getting there involves several hours of waiting in traffic. So we opted to spend the weekend in a town called Tepoztlán, an hour south of the city. Here, on the Day of the Dead there is a tradition of the residents creating offerings in their houses and opening their doors to the public. We had already made a trip there a few times before to walk up Tepozteco, a mountain above the town with the ruins of an Aztec pyramid at its peak.

This town is considered holy for many indigenous Mexicans as it is said to be the birthplace of the feathered serpent god Quetzalcóatl. Many of the town's inhabitants are traditional Nahuas, who co-exist with a large population of Mexican and international new-agers, or *'papayas cósmicas'* as they are known in Mexico. It is unclear whether they were attracted to the town by the frequently reported sightings of UFOs, or whether these sightings began only after the cosmic papayas had already settled there. One resident of Tepoztlán, a photographer named Carlos Díaz, believes he was abducted by one of these UFOs, and his case is said to be the most well documented in the history of the phenomenon.

We arrived in the town at dusk and the air already smelled of bonfire. We drove past the local cemetery, which was bustling with families. They sat around the graves, which glowed with marigolds and candlelight. We parked somewhere near the town centre and walked up to Govinda Ram's Ayurvedic Restaurant to meet my old friend Buck, who had moved here a few months before.

'The thing about urine therapy is it really makes you eat healthy . . . Because, if you don't eat healthy, the taste is just unbearable,' he explained over a bowl of brown rice and lentils. He seemed much happier and more relaxed than he had been when he'd lived in the Centro Histórico. Even though what he was drinking may have been controversial for some, he knew all the historical precedents in traditional Chinese and Indian medicine – and it seemed to be working for him. After eating, the three of us walked outside and became part of a large group of elegantly dressed skeletons and spirits who were strolling merrily along the narrow cobbled streets. Their costumes were creative and spectacular. Young women skeletons, in full-brimmed hats intricately embroidered with cobwebs and flowers, pranced along the street holding up the skirts of their ballgowns, which were also dripping with cobwebs. Unadorned skeletons, in lycra body suits and huge papier-mâché masks, towered above us on stilts. Many of them were children, but they weren't in the majority.

We followed a group of whimsical characters in through the door of a house left wide open and decorated with flowers and lanterns. Walking through to the back garden, we found a group of larger-than-life-sized skeletons wearing papier-mâché masks and riding gigantic bicycles with crazed expressions of joy. Our hosts, a smiling old couple, stood behind a table dishing out a hot punch made from fruit, cinnamon and rum to their guests. We commended them on their creations and made our way to the next house.

Each offering we saw was original and imaginative. Most of them involved skeletons in some form – dancing, singing, baking bread, sitting down to dinner, playing musical instruments, engaged in *lucha libre* wrestling.

Makeshift stages had been set up, where children were acting out ghost stories.

With each home we visited, we fell further into a warm, punch-induced lull of tipsiness. We chatted with our hosts and the people around us – grandparents, teenagers, children, everyone was included. It was a sensation I had never experienced before. The whole community was getting together and celebrating – not in small groups, but as one entity. Everyone was interacting with everyone else, there were no barriers. It was as if the presence of the imagery of death was reminding us of the one thing that we all had in common, mortality. Why not celebrate? We won't be here together like this for very long.

❧

This is what the great Poet King of Texcoco, Netzahualcóyotl, had written about.

> *Not forever on earth,*
> *Only a little while here.*
> *Though it be jade it falls apart,*
> *Though it be gold it wears away,*
> *Though it be quetzal plumage it is torn asunder.*
> *Not forever on earth,*
> *Only a little while here.*

❧

At the end of the night, the sky opened and the three of us were running back along the slippery cobbled streets towards Buck's cabin on the edge of the forest. Suddenly Buck blurted something out in English. 'Man, the energy of this place is incredible!' And it was at this moment – after a split second of confusion, while my brain processed the unfamiliar phonemes he had uttered – that I realised that I had been speaking in Spanish the whole night without being consciously aware of it.

And so it dawned on me that my mission was finally complete. It wasn't that I was speaking without grammatical errors – it was more that it just felt natural now. Instead of thinking about the grammatical structures of the sentences, I was now just thinking about what it was that I was saying and hearing.

The goal that had had me spending lonely Saturday nights writing out verb tables – that had turned me into a nervous self-hating wreck, and had had me screaming obscenities at old men and bursting into tears – had finally been reached.

❦ 17 ❦

Taking Off

Two hours to go before we have to be at the airport. The floor is still covered in boxes and piles of books and papers. Where the hell is Ricardo? He left to go to the dentist at nine this morning – it's now 2 pm. He's not answering his phone.

My slight hangover adds to my irritation. Last night Fifth Avenue Polanco threw me a farewell party. Nearly all the students turned up and Charlie, the illiterate but politically switched-on chauffeur, brought along an unusually strong bottle of tequila. This may have been what caused Elvira to try out some truly explosive moves on the dance floor, shaking her magnificent curves.

All the members of the First Wives' Breakfast Club are now divorced, including Concepción, who is in her seventies, and has eight grandchildren. Marisol will soon be moving to Texas with her gringo boyfriend, who was

315

with her last night. They have applied for a de facto visa, because she won't be getting married again. I knew I would miss this gang of strong, spirited women, who had experienced so many hardships yet were some of the most cheerful people I had ever met.

Ofelia came along as well – she's now an honorary member of the Club. 'So I told him,' she slurred, '"Silvio, this is my life . . . And if you can't deal with it, well, you don't have to. Because I want a divorce."' Silvio's charm and good looks had not been enough to make up for his annoying tendency to be compulsively and irrationally jealous and controlling. Ofelia had accepted a job in an international law firm which would require her to travel all over the world.

We all promised to stay in contact, and I hurried home to continue packing up my Mexican life.

Now I am reaching for a pile of papers in order to start sorting through it; but Shell, the tortoiseshell cat, proceeds to sit on it. When I try to move her, she pounces on my hand as if it were a bird. This is her way of grappling with the unwelcome reality that she will be forced to move back in with Carmen and all the other cats. Carmen would also be re-adopting our dog, Camilo, who had always really belonged to her, except that he lived on our terrace and we had become his designated walkers.

The small white cat, Neige, has not been lucky enough to be accepted by Carmen. First, because one of the other cats was constantly trying to kill her; and second, because her health problems are too complicated. After opening her up, the vet discovered she did not have bladder stones after all; he attributed her compulsive urinating to 'trauma-induced neuroses', for which he prescribed an expensive cat-Valium drug. This was not a convenient diagnosis for her to have been given just before going out for adoption.

If it wasn't for Buck's friend Luna, the local Reiki practitioner at Tepoztlán, Neige would be going back onto the streets. We drove her out to her new home a few days ago. 'Don't worry,' Luna assured us as I attempted to hand her two months' worth of cat-Valium, 'there's healing energy in this place. She won't be needing all those chemicals.' Neige looked suspicious, but I hope Luna's right. The cats have been such loyal companions to me over the last few years, comforting me during some of my loneliest moments.

☙

The drugs are still in my handbag. I wonder if the effect would be very different from human Valium – if Ricardo doesn't get back soon, I may have to try them out.

Focus on the piles, I tell myself. I lift Shell off a pile of exercise books. I open the one at the top – pages and pages of repetitive sentences, verb conjugations, vocabulary lists and endless grammar rules. One exercise book is devoted entirely to 'Uses of the Subjunctive'. What should I do with them all? Over two years of learning to talk. It seems terrible just to throw them all out – they represent so much work – but I can't justify lugging them to the other side of the world. I console myself with the thought that it is all in my head now anyway. And Mexico itself is inside my head; I guess that's how I can bear to leave it behind now.

Carmen's front door opens and I rush to close the curtains so she can't see the extent of the chaos inside. But she pops her head through the curtains.

'What time's your flight?' she asks.

'Soon,' I tell her. I don't want to think about it.

'Where's Ricardo?' she inquires.

'He went to the dentist.'

'What? But he left to go there about five hours ago!'

Suddenly the gate opens. Ricardo is back. I brace myself to shout at him for arriving so late, but I stop short when I see that his face is covered in bruises and is horribly swollen. 'What the hell!' Carmen and I stare at him as he gets out of the car. 'Eeaaaaaaaaaaaaaooooooo,' he says. It eventually becomes clear that the dentist had to do more work on his teeth than expected.

We throw everything in the car that we can't bear to throw out – the lot will now be stashed away for eternity in a box in Ricardo's family's flat, where we will stop off on the way to the airport. The car will be left to Ricardo's little brother, Ángel. Ricardo squashes our bags into the car.

I look at the time – we should have left half an hour ago. I grab the broom and give the place one last frenzied sweep.

Carmen is waiting for us on the steps. We hand her a bottle of wine and the keys to the house. She doesn't say anything. I am worried that my final sweep-up was below standard. But when she looks up, her eyes are filled with tears.

Tonyo, Tonyo Grande and Jacquelíne are waiting for us outside. We haven't told them we are leaving, but they know. Somehow *viene-vienes* always know everything.

'Hey, güera,' Jacquelíne asks. 'Are you bringing the car with you where you're going?'

'No, we're going by plane,' I tell her.

'Pity. I've got these mufflers . . .'

We say goodbye and thank them for everything. They wave as we drive away, and in the rear-vision mirror I catch one last flash of golden teeth as Tonyo grins.

§

It's dark by the time the plane takes off.

'Hey, that's the Zócalo!'

Ricardo points out the window to a large black square amid a sea of golden lights. From there I make out a straight line of white lights stretching diagonally across the city. It's Paseo de la Reforma, the road which turned into a giant festival camping ground after the election results. It leads to Polanco, the sleek *fresa* suburb where I went to work every morning. Another line of white lights cuts through the middle of Reforma. It's Calle

Insurgentes, connecting the north of the city to the south, and connecting Colonia Roma, where I first lived, to Guadalupe Inn, where I had my first real home. Further south, the white light leads to a circular patch of black, the forest surrounding the National University.

We rise above the volcanoes and mountains surrounding the valley of Mexico, and the map of my life over the past two years shrinks and disappears as we go up into the black infinity. Below me, the second most dangerous city in the world for kidnapping statistics continues on without my watching eyes.

Epilogue

Our flight lands in Sydney late at night. We sleep on the fold-out sofa at my parents' small flat in Bondi. The change of time zone tricks us into waking at dawn, and we zigzag our way down the hill towards the ocean. The tree-lined streets are empty. We peer into people's front yards. They are landscaped with native flora and small magnolia trees, with serried lines of glazed pots containing drought-friendly architectural plants. They seem so open, so exposed. I realise that front yards are invisible in Mexico City – the sorts of houses that have front yards are hidden behind razor-wire-covered walls which are fitted with surveillance cameras and intercom systems.

The sun is almost halfway into the sky by the time we get to the beach. We throw off our clothes and walk towards the surf, dodging the semi-naked runners who seem to be coming at us from every angle. Black rubber wetsuits cling to strong young bodies as they charge past us into the ocean carrying surfboards three times their own size. We feel we are surrounded by superhumans. A young girl powers by. She has a lithe muscular body and long shining hair and is wearing nothing but an olive-green bikini. But no one is staring at her. And there are hundreds of other girls like her; almost naked, strong and proud. Ricardo and I splash into the white foam and I open my eyes underwater to see the bubbles and the turquoise.

Oh Australia!

Walking back up the hill, more joggers have appeared on the footpaths. Some are running with high-tech strollers containing wildly alert babies. Others are followed by panting dogs on leads. Ricardo is intrigued by the amount of exercise that is going on. 'Don't people here have to go to work?' he asks. A band of kids in school uniforms are racing each other on scooters down the street. We stop and stare at them. It takes me a few moments to register why we find this scene so odd. Where are their parents? I wonder. In Mexico City the only kids you see on the street are street kids. Like front yards, middle-class children are generally kept behind walls.

§

Ricky was rocketed into my world of family and friends. Christmas was coming and everyone was gathering from far and wide. He dealt with the joyful homecoming drama warmly, as if he had been in my crazy family for ever. We found an affordable flat near Bondi Beach in a grungy building tenanted with British backpackers. Their daily drunkenness peaks in the early morning hours and climaxes with the Spice Girls at full volume while they beat each other up and then vomit. But from the bedroom window, looking out over a terracotta roof, we see the blue sky and the blue ocean. And from the kitchen window we look right into the middle of a large gum tree, the boudoir of white cockatoos and rainbow lorikeets whose hectic and immodest breeding program takes place before our eyes while we eat breakfast, like a documentary. This makes us think of Ricky's dad, and his love of the Discovery channel. Sitting at the table there I began to write my memories of Mexico.

*

I found a job teaching English again, this time to Jordanians, Indians, Koreans and Slovakians, and started a Masters degree. Ricardo gives private Spanish lessons in our flat, and is beloved by an eclectic cross-section of students, and sings Mexican songs at our local bar. He eventually found a nine-to-five job, interpreting at a television company, but continues giving classes and singing on the weekends. Although he had one or two challenging moments in the surf, *Bondi Rescue* – the reality TV show that films swimmers in the throes of drowning and then being saved by hunky lifesavers – was fortunately not scheduled to shoot on those days. Now he is confident in the ocean. The slow-cooked lamb recipes are inching towards perfection; made with Australian lamb, they have a distinctly different taste to those made with Mexican mutton.

§

'When will Australians understand that a taco is not a sandwich?' Ricardo says as he carefully removes the felonious piece of lettuce from the pork taco in front of him. A Mexican's reaction to the inclusion of lettuce in a taco is akin to the horror a Japanese person would feel if tomato sauce were squirted onto sashimi. We had given up on Mexican restaurants in Sydney. But tonight is 16 September 2010, the 200th anniversary of the Mexican war of independence from Spain. And as it is so important for Mexicans to be together at such special times, we had joined a table full of Sydney-based Mexicans to celebrate. Privately we were also celebrating that I had just that day typed 'THE END' on this memoir.

At the restaurant we are enfolded in a vague fantasy of Mexico, a well-meaning anthology of bland recipes and Tex-Mex music. It smells of corn chips. The waiters are dressed in embroidered white blouses and the walls are decorated with sombreros and a mismatch of souvenirs from all over Latin America. Just as for most Mexicans, Australia could be Austria; for most Australians, Mexico is anything involving beans and blankets with rainbow-coloured stripes. We are drinking sangria, which most Mexicans have never heard of.

Earlier that day an enlightening piece on www.guardian.co.uk revealed that President Calderón had spent hundreds of millions of American dollars on tonight's celebrations, in a ceremony designed by Australian Ric Birch – fireworks, marching mariachi bands, laser light displays and a 20-metre-tall figure of a moustachioed revolutionary made from steel and plastic, who would be lifted to his feet by cranes in the Zócalo. After all, Mexicans deserved it – what with 70 per cent of them balancing on the poverty line and 5 000 000 newly impoverished from the global financial crisis. The only solid remaining pillar of the Mexican economy is the drug trade, which employs over 1 000 000 people. But that employment is hardly secure; 28 000 Mexicans have been violently killed since Calderón announced the War on Drugs in 2006. So despite the expensive joy of the celebrations, right now Mexico risks becoming a 'failed state'. I remembered the radical students and professors at university in Mexico City muttering that the country was due for another revolution. Perhaps the erection of a colossal generic revolutionary in the Zócalo is asking for trouble.

❧

We all charge our glasses from a jug of sangria in which slices of orange are floating.

'*¡Viva México!*' shouts a Mexican–American architect married to an Italian–Australian, and we all join in. Meanwhile, back in Mexico City, President Calderón is standing on the balcony of the presidential palace and shouting '*¡Viva México!*'. The hundreds of thousands of Mexicans who have managed to find a place in the Zócalo, respond with a huge roar, '*¡Viva!*' And the millions of dollars worth of fireworks explode, dangerously close to the crowd.

Acknowledgements

I thank my mother Julie for giving me the confidence and support to take on the first major writing project I have ever attempted. And I feel immense gratitude to my three significant Richards; my father Richard for his encouragement, Richard Walsh for commissioning this book and all his meticulous help along the way, and my partner Ricardo for his endless patience. To Susie Walsh, who came up with the idea, I am deeply indebted.

My editors Siobhán Cantrill and Clara Finlay worked generously to improve this book and I thank them, along with my publisher Louise Thurtell, for their commitment. Lisa White designed the book cover of my dreams.

And of course, I wish to state my gratitude to the friends, students and colleagues in Mexico who I have written about, some of whom are referred to by different names in order to protect their privacy. This book could not have been written without them. Also I would like to apologise in advance for any mistakes I have made or wrong conclusions I have drawn in this description of my time in Mexico, a country into which I was so graciously welcomed and whose amazing history and culture I so admire.

I also acknowledge some wonderful books which have deepened my understanding of Mexico and from which I have drawn, or made reference to, in this book:

The Conquest of New Spain by Bernal Díaz del Castillo; *The Mexican Dream: Or, The Interrupted Thought of the Amerindian Civilizations* by J.M.G. Le Clézio; *The Labyrinth of Solitude* by Octavio Paz; *Looking for History: Dispatches from Latin America* by Alma Guillermoprieto; *Opening Mexico: The Making of a Democracy* by Julia Preston, Samuel Dillon and Joanne J. Myers.